SCIENCE AND EDUCATION;

SCIENCE AND EDUCATION;

Thomas Henry Huxley

www.General-Books.net

Publication Data:

Title: Science and Education
Author: Thomas Henry Huxley
General Books publication date: 2009
Original publication date: 1902
Original Publisher: American Home Library
Subjects: Education
Science
Education / Teaching Methods Materials / Science Technology
Science / General
Science / Environmental Science
Science / Study Teaching
Science / Philosophy Social Aspects

CONTENTS

1

SECTION 1

Literary Editor of the New York Mail and Express. HENRY VAN DYKE, D. D., LL. D., author of "Little Rivers," etc.;

Professor of English Literature at Princeton University.   THOMAS NELSON PAGE, LL. D., Litt. D., author of "Red Rock," etc.

ORATIONS

HON. HENRY CABOT LODGE, A. B., LL. B., author of "Life of Daniel Webster," etc.; U. S. Senator from Massachusetts.

HON. JOHN R. PROCTOR, President U. S. Civil Service Commission.

MORRIS HICKEY MORGAN, Ph.   D., LL. D., Professor in Latin, Harvard University.

2

SECTION 2

PREFACE

An apology must be here offered for the occurrence of repetitions in this volume. But it could hardly be otherwise with speeches and essays, on the same topic, addressed at intervals, during more than thirty years, to widely distant and different hearers and readers. The oldest piece, that "On the Educational Value of the Natural History Sciences," contains some crudities, which I repudiated when the lecture was first reprinted, more than twenty years ago; but it will be seen that much of what I have had to say, later on in life, is merely a development of the propositions enunciated in this early and sadly-imperfect piece of work.

In view of the recent attempt to disturb the compromise about the teaching of dogmatic theology, solemnly agreed to by the first School Board for London, the fifteenth Essay, and, more particularly, the note on page

, may be found interesting. T. H. JBL.

Hodeslea, Eastbournb,

September 4, 1898.

SCIENCE AND EDUCATION

JOSEPH PRIESTLEY

[1874]

IF THE man to perpetuate whose memory we have this day raised a statue had been asked on what part of his busy life's work he set the highest value, he would undoubtedly have pointed to his voluminous contributions to theology. In season and out of season, he was the steadfast champion of that hypothesis respecting the Divine nature which is termed Unitarianism by its friends and Socinianism by its foes. Regardless of odds, he was ready to do battle with all comers in that cause; and if no adversaries entered the lists, he would sally forth to seek them.

To this, his highest ideal of duty, Joseph Priestley sacrificed the vulgar prizes of life, which, assuredly, were within easy reach of a man of his singular energy and varied abilities. For this object he put aside, as of secondary importance, those scientific investigations which he loved so well, and in which he showed himself so competent to enlarge the boundaries of natural knowledge and to win fame. In this cause he not only cheerfully suffered obloquy from the bigoted and the unthinking, and came within sight of martyrdom; but bore with thatwhich is much harder to be borne than all these, the unfeigned astonishment and hardly disguised contempt of a brilliant society, composed of men whose sympathy and esteem must have been most dear to him, and to whom it was simply incomprehensible that a philosopher should seriously occupy himself with any form of Christianity.

It appears to me that the man who, setting before himself such an ideal of life, acted up to it consistently, is worthy of the deepest respect, whatever opinion may be entertained as to the real value of the tenets which he so zealously propagated and defended.

But I am sure that I speak not only for myself, but for all this assemblage, when I say that our purpose today is to do honor, not to Priestley, the Unitarian divine, but to Priestley, the fearless defender of rational freedom in thought and in action: to Priestley, the philosophic thinker; to that Priestley who held a foremost place among "the swift runners who hand over the lamp of life," ' and transmit from one generation to another the fire kindled, in the childhood of the world, at the Promethean altar of Science.

The main incidents of Priestley's life are so well known that I need dwell upon them at no great length.

Born in 1783, at Fieldhead, near Leeds, and brought up among Calvinists of the straitest orthodoxy, the boy's striking natural ability led to his being devoted to the profession of a minister of religion; and, in 1752, he was sent to the Dissenting Academy at Daventry – an institution which authority left undisturbed, though its existence contravened the law. The teachers under whose instruction and influence the young man came at Daven- try carried out to the letter the injunction to "try all things: hold fast that which is good," and encouraged the discussion of every imaginable proposition with complete freedom, the leading professors taking opposite sides; a discipline which, admirable as it may be from a purely scientific point of view, would seem to be calculated to make acute, rather than sound, divines. Priestley tells us, in his "Autobiography," that he generally found himself on the unorthodox side: and, as he grew older, and his faculties attained their maturity, this native tendency toward heterodoxy grew with his growth and strengthened with his strength. He passed from Calvinism to Arianism; and finally, in middle life, landed in that very broad form of

Unitarianism by which his craving after a credible and consistent theory of things was satisfied.

1 "Quasi eursores, vitai lampada tradunt." – Lucr. "De Berum Nat"

On leaving Daventry, Priestley became minister of a congregation, first at Needham Market, and secondly at Nantwich; but whether on account of his heterodox opinions or of the stuttering which impeded his expression of them in the pulpit, little success attended his efforts in this capacity. In 1761, a career much more suited to his abilities became open to him. He was appointed "tutor in the languages" in the Dissenting Academy at Warrington, in which capacity, besides giving three courses of lectures, he taught Latin, Greek, French, and Italian, and read lectures on the theory of language and universal grammar, on oratory, philosophical criticism, and civil law. And it is interesting to observe that, as a teacher, he encouraged and cherished in those whom he instructed the freedom which he had enjoyed, in his own student days, at Daventry. One of his pupils tells us that,

"At the conclusion of his lecture, he always encouraged his students to express their sentiments relative to the subject of it, and to urge any objections to what he had delivered, without reserve. It pleased him when any one commenced such a conversation. In order to excite the freest discussion, he occasionally invited the students to drink tea with him, in order to canvass the subjects of his lectures. I do not recollect that he ever showed the least displeasure at the strongest objections that were made to what he delivered, but I distinctly remember the smile of approbation with which he usually received them: nor did he fail to point out, in a very encouraging manner, the ingenuity or force of any remarks that were made, when they merited these characters. His object, as well as Dr. Aikin's, was to engage the students to examine and decide for themselves, uninfluenced by the sentiments of any other persons." '

It would be difficult to give a better description of a model teacher than that conveyed in these words.

From his earliest days, Priestley had shown a strong bent toward the study of nature; and his brother Timothy tells us that the boy put spiders into bottles, to see how long they would live in the same air – a curious anticipation of the investigations of his later years. At Nantwich, where he set up a school, Priestley informs us that he bought an air pump, an electrical machine, and other instruments, in the use of which he instructed his scholars. But he does not seem to have devoted himself seriously to physical science until 1766, when he had the great good fortune to meet Benjamin Franklin, whose friendship he ever afterward enjoyed. Encouraged by Franklin, he wrote a "History of Electricity," which Wp. s published in 1767, and appears to have met with considerable success.

1 "Life and Correspondence of Dr. Priestley," by J. T. Butt. Vol. i., 1 "Autobiography," §§ 100, 101.

In the same year, Priestley left Warrington to become the minister of a congregation at Leeds; and here, happening to live next door to a public brewery, as he says,

"I, at first, amused myself with making experiments ou the fixed air which I found ready-made in the process of fermentation. When I removed from that house I was under the necessity of making fixed air for myself; and one experiment leading to another, as I have distinctly and faithfully noted in my various publications on the subject, I by degrees contrived a convenient apparatus for the purpose, but of the cheapest kind.

"When I began these experiments I knew very little of *chemistry,* and had, in a manner, no idea on the subject before I attended a course of chemical lectures, delivered in the Academy at Warrington, by Dr. Turner of Liverpool. But I have often thought that, upon the whole, this circumstance was no disadvantage to me; as, in this situation, I was led to devise an apparatus and processes of my own, adapted to my peculiar views; whereas, if I had been previously accustomed to the usual chemical processes, I should not have so easily thought of any other, and without new modes of operation I should hardly have discovered anything materially new." '

The first outcome of Priestley's chemical work, published in 1772, was of a very practical character. He discovered the way of impregnating water with an excess of "fixed air," or carbonic acid, and thereby producing what we now know as "soda water" – a service to naturally, and still more to artificially, thirsty souls, which those whose parched throats and hot heads are cooled by morning draughts of that beverage cannot too gratefully acknowledge. In the same year, Priestley communicated the extensive series of observations which his industry and ingenuity had accumulated, in the course of four years, to the Royal Society, under the title of "Observations on Different Kinds of Air" – a memoir which was justly regarded of so much merit and importance that the Society at once conferred upon the author the highest distinction in their power, by awarding him the Copley Medal.

In 1771 a proposal was made to Priestley to accompany Captain Cook in his second voyage to the South Seas. He accepted it, and his congregation agreed to pay an assistant to supply his place during his absence. But the appointment lay in the hands of the Board of Longitude, of which certain clergymen were members; and whether these worthy ecclesiastics feared that Priestley's presence among the ship's company might expose his Majesty's sloop "Resolution" to the fate which aforetime befell a certain ship that went from Joppa to Tarshish; or whether they were alarmed lest a Socinian should undermine that piety which, in the days of Commodore Trunnion, so strikingly characterized sailors, does not appear; but, at any rate, they objected to Priestley "on account of his religious principles," and appointed the two Fors- ters, whose "religious principles," if they had been known to these well-meaning but not farsighted persons, would probably have surprised them.

In 1772 another proposal was made to Priestley. Lord Shelburne, desiring a "literary companion," had been brought into communication with Priestley by the good offices of a friend of both, Dr. Price; and offered him the nominal post of librarian with a good house and appointments, and an annuity in case of the termination of the engagement. Priestley accepted the offer, and remained with Lord Shelburne for seven years, sometimes residing at Calne, sometimes travelling abroad with the Earl.

Why the connection terminated has never been exactly known; but it is certain that Lord Shelburne behaved with the utmost consideration and kindness toward Priestley; that he fulfilled his engagements to the letter; and that, at a later period, he expressed a desire that Priestley should return to his old footing in his house. Probably enough, the politician, aspiring to the highest offices in 'the State, may have found the position of the protector of a man who was being denounced all over the country as an infidel and an atheist somewhat embarrassing. In fact, a passage in Priestley's "Autobiography" on the occasion of the publication of his "Disquisitions relating to Matter and Spirit," which took place in 1777, indicates pretty clearly the state of the case:

"(126) It being probable that this publication would be unpopular, and might be the means of bringing odium on my patron, several attempts were made by his friends, though none by himself, to dissuade me from persisting in it. But being, as I thought, engaged in the cause of important truth, I proceeded without regard to any consequences, assuring them that this publication should not be injurious to his lordship."

It is not unreasonable to suppose that his lordship, as a keen, practical man of the world, did not derive much satisfaction from this assurance. The "evident marks of dissatisfaction" which Priestley says he first perceived in his patron in 1778, may well have arisen from the peer's not unnatural uneasiness as to what his domesticated, but not tamed, philosopher might write next, and what storm might thereby be brought down on his own head; and it speaks very highly for Lord Shelburne's delicacy that, in the midst of such perplexities, he made not the least attempt to interfere with Priestley's freedom of action. In 1780, however, he intimated to Dr. Price that he should be glad to establish Priestley on his Irish estates: the suggestion was interpreted, as Lord Shelburne probably intended it should be, and Priestley left him, the annuity of $150 a year, which had been promised in view of such a contingency, being punctually paid.

After leaving Calne, Priestley spent some little time in London, and then, having settled in Birmingham at the desire of his brother-in-law, he was soon invited to become the minister of a large congregation. This settlement Priestley considered, at the time, to be "the happiest event of his life." And well he might think so; for it gave him competence and leisure; placed him within reach of the best makers of apparatus of the day; made him a member of that remarkable "Lunar Society," at whose meetings he could exchange thoughts with such men as Watt, Wedgwood, Darwin and Boulton; and threw open to him the pleasant house of the Galtons of Barr, where these men, and others of less note, formed a society of exceptional charm and intelligence.[1]

1 See "The Life of Mary Anne Schimmelpenninok." Mrs. Schimmelpenninck (nee Gallon) remembered Priestley very well, and her description of him is worth quotation – "A man of admirable simplicity, gentleness and kindness of heart, united with great acuteness of intellect. I can never forget the impression produced on me by the serene expression of his countenance. He, indeed, seemed present with God by recollection, and with man by cheerfulness. I remember that, in the assembly of these distinguished men, among whom Mr. Boulton, by his noble manner, his fine countenance (which much resembled that of Louis XIV.), and princely munificence, stood pre-eminently as the great Mecsenas; even as a child, I used to feel, when Dr. Priestley entered after him, that the glory of the one was terrestrial, that of the other celestial; and utterly far as I am removed from a belief in the sufficiency of Dr. Priestley's theological creed, I cannot but here record this evidence of the eternal power of any portion of the truth held in its vitality."

But these halcyon days were ended by a bitter storm. The French Revolution broke out. An electric shock ran through the nations; whatever there was of corrupt and retrograde, and, at the same time, a great deal of vhat there was of best and noblest, in European society shuddered at the outburst of long-pent-up social fires. Men's feelings were excited in a way that we, in this generation, can hardly comprehend. Party wrath and virulence were expressed in a manner unparalleled, and it is to be hoped impossible, in our times; and Priestley and his friends were held up to public scorn, even in Parliament, as fomenters of sedition. A "Church-aud-King" cry was raised against the Liberal Dissenters; and, in Birmingham, it was intensified and specially directed toward Priestley by a local controversy, in which he had engaged with his usual vigor. In 1791, the celebration of the second anniversary of the taking of the Bastille by a public dinner, with which Priestley had nothing whatever to do, gave the signal to the loyal and pious mob, who, unchecked, and indeed to some extent encouraged, by those who were responsible for order, had the town at their mercy for three days. The chapels and housesof the leading Dissenters were wrecked, and Priestley and his family had to fly for their lives, leaving library, apparatus, papers, and all their possessions, a prey to the flames.

Priestley never returned to Birmingham. He bore the outrages and losses inflicted upon him with extreme patience and sweetness,' p, nd betook himself to London. But even his scientific colleagues gave him a cold shoulder; and though he was elected minister of a congregation at Hackney, he felt his position to be insecure, and finally determined on emigrating to the United States. He landed in America in 1794; lived quietly with his sons at Northumberland, in Pennsylvania, where his posterity still flourish; and, clear-headed and busy to the last, died on the 6th of February, 1804.

Such were the conditions under which Joseph Priestley did the work which lay before him, and then, as the Norse Sagas say, went out of the story. The work itself was of the most varied kind. No human interest was without its attraction for Priestley, and few men have ever had so many irons in the fire at once; but, though he may have burned his fingers a little, very few who have tried that operation have burned their fingers so little. He made admirable discoveries in science; his philosophical treatises are still well worth reading; his political works are full of insight and replete with the spirit of freedom; and while all these sparks flew off from his anvil, the controversial hammer rained a hailof blows on orthodox priest and bishop. While thus engaged, the kindly, cheerful doctor felt no more wrath or uncharitableness toward his opponents than a smith does toward his iron. But if the iron could only speak! – and the priests and bishops took the point of view of the iron. No doubt what Priestley's friends repeatedly urged upon him – that he would have escaped the heavier trials of his life and done more for the advancement of knowledge, if he had confined himself to his scientific pursuits and let his fellowmen go their way – was true. But it seems to have been Priestley's feeling that he was a man and a citizen before he was a philosopher, and that the duties of the two former positions are at least as imperative as those of the latter. Moreover, there are men (and I think Priestley was one of them) to whom the satisfaction of throwing down a triumphant fallacy is as great as that which attends the discovery of a new truth; who feel better satisfied with the government of the world, when they have been helping Providence by knocking an imposture on the head; and who care even more for freedom of thought than for mere advance of knowledge. These men are the Garnots who organize victory for truth, and they are, at least, as important as the generals who visibly fight her battles in the field.

1 Even Mrs. Priestley, who might be forgiven for regarding the destroyers of her household gods with some asperity, contents herself, in writing to Mrs. Barbauld, with the sarcasm that the Birmingham people "will scarcely find so many respectable characters, a second time, to make a bonfire of."

Priestley's reputation as a man of science rests upon bis numerous and important contributions to the chemistry of gaseous bodies; and to form a just estimate of the value of his work – of the extent to which it advanced the knowledge of fact and the development of sound theoretical views – we must reflect what chemistry was in the first half of the eighteenth century.

The vast science which now passes under that name bad no existence. Air, water, and fire were still counted among the elemental bodies; and though Van Helmont, a century before, had distinguished different kinds of air as *gas ventosum* and *gas sylvestre,* and Boyle and Hales had experimentally defined the physical properties of air, and discriminated some of the various kinds of aeriform bodies, no one suspected the existence of the numerous totally distinct gaseous elements which are now known, or dreamed that the air we breathe and the water we drink are compounds of gaseous elements.

But, in 1754, a young Scotch physician, Dr. Black, made the first . clearing in this tangled backwood of knowledge. And it gives one a wonderful impression of the juvenility of scientific chemistry to think that Lord Brougham, whom so many of us recollect, attended Black's lectures when he was a student in Edinburgh. Black's researches gave the world the novel and startling conception of a gas that was a permanently elastic fluid like air, but that differed from common air in being much heavier, very poisonous, and in having the properties of an acid, capable of neutralizing the strongest alkalies; and it took the world some time to become accustomed to the notion.

A dozen years later, one of the most sagacious and accurate investigators who has adorned this, or any other, country, Henry Cavendish, published a memoir in the "Philosophical Transactions," in which he deals not only with the "fixed air" (now called carbonic acid or carbonic anhydride) of Black, but with "inflammable air," or what we now term hydrogen.

By the rigorous application of weight and measure toall his processes, Cavendish implied the belief subsequently formulated by Lavoisier, that, in chemical processes, matter is neither created nor destroyed, and indicated the path along which all future explorers must travel. Nor did he himself halt until this path led him, in 1784, to the brilliant and fundamental discovery that water is composed of two gases united in fixed and constant proportions.

It is a trying ordeal for any man to be compared with Black and Cavendish, and Priestley cannot be said to stand on their level. Nevertheless his achievements are not only great in themselves, but truly wonderful, if we consider the disadvantages under which he labored. Without the careful scientific training of Black, without the leisure and appliances secured by the wealth of Cavendish, he scaled the walls of science as so many Englishmen have done before and since his day; and trusting to mother wit to supply the place of training, and to ingenuity to create apparatus out of washing tubs, he discovered more new gases than all his predecessors put together had done. He laid the foundations of gas analysis; he discovered the complementary actions of animal and vegetable life upon the constituents of the atmosphere; and, finally, he crowned his work, this day one hundred years ago, by the discovery of that "pure dephlogisticated air" to which the French chemists subsequently gave the name of oxygen. Its importance, as the constituent of the atmosphere which disappears in the processes of respiration and combustion, and is restored by green plants growing in sunshine, was proved somewhat later. For these brilliant discoveries, the Royal Society elected Priestley a fellow and gave him theirmedal, while the Academies of Paris and St. Petersburg conferred their membership upon him. Edinburgh had made him an honorary doctor of laws at an early period of his career; but, I need hardly add, that a man of Priestley's opinions received no recognition from the universities of his own country.

That Priestley's contributions to the knowledge of chemical fact were of the greatest importance, and that they richly deserve all the praise that has been awarded to them, is unquestionable; but it must, at the same time, be admitted that he had no comprehension of the deeper significance of his work; and, so far from contributing anything to the theory of the facts which he discovered, or assisting in their rational explanation, his influence to the end of his life was warmly exerted in favor of error. From first to last, he was a stiff adherent of the phlogiston doctrine which was prevalent when his studies commenced; and, by a curious irony of fate, the man who by the discovery of what he called "dephlogis- ticated air" furnished the essential datum for the true theory of combustion, of respiration, and of the composition of water, to the end of his days fought against the inevitable corollaries from his own labors. His last scientific work, published in 1800, bears the title, "The Doctrine of Phlogiston established, and that of the Composition of Water refuted."

When Priestley commenced his studies, the current belief was that atmospheric air, freed from accidental impurities, is a simple elementary substance, indestructible and unalterable, as water was supposed to be. When a combustible burned, or when an animal breathed in air, it was supposed that a substance, "phlogiston," thematter of heat and light, passed from the burning or breathing body into it, and destroyed its powers of supporting life and combustion. Thus, air contained in a vessel in which a lighted candle had gone out, or a living animal had breathed until it could breathe no longer, was called "phlogisticated." The same result was supposed to be brought about by the addition of what Priestley called "nitrous gas" to common air.

In the course of his researches, Priestley found that the quantity of common air which can thus become "phlogisticated," amounts to about one-fifth the volume of the whole quantity submitted to experiment. Hence it appeared that common air consists, to the extent of four-fifths of its volume, of air which is already "phlogisticated"; while the other fifth is free from phlogiston, or "dephlogisticated." On the other hand, Priestley found that air "phlogisticated" by combustion or respiration could be "dephlogisticated," or have the properties of pure common air restored to it, by the action of green plants in sunshine. The question, therefore, would naturally arise – as common air can be wholly phlogisticated by combustion, and converted into a substance which will no longer support combustion, is it possible to get air that shall be less phlogisticated than common air, and consequently support combustion better than common air does?

Now, Priestley says that, in 1774, the possibility of obtaining air less phlogisticated than common air had not occurred to him.1 But in pursuing his experiments on the evolution of air from various bodies by meansof heat, it happened that, on the 1st of August, 1774, he '

1 "Experiments and Observations on Different Kinds of Air," vol. ii. p. 81.

threw the beat of the sun, by means of a large burning w
glass which he had recently obtained, upon a substance "
which was then called *mercurius calcinatus per se,* and
which is commonly known as red precipitate. i to
! it "I presently found that, by means of this lens, air was
expelled from it very readily. Having got about three or I four times as much as the bulk of my materials, I admitted water to it, and found that it was not imbibed by it. But B what surprised me more than I can well express was that a

candle burned in this air with a remarkably vigorous flame, ' p very much like that enlarged flame with which a candle ; , burns in nitrous air, exposed to iron or lime of sulphur; but ! as I had got nothing like this remarkable appearance from any kind of air besides this particular modification of nitrous air, and I knew no nitrous acid was used in the preparation of *mercurius calcinatus,* I was utterly at a loss how to account for it.

"In this case also, though I did not give sufficient attention to the circumstance at that time, the flame of the candle, besides being larger, burned with more splendor and heat than in that species of nitrous air; and a piece of red- hot wood sparkled in it, exactly like paper dipped in a solution of nitre, and it consumed very fast – an experiment which I had never thought of trying with nitrous air." '

Priestley obtained the same sort of air from red lead, but, as he says himself, he remained in ignorance of the properties of this new kind of air for seven months, or until March, 1775, when he found that the new air behaved with "nitrous gas" in the same way as the deph- logisticated part of common air does;" but that, insteadof being diminished to four-fifths, it almost completely vanished, and, therefore, showed itself to be "between five and six times as good as the best common air I have ever met with." ' As this new air thus appeared to be completely free from phlogiston, Priestley called it "dephlogisticated air."

1 "Experiments and Observations on Different Kinds of Air," vol. ii, pp. 84, 35.
8 Ibid. vol. i. p. 40.

What was the nature of this air? Priestley found that the same kind of air was to be obtained by moistening with the spirit of nitre (which he terms nitrous acid) any kind of earth that is free from phlogiston, and applying heat; and consequently he says: "There remained no doubt on my mind but that the atmospherical air, or the thing that we breathe, consists of the nitrous acid and earth, with so much phlogiston as is necessary to its elasticity, and likewise so much more as is required to bring it from its state of perfect purity to the mean condition in which we find it."

Priestley's view, in fact, is that atmospheric air is a kind of saltpetre, in which the potash is replaced by some unknown earth. And in speculating on the manner in which saltpetre is formed, he enunciates the hypothesis, "that nitre is formed by a real *decomposition of the air itself,* the *bases* that are presented to it having, in such circumstances, a nearer affinity with the spirit of nitre than that kind of earth with which it is united in the atmosphere."'

It would have been hard for the most ingenious person to have wandered further from the truth than Priestley does in this hypothesis; and, though Lavoisier undoubtedly treated Priestley very ill, and pretended to have discovered dephlogisticated air, or oxygen, as he called it, independently, we can almost forgive him when we reflect how different were the ideas which the great French chemist attached to the body which Priestley discovered.

1 "Experiments and Observations on Different Kinds of Air," vol. n. p. 48.

Ibid. p. 55.

Ibid. p. 60. The italics are Priestley's own.

– Science – 2

They are like two navigators of whom the first sees a new country, but takes clouds for mountains and mirage for lowlands; while the second determines its length and breadth, and lays down on a chart its exact place, so that, thenceforth, it serves as a guide to his successors, and becomes a secure outpost whence new explorations may be pushed.

Nevertheless, as Priestley himself somewhere remarks, the first object of physical science is to ascertain facts, and the service which he rendered to chemistry by the definite establishment of a large number of new and fundamentally important facts, is such as to entitle him to a very high place among the fathers of chemical science.

It is difficult to say whether Priestley's philosophical, political, or theological views were most responsible for the bitter hatred which was borne to him by a large body of his countrymen,1 and which found its expression in the malignant insinuations in which Burke, to his

1 "In all the newspapera and most of the periodical publications I was represented as an unbeliever in Revelation, and no better than an atheist." – "Autobiography," Rutt, vol. i. p. 124. "On the walls of houses, etc., and especially where I usually weut, were to be seen, in large characters, "madan Forever; Damn Priestley; No Presbyterianism; Damn The PresbyteRians,' etc., etc.; and, at one time, I was followed by a number of boys, who left their play, repeating what they had seen on the walls, and shouting out, 'Damn Priestley; damn him, damn him, forever, forever,' etc., etc. This was no doubt a lesson which they had been taught by their parents, and what they, I fear, had learned from their superiors/' – "Appeal to the Public on the Subject of the Riots at Birmingham."

everlasting shame, indulged in the House of Commons.

Without containing much that will be new to the readers of Hobbs, Spinoza, Collins, Hume, and Hartley, and, indeed, while making no pretensions to originality, Priestley's "Disquisitions relating to Matter and Spirit," and his "Doctrine of Philosophical Necessity Illustrated," are among the most powerful, clear, and unflinching expositions of materialism and necessarianism which exist in the English language, and are still well worth reading.

Priestley denied the freedom of the will in the sense of its self-determination; he denied the existence of a soul distinct from the body; and as a natural consequence, he denied the natural immortality of man.

In relation to these matters English opinion, a century ago, was very much what it is now.

A man may be a necessarian without incurring graver reproach than that implied in being called a gloomy fanatic, necessarianism, though very shocking, having a note of Calvinistic orthodoxy; but, if a man is a materialist; or, if good authorities say he is and must be so, in spite of his assertion to the contrary; or, if he acknowledge himself unable to Bee good reasons for believing in the natural immortality of man, respectable folk look upon him as an unsafe neighbor of a cashbox, as an actual or potential sensualist, the more virtuous in outward seeming, the more certainly loaded with secret "grave personal sins."

Nevertheless, it is as certain as anything can be, that Joseph Priestley was no gloomy fanatic, but as cheerful and kindly a soul as ever breathed, the idol of children; a man who was hated. only by those who did not knowhim, and who charmed away the bitterest prejudices in personal intercourse; a man who never lost a friend, and the best testimony to whose worth is the generous and tender warmth with which his many friends vied with one another in rendering him substantial help, in all the crises of his career.

The unspotted purity of Priestley's life, the strictness of his performance of every duty, his transparent sincerity, the unostentatious and deep-seated piety which breathes through all his correspondence, are in themselves a sufficient refutation of the hypothesis, invented by bigots to cover uncharitableness, that such opinions as his must arise from moral defects. And his statue will do as good service as the brazen image' that was set upon a pole before the Israelites, if those who have been bitten by the fiery serpents of sectarian hatred, which still haunt this wilderness of a world, are made whole by looking upon the image of a heretic who was yet a saint.

Though Priestley did not believe in the natural immortality of man, he held with an almost naï've realism that man would be raised from the dead by a direct exertion of the power of God, and thenceforward be immortal. And 'it may be as well for those who may be shocked by this doctrine to know that views substantially identical with Priestley's have been advocated, since his time, by two prelates of the Anglican Church: by Dr. Whately, Archbishop of Dublin, in his well- known "Essays";1 and by Dr. Courtenay, Bishop of Kingston in Jamaica, the first edition of whose remarkable book "On the Future States," dedicated to Archbishop Whately, was published in 1843 and the second in 1857. According to Bishop Courtenay,

1 First Series. "On Some of the Peculiarities of the Christian Religion." Essay I.: "Revelation of a Future State."

"The death of the body will cause a cessation of all the activity of the mind by way of natural consequence; to continue forever Unless the Creator should interfere."

And again: –

"The natural end of human existence is the 'first death,' the dreamless slumber of the grave, wherein man lies spellbound, soul and body, under the dominion of sin and death – that whatever modes of conscious existence, whatever future states of 'life' or of 'torment' beyond Hades are reserved for man, are results of our blessed Lord's victory over sin and death; that the resurrection of the dead must be preliminary to their entrance into either of the future states, and that the nature and even existence of these states, and even the mere fact that there is a futurity of consciousness, can be known *only* through God's revelation of Himself in the Person and the Gospel of His Son." – Page 389.

And now hear Priestley: –

"Man, according to this system (of materialism), is no more than we now see of him. His being commences at the time of his conception, or perhaps at an earlier period. The corporeal and mental faculties, in being in the same substance, grow, ripen, and decay together; and whenever the system is dissolved it continues in a state of dissolution till it shall please that Almighty Being who called it into existence to restore it to life again." – "Matter and Spirit," page 49.

And again: –

"The doctrine of the Scripture is, that God made man of the dust of the ground, and by simply animating this organized matter made man that living percipient and intelligentbeing that he is. According to Kevelation, *death* is a state of rest and insensibility, and our only though sure hope of a future life is founded on the doctrine of the resurrection of the whole man at some distant period; this assurance being sufficiently confirmed to us both by the evident tokens of a Divine commission attending the persons who delivered the doctrine, and especially by the actual resurrection of Jesus Christ, which is more authentically attested than any other fact in history." – Ibid., page 247.

We all know that "a saint in crape is twice a saint in lawn"; but it is not yet admitted that the views which are consistent with such saintliness in lawn, become diabolical when held by a mere dissenter.'

I am not here either to defend or to attack Priestley's philosophical views, and I cannot say that I am personally disposed to attach much value to episcopal authority in philosophical questions; but it seems right to call attention to the fact that those of Priestley's opinions which have brought most odium upon him have been openly promulgated, without challenge, by persons occupying the highest positions in the State Church.

I must confess that what interests me most about Priestley's materialism is the evidence that he saw dimly the seed of destruction which such materialism carries within its own bosom. In the course of his reading forhis "History of Discoveries relating to Vision, Light, and Colors," he had come upon the speculations of Boscovich and Michell, and had been led to admit the sufficiently obvious truth that our knowledge of matter is a knowledge of its properties; and that of its substance – if it have a substance – we know nothing. And this led to the further admission that, so far as we can know, there may be no difference between the substance of matter and the substance of spirit ("Disquisitions," page 16). A step further would have shown Priestley that his materialism was, essentially, very little different from the Idealism of his contemporary, the Bishop of Cloyne.

1 Not only is Priestley at one with Bishop Courtenay in this matter, but with Hartley and Bonnet, both of them stout champions of Christianity. Moreover, Archbishop

Whately's essay is little better than an expansion of the first paragraph of Hume's famous essay on the Immortality of the Soul: "By the mere light of reason it seems difficult to prove the immortality of the soul; the arguments for it are commonly derived either from metaphysical topics, or moral, or physical. But it is in reality the Gospel, and the Gospel alone, that has brought *life and immortality to light.*" It is impossible to imagine that a man of Whately's tastes and acquirements had not read Hume or Hartley, though he refers to neither.

As Priestley's philosophy is mainly a clear statement of the views of the deeper thinkers of his day, so are his political conceptions based upon those of Locke. Locke's aphorism that "the end of government is the good of mankind," is thus expanded by Priestley:

"It must necessarily be understood, therefore, whether it be expressed or not, that all people live in society for their mutual advantage; so that the good and happiness of the members, that is, of the majority of the members, of any state, is the great standard by which everything relating to that state must finally be determined." '

The little sentence here interpolated, "that is, of the majority of the members of any state," appears to be that passage which suggested to Bentham, according to his own acknowledgment, the famous "greatest happiness" formula, which, by substituting "happiness" for "good," has converted a noble into an ignoble principle. But I do not call to mind that there is any utterance in Locke quite so outspoken as the following passage in the "Essay on the First Principles of Government." After laying down, as "a fundamental maxim in all Governments," the proposition that "kings, senators, and nobles" are "the servants of the public," Priestley goes on to say:

1 "Essay on the First Principles of Government," Second Edition, 1771, p. 13.

"But in the largest states, if the abuses of the government should at any time be great and manifest; if the servants of the people, forgetting their masters and their masters' interest, should pursue a separate one of their own; if, instead of considering that they are made for the people, they should consider the people as made for them; if the oppressions and violation of right should be great, flagrant, and universally resented; if the tyrannical governors should have no friends but a few sycophants, who had long preyed upon the vitals of their fellow-citizens, and who might be expected to desert a government whenever their interests should be detached from it: if, in consequence of these circumstances, it should become manifest that the risk which would be run in attempting a revolution would be trifling, and the evils which might be apprehended from it were far less than those which were actually suffered and which were daily increasing; in the name of God, I ask, what principles are those which ought to restrain an injured and insulted people from asserting their natural rights, and from changing or even punishing their governors – that is, their servants – who had abused their trust, or from altering the whole form of their government, if it appeared to be of a structure so liable to abuse?"

As a Dissenter, subject to the operation of the Corporation and Test Acts, and as a Unitarian excluded from the benefit of the Toleration Act, it is not surprising to find that Priestley had very definite opinions about Ecclesiastical Establishments; the only wonder is that these opinions were so moderate as the following passages show them to have been:

"Ecclesiastical authority may have been necessary in the infant state of society, and, for the same reason, it may perhaps continue to be, in some degree, necessary as long as society is imperfect; and therefore may not be entirely abolished till civil governments have arrived at a much greater degree of perfection. If, therefore, I were asked whether I should approve of the immediate dissolution of all the ecclesiastical establishments in Europe, I should answer, No. . . . Let experiment be first made of *alterations,* or, which is the same thing, of *better establishments* than the present. Let them be reformed in many essential articles, and then not thrown aside entirely till it be found by experience that no good can be made of them."

Priestley goes on to suggest four such reforms of a capital nature:

"1. Let the Articles of Faith to be subscribed by candidates for the ministry be greatly reduced. In the formulary of the Church of England, might not thirty-eight out of the thirty-nine be very well spared ? It is a reproach to any Christian establishment if every man cannot claim the benefit of it who can say that he believes in the religion of Jesus Christ as it is set forth in the New Testament. You say the terms are so general that even Deists would quibble and insinuate themselves. I answer that all the articles which are subscribed at present by no means exclude Deists who will prevaricate; and upon this scheme you would at least exclude fewer honest men." '

The second reform suggested is the equalization, in proportion to work done, of the stipends of the clergy; the third, the exclusion of the Bishops from Parliament; and the fourth, complete toleration, so that every man may enjoy the rights of a citizen, and be qualified to serve his country, whether he belong to the Established Church or not.

1 "Utility of Establishments," in "Essay on First Principles of Government," p. 198, 1771.

Opinions such as those I have quoted, respecting the duties and the responsibilities of governors, are the commonplaces of modern Liberalism; and Priestley's views on Ecclesiastical Establishments would, I fear, meet with but a cool reception, as altogether too conservative, from a large proportion of the lineal descendants of the people who taught their children to cry "Damn Priestley"; and with that love for the practical application of science, which is the source of the greatness of Birmingham, tried to set fire to the doctor's house with sparks from his own electrical machine; thereby giving the man they called an incendiary and raiser of sedition against Church and King an appropriately experimental illustration of the nature of arson and riot.

If I have succeeded in putting before you the main features of Priestley's work, its value will become apparent when we compare the condition of the English nation, as he knew it, with its present state.

The fact that France has been for eighty-five years trying, without much success, to right herself after the great storm of the Revolution, is not infrequently cited among us as an indication of some inherent incapacity for self-government among the French people. I think, however, that Englishmen who argue thus forget that, from the meeting of the Long Parliament, in 1640, to the last Stuart rebellion, in 1745, is a hundred and five years, and that, in the middle of the last century, we had but just safely freed ourselves from our Bourbons and all that they represented. The corruption of our state was as bad as that of the Second Empire. Bribery was the instrument of government, and peculation its reward. Four-fifths of the seats in the House of Commons were more or less openly dealt with as property. A minister had to consider the state of the vote market, and the sovereign secured a sufficiency of "king's friends" by payments allotted with retail, rather than royal, sagacity.

Barefaced and brutal immorality and intemperance pervaded the land, from the highest to the lowest classes of society. The Established Church was torpid, as far as it was not a scandal; but those who dissented from it came within the meshes of the Act of Uniformity, the Test Act, and the Corporation Act. By law, such a man as Priestley, being a Unitarian, could neither teach nor preach, and was liable to ruinous fines and long imprisonment.1 In those days the guns that were pointed by the Church against the Dissenters were shotted. The law was a cesspool of iniquity and cruelty. Adam Smith was a new prophet whom few regarded, and commerce was hampered by idiotic impediments, and ruined by still more absurd help, on the part of government.

Birmingham, though already the centre of a considerable industry, was a mere village as compared with its present extent. People who travelled went about armed, by reason of the abundance of highwaymen and the paucity and inefficiency of the police. Stage coaches had not reached Birmingham, and it took three days to get toLondon. Even canals were a recent and much opposed invention.

1 In 1732 Doddridge was cited for teaching, without the Bishop's leava, at Northampton.

Newton had laid the foundation of a mechanical conception of the physical universe; Hartley, putting a modern face upon ancient materialism, had extended that mechanical conception to psychology; Linnaeus and Haller were beginning to introduce method and order into the chaotic accumulation of biological facts. But those parts of physical science which deal with heat, electricity, and magnetism, and above all, chemistry, in the modern sense, can hardly be said to have had an existence. No one knew that two of the old elemental bodies, air and water, are compounds, and that a third, fire, is not a substance but a motion. The great industries that have grown out of the applications of modern scientific discoveries had no existence, and the man who should have foretold their coming into being in the days of his son would have been regarded as a mad enthusiast.

In common with many other excellent persons, Priestley believed that man is capable of reaching, and will eventually attain, perfection. If the temperature of space presented no obstacle, I should be glad to entertain the same idea; but, judging from the past progress of our species, I am afraid that the globe will have cooled down so far, before the advent of this natural millennium, that we shall be, at best, perfected Esquimaux. For all practical purposes, however, it is enough that man may visibly improve his condition in the course of a century or so. And, if the picture of the state of things in Priestley's time, which I have just drawn, have any pretence to accuracy, I think it must be admitted that there has been a considerable change for the better.

I need not advert to the well-worn topic of material

advancement, in a place in which the very atones testify to that progress – in the town of Watt and of Boulton. I will only remark, in passing, that material advancement has its share in moral and intellectual progress. Becky Sharp's acute remark that it is not difficult to be virtuous on ten thousand a year has its application to nations; and it is futile to expect a hungry and squalid population to be anything but violent and gross. But as regards other than material welfare, although perfection ia not yet in sight – even from the masthead – it is surely true that things are much better than they were.

Take the upper and middle classes as a whole, and it may be said that open immorality and gross intemperance have vanished. Four and six bottle men are as extinct as the dodo. Women of good repute do not gamble, and talk modelled upon Dean Swift's "Art of Polite Conversation" would be tolerated in no decent kitchen.

Members of the legislature are not to be bought; and constituents are awakening to the fact that votes must not be sold – even for such trifles as rabbits and tea and cake. Political power has passed into the hands of the masses of the people. Those whom Priestley calls their servants have recognized their position, and have requested the master to be so good as to go to school and fit himself for the administration of his property. In ordinary life, no civil disability attaches to any one on theological grounds, and high offices of the state are open to Papist, Jew, and Secularist.

Whatever men's opinions as to the policy of Establishment, no one can hesitate to admit that the clergy of the Church are men of pure life and conversation, zealous inthe discharge of their duties; and at present, apparently, more bent on prosecuting one another than on meddling with Dissenters. Theology itself has broadened so much that Anglican divines put forward doctrines more liberal than those of Priestley; and, in our state-supported churches, one listener may hear a sermon to which Bossuet might have given his approbation, while another may hear a discourse in which Socrates would find nothing new.

But great as these changes may be, they sink into insignificance beside the progress of physical science, whether we consider the improvement of methods of investigation, or the increase in bulk of solid knowledge. Consider that the labors of Laplace, of Young, of Davy, and of Faraday; of Cuvier, of Lamarck, and of Robert Brown; of Von Baer, and of Schwann; of Smith and of Hutton, have all been carried on since Priestley discovered oxygen; and consider that they are now things of the past, concealed by the industry of those who have built upon them, as the first founders of a coral reef are hidden beneath the life's work of their successors; consider that the methods of physical science are slowly spreading into all investigations, and that proofs as valid as those required by her canons of investigation are being demanded of all doctrines which ask for men's assent; and you will have a faint image of the astounding difference in this respect between the nineteenth century and the eighteenth.

If we ask what is the deeper meaning of all these vast changes, I think there can be but one reply. They mean that reason has asserted and exercised her primacy over all provinces of human activity; that ecclesiasticalauthority has been relegated to its proper place; that the good of the governed has been finally recognized as the end of government, and the complete responsibility of governors to the people as its means; and that the dependence of natural phenomena in general on the laws of action of what we call matter has become an axiom.

But it was to bring these things about, and to enforce the recognition of these truths, that Joseph Priestley labored. If the nineteenth century is other and better than the eighteenth, it is, in great measure, to him, and to such men as he, that we owe the change. If the twentieth century is to be better than the nineteenth, it will be because there are among us men who walk in Priestley's footsteps.

Such men are not those whom their own generation delights to honor; such men, in fact, rarely trouble themselves about honor, but ask, in another spirit than Fal- staff's, "What is honor? Who hath it? He that died o' Wednesday." But whether Priestley's lot be theirs, and a future generation, in justice and in gratitude, set up their statues; or whether their names and fame are blotted out from remembrance, their work will live as long as time endures. To all eternity, the sum of truth and right will have been increased by their means; to all eternity, falsehood and injustice will be the weaker because they have lived.

3

SECTION 3

II
ON THE EDUCATIONAL VALUE OF THE NATURAL HISTORY SCIENCES
[1854]

THE subject to which I have to beg your attention during the ensuing hour is "The Relation of Physiological Science to other branches of Knowledge."

Had circumstances permitted of the delivery, in their strict logical order, of that series of discourses of which the present lecture is a member, I should have preceded my friend and colleague, Mr. Henfrey, who addressed you on Monday last; but while, for the sake of that order, I must beg you to suppose that this discussion of the Educational bearings of Biology in general *does* precede that of Special Zoology and Botany, I am rejoiced to be able to take advantage of the light thus already thrown upon the tendency and methods of Physiological Science.

Regarding Physiological Science, then, in its widest sense – as the equivalent of *Biology* – the Science of Individual Life – we have to consider in succession:

1. Its position and scope as a branch of knowledge.
2. Its value as a means of mental discipline.
3. Its worth as practical information. And lastly,
4. A-t what period it may best be made a branch of Education.

Our conclusions on the first of these heads must depend, of course, upon the nature of the subject-matter of Biology; and I think a few preliminary considerations will place before you in a clear light the vast difference which exists between the living bodies with which Physiological science is concerned, and the remainder of the universe: – between the phenomena of Number and Space, of Physical and of Chemical force, on the one hand, and those of Life on the other.

The mathematician, the physicist, and the chemist contemplate things in a condition of rest; they look upon a state of equilibrium as that to which all bodies normally tend.

The mathematician does not suppose that a quantity will alter, or that a given point in space will change, its direction, with regard to another point, spontaneously. And it is the same with the physicist. When Newton saw the apple fall, he concluded at once that the act of falling was not the result of any power inherent in the apple, but that it was the result of the action of something else on the apple. In a similar manner, all physical force is regarded as the disturbance of an equilibrium to which things tended before its exertion – to which they will tend again after its cessation.

The chemist equally regards chemical change in a body as the effect of the action of something external to the body changed. A chemical compound once formed would persist forever, if no alteration took place in surrounding conditions.

But to the student of Life the aspect of Nature is reversed. Here, incessant, and, so far as we know, spontaneous change is the rule, rest the exception – the anomaly to be accounted for. Living things have no inertia, and tend to no equilibrium.

Permit me, however, to give more force and clearness to these somewhat abstract considerations by an illustration or two.

Imagine a vessel full of water, at the ordinary temperature, iti an atmosphere saturated with vapor. The *quantity* and the *figure* of that water will not change, so far as we know, forever.

Suppose a lump of gold be thrown into the vessel – motion and disturbance of figure exactly proportional to the momentum of the gold will take place. But after a time the effects of this disturbance will subside – equilibrium will be restored, and the water will return to its passive state.

Expose the water to cold, it will solidify, and in so doing its particles will arrange themselves in definite crystalline shapes. But once formed, these crystals change no further.

Again, substitute for the lump of gold some substance capable of entering into chemical relations with the water – say, a mass of that substance which is called "protein" – the substance of flesh – a very considerable disturbance of equilibrium will take place – all sorts of chemical compositions and decompositions will occur; but in the end, as before, the result will be the resumption of a condition of rest.

Instead of such a mass of *dead* protein, however, take a particle of *living* protein – one of those minute microscopic living things which throng our pools, and are known as Infusoria – such a creature, for instance, as a Euglena – and place it in our vessel of water. It isa round mass provided with a long filament, and, except in this peculiarity of shape, presents no appreciable physical or chemical difference whereby it might be distinguished from the particle of dead protein.

But the difference in the phenomena to which it will give rise is immense: in the first place it will develop a vast quantity of physical force – cleaving the water in all directions with considerable rapidity by means of the vibrations of the long filament or cilium.

Nor is the amount of chemical energy which the little creature possesses less striking. It is a perfect laboratory in itself, and it will act and react upon the water and the matters contained therein; converting them into new compounds resembling its own substance, and at the same time giving up portions of its own substance which have become effete.

Furthermore, the Euglena will increase in size; but this increase is by no means unlimited, as the increase of a crystal might be. After it has grown to a certain extent it divides, and each portion assumes the form of the original, and proceeds to repeat the process of growth and division.

Nor is this all. For after a series of such divisions and subdivisions, these minute points assume a totally new form, lose their long tails – round themselves, and secrete a sort of envelope or box, in which they remain shut up for a time, eventually to resume, directly or indirectly, their primitive mode of existence.

Now, so far as we know, there is no natural limit to the existence of the Euglena, or of any other living germ. A living species once launched into existence tends to live forever.

Consider how widely different this living particle is from the dead atoms with which the physicist and chemist have to do!

The particle of gold falls to the bottom and rests – the particle of dead protein decomposes and disappears – it also rests: but the *living* protein mass neither tends to exhaustion of its forces nor to any permanency of form, but is essentially distinguished as a disturber of equilibrium so far as force is concerned – as undergoing continual metamorphosis and change, in point of form.

Tendency to equilibrium of force and to permanency of form, then, are the characters of that portion of the universe which does not live – the domain of the chemist and physicist.

Tendency to disturb existing equilibrium – to take on forms which succeed one another in definite cycles – is the character of the living world.

What is the cause of this wonderful difference between the dead particle and the living particle of matter appearing in other respects identical? that difference to which we give the name of Life?

I, for one, cannot tell you. It may be that, by and by, philosophers will discover some higher laws of which the facts of life are particular cases – very possibly they will find out some bond between physico-chemical phenomena on the one hand, and vital phenomena on the other. At present, however, we assuredly know of none; and I think we shall exercise a wise humility in confessing that, for us at least, this successive assumption of different states – (external conditions remaining the same) – this *spontaneity of action* – if I may use a term which implies more than I would be answerable for – which constitutes so vast and plain a practical distinction between living bodies and those which do not live, is an ultimate fact; indicating as such the existence of a broad line of demarcation between the subject-matter of Biological and that of all other sciences.

For I would have it understood that this simple Eu- glena is the type of *all* living things, so far as the distinction between these and inert matter is concerned. That cycle of changes, which is constituted by perhaps not more than two or three steps in the Euglena, is as clearly manifested in the multitudinous stages through which the germ of an oak or of a man passes. Whatever forms the Living Being may take on, whether simple or complex, *production, growth, reproduction,* are the phenomena which distinguish it from that which does not live.

If this be true, it is clear that the student, in passing from the physico-chemical to the physiological sciences, enters upon a totally new order of facts; and it will next be for us to consider how far these new facts involve *new* methods, or require a modification of those with which he is already acquainted. Now a great deal is said about the peculiarity of the scientific method in general, and of the different methods which are pursued in the different sciences. The Mathematics are said to have one special method; Physics another, Biology a third, and so forth. For my own part, I must confess that I do not understand this phraseology.

So far as I can arrive at any clear comprehension of the matter, Science is not, as many would seem to suppose, a modification of the black art, suited to the tastes of the nineteenth century, and flourishing mainly in consequence of the decay of the Inquisition.

Science is, I believe, nothing but *trained and organized common-sense,* differing from the latter only as a veteran may differ from a raw recruit: and its methods differ from those of common-sense only so far as the guardsman's cut and thrust differ from the manner in which a savage wields his club. The primary power is the same in each case, and perhaps the untutored savage has the more brawny arm of the two. The *real* advantage lies in the point and polish of the swordsman's weapon; in the trained eye quick to spy out the weakness of the adversary; in the ready hand prompt to follow it on the instant. But, after all, the sword exercise is only the hewing and poking of the clubman developed and perfected.

So, the vast results obtained by Science are won by no mystical faculties, by no mental processes, other than those which are practiced by every one of us, in the humblest and meanest affairs of life. A detective policeman discovers a burglar from the marks made by his shoe, by a mental process identical with that by which Cuvier restored the extinct animals of Montmartre from fragments of their bones. Nor does that process of induction and deduction by which a lady, finding a stain of a peculiar kind upon her dress, concludes that somebody has upset the inkstand thereon, differ in any way, in kind, from that by which Adams and Leverrier discovered a new planet.

The man of science, in fact, simply uses with scrupulous exactness the methods which we all, habitually and at every moment, use carelessly; and the man of business must as much avail himself of the scientific method – must be as truly a man of science – as the veriest bookworm of us all; though I have no doubt that the man of businesswill find himself out to be a philosopher with as much surprise as M. Jourdain exhibited when he discovered that he had been all his life talking prose. If, however, there be no real -difference between the methods of science and those of common life, it would seem, on the face of the matter, highly improbable that there should be any difference between the methods of the different sciences; nevertheless, it is constantly taken for granted that there is a very wide difference between the Physiological and other sciences in point of method.

In the first place it is said – and I take this point first, because the imputation is too frequently admitted by Physiologists themselves – that Biology differs from the Physico-chemical and Mathematical sciences in being "inexact."

Now, this phrase "inexact" must refer either to the *methods* or to the *results* of Physiological science.

It cannot be correct to apply it to the methods; for, as I hope to show you by and by, these are identical in all sciences, and whatever is true of Physiological method is true of Physical and Mathematical method.

Is it then the *results* of Biological science which are "inexact"? I think not. If I say that respiration is performed by the lungs; that digestion is effected in the stomach; that the eye is the organ of sight; that the jaws of a vertebrated animal never open sidewise, but always up and down; while those of an annulose animal always open sidewise, and never up and down – I am enumerating propositions which are as exact as anything in Euclid. How then has this notion of the inexactness of Biological science come about? I believe from two causes: first, because, in consequence of the great complexity of thescience and the multitude of interfering conditions, we are very often only enabled to predict approximately what will occur under given circumstances; and secondly, because, on account of the comparative youth of the Physiological sciences, a great many of their laws are still imperfectly worked out. But, in an educational point of view, it is most important to distinguish between the essence of a science and the accidents which surround it; and essentially, the methods and results of Physiology are as exact as those of Physics or Mathematics.

It is said that the Physiological method is especially *comparative;*' and this dictum also finds favor in the eyes of many. I should be sorry to suggest that the speculators on scientific classification have been misled by the accident of the name of one leading branch of Biology   *Comparative Anatomy ;* but I would ask whether *comparison,* and that classification which is the result of comparison, are not the essence of every science whatsoever? How is it possible to discover a relation of cause and effect of *any* kind without comparing a series of cases together in which the supposed cause and effectoccur singly, or combined ? So far from comparison being in any way peculiar to Biological science, it is, I think, the essence of every science.

1 "In the third place, we have to review the method of Comparison, which is so specially adapted to the study of living bodies, and by which, above all others, that study must be advanced. In Astronomy, this method is necessarily inapplicable; and it is not till we arrive at Chemistry that this third means of investigation can be used, and then only in subordination to the two others. It is in the study, both statical and dynamical, of living bodies that it first acquires its full development; and its use elsewhere can be only through its application here." – Comte's "Positive Philosophy," translated by Miss Mar- tineau. Vol. i. p. 372.

By what method does M. Comte suppose that the equality or inequality of forces and quantities and the dissimilarity or similarity of forms – points of some slight importance not only in Astronomy and Physics, but even in Mathematics – are ascertained, if not by Comparison?

A speculative philosopher again tells us that the Biological sciences are distinguished by being sciences of observation ana not 01 experiment 1'

Of all the strange assertions into which speculation without practical acquaintance with a subject may lead even an able man, I think this is the very strangest. Physiology not an experimental science ? Why, there is not a function of a single organ in the body which has not been determined wholly and solely by experiment? How did Harvey determine the nature of the circulation, except by experiment? How did Sir Charles Bell determine the functions of the roots of the spinal nerves, save by experiment ? How do we know the use of a nerve at all, except by experiment? Nay, how do you know even that your eye is your seeing apparatus, unless you make the experiment of shutting it; or that your ear is your hearing apparatus, unless you close it up and thereby discover that you become deaf ?

It would really be much more true to say that Physiology is *the* experimental science *par excellence* of all sciences; that in which there is least to be learned by mereobservation, and that which affords the greatest field for the exercise of those faculties which characterize the experimental philosopher. I confess, if any one were to ask me for a model application of the logic of experiment, I should know no better work to put into his hands than Bernard's late Researches on the Functions of the Liver.1

1 "Proceeding to the second class of means – Experiment cannot but be less and less decisive, in proportion to the complexity o$ the phenomena to be explored ; and therefore we saw this resource to be less effectual in chemistry than in physics: and we now find that it is eminently useful in chemistry in comparison with physiology. *In fact, the nature of the phenomena seems to ojjer almost insurmountable impediments to any extensive and prolific application of such a procedure in biology."* – Comte, vol. i. p. 367.

M. Comte, as his manner is, contradicts himself two pages further on, but that will hardly relieve him from the responsibility of such a paragraph as the above.

– Science – 3

Not to give this lecture a too controversial tone, however, I must only advert to one more doctrine, held by a thinker of our own age and country, whose opinions are worthy of all respect. It is, that the Biological sciences differ from all others, inasmuch as in *them* classification takes place by type and not by definition."

It is said, in short, that a natural-history class is not capable of being defined – that the class Rosaceas, for instance, or the class of Fishes, is not accurately and absolutely definable, inasmuch as its members will present exceptions to every possible definition; and that the members of the class are united together only by the circumstance that they are all more like some imaginary average rose or average fish than they resemble anything else.

But here, as before, I think the distinction has arisen entirely from confusing a transitory imperfection with anessential character. So long as our information concerning them is imperfect, we class all objects together according to resemblances which we *feel,* but cannot *define;* we group them round *types,* in short. Thus if you ask an ordinary person what kinds of animals there are, he will probably say, beasts, birds, reptiles, fishes, insects, etc. Ask him to define a beast from a reptile, and he cannot do it; but he says, things like a cow or a horse are beasts, and things like a frog or a lizard are reptiles. You see *he does* class by type, and not by definition. But how does this classification differ from that of the scientific Zoologist ? How does the meaning of the scientific class-name of "Mammalia" differ from the unscientific of "Beasts"?

1 *NouveUe Function du Foie considers comme organs producteur de matiere sucree chez VHomme et les Animaux, par* M. Claude Bernard.

"*Natural Groups given by Type, not by Definition.* . . . The class ia steadily fixed, though not precisely limited; it is given, though not circumscribed; it is determined, not by a boundary-line without, but by a central point within; not by what it strictly excludes, but what it eminently includes; by an example, not by a precept; in short, instead of Definition we have a *Type* for our director. A type is an example of any class, for instance, a species of a genus, which is considered as eminently possessing the characters of the class. All the species which have a greater affinity with this type species than with any others, form the genus, and are ranged about it, deviating from it in various directions and different degrees." – Whewell, "The Philosophy of the Inductive Sciences," vol. i. pp. 476, 477.

Why, exactly because the former depends on a definition, the latter on a type. The class Mammalia is scientifically defined as "all animals which have a verte-brated skeleton and suckle their young." Here is no reference to type, but a definition rigorous enough for a geometrician. And such is the character which every scientific naturalist recognizes as that to which his classes must aspire – knowing, as he does, that classification by type is simply an acknowledgment of ignorance and a temporary device.

So much in the way of negative argument as against the reputed differences between Biological and other methods. No such differences, I believe, really exist. The subject-matter of Biological science is different from that of other sciences, but the methods of all are Identical; and these methods are:

1. *Observation* of facts – including under this head that *artificial observation* which is called *experiment.*

2. That process of tying up similar facts into bundles, ticketed and ready for use, which is called *Comparison* and *Classification* – the results of the process, the ticketed bundles, being named *General propositions.*

3. *Deduction,* which takes us from the general proposition to facts again – teaches us, if I may so say, to anticipate from the ticket what is inside the bundle. And finally –

4. *Verification,* which is the process of ascertaining whether, in point of fact, our anticipation is a correct one.

Such are the methods of all science whatsoever; but perhaps you will permit me to give you an illustration of their employment in the science of Life; and I will take as a special case the establishment of the doctrine of the *Circulation of the Blood.*

In this case, *simple observation* yields us a knowledge of the existence of the blood from some accidental hemorrhage, we will say; we may even grant that it informs us of the localization of this blood in particular vessels, the heart, etc., from some accidental cut or the like. It teaches also the existence of a pulse in various parts of the body, and acquaints us with the structure of the heart and vessels.

Here, however, *simple observation* stops, and we must have recourse to *experiment.*

You tie a vein, and you find that the blood accumulates on the side of the ligature opposite the heart. You tie an artery, and you find that the blood accumulates on the side near the heart. Open the chest, and you see the heart contracting with great force. Make openings into its principal cavities, and you will find that all the blood flows out, and no more pressure is exerted on either side of the arterial or venous ligature.

Now all these facts, taken together, constitute the evidence that the blood is propelled by the heart through the arteries, and returns by the veins – that, in short, the blood circulates.

Suppose our experiments and observations have been made on horses, then we group and ticket them into a genera] proposition, thus – *all horses have a circulation of their blood.*

Henceforward a horse is a sort of indication or label, telling us where we shall find a peculiar series of phenomena called the circulation of the blood.

Here is our *general proposition,* then.

How, and when, are we justified in making our next step – a *deduction* from it?

Suppose our physiologist, whose experience is limited to horses, meets with a zebra for the first time – will he suppose that this generalization holds good for zebras also ?

That depends very much on his turn of mind. But we will suppose him to be a bold man. He will say, "The zebra is certainly not a horse, but it is very like one – so like that it must be the 'ticket' or mark of a blood-circulation also; and, I conclude that the zebra has a circulation."

That is a deduction, a very fair deduction, but by no means to be considered scientifically secure. This last quality in fact can only be given by *verification* – that is, by making a zebra the subject of all the experiments performed on the horse. Of course, in the present case, the *deduction* would be *confirmed* by this process of verification, and the result would be, not merely a positive widening of knowledge, but a fair increase of confidence in the truth of one's generalizations in other cases.

Thus, having settled the point in the zebra and horse, our philosopher would have great confidence in the existence of a circulation in the ass. Nay, I fancy most persons would excuse him, if in this case he did not take the trouble to go through the process of verification at all; and it would not be without a parallel in the history of the human mind if our imaginary physiologist now maintained that he was acquainted with asinine circulation *d priori.*

However, if J might impress any caution upon your minds, it is, the utterly conditional nature of all our knowledge – the danger of neglecting the process of verification under any circumstances; and the film upon which we rest, the moment our deductions carry us beyond the reach of this great process of verification. There is no better instance of this than is afforded by the history of our knowledge of the circulation of the blood in the animal kingdom until the year 1824. In every animal possessing a circulation at all, which had been observed up to that time, the current of the blood was known to take one definite and invariable direction. Now, there is a class of animals called *Ascidians,* which possess a heart and a circulation, and, up to the period of which I speak, no one would have dreamed of questioning the propriety of the deduction that these creatures have a circulation in one direction; nor would any one have thought it worth while to verify the point. But, in that year, M. von Hasselt, happening to examine a transparent animal of this class, found, to his infinite surprise

that after the heart had beat a certain number of times it stopped, and then began beating the opposite way – so as to reverse the course of the current, which returned by and by to its original direction.

I have myself timed the heart of these little animals. I found it as regular as possible in its periods of reversal: and I know no spectacle in the animal kingdom more wonderful than that which it presents – all the more wonderful that to this day it remains a unique fact, peculiar to this class among the whole animated world. At the same time I know of no more striking case of the necessity of the *verification* of even those deductions which seem founded on the widest and safest inductions.

Such are the methods of Biology – methods which are obviously identical with those of all other sciences, and therefore wholly incompetent to form the ground of any distinction between it and them.'

But I shall be asked at once, Do you mean to say that there is no difference between the habit of mind of a mathematician and that of a naturalist? Do you imagine that Laplace might have been put into the Jardin des Plantes, and Cuvier into the Observatory, with equal advantage to the progress of the sciences they professed ?

To which I would reply that nothing could be further from my thoughts. But different habits and various special tendencies of two sciences do not imply different methods. The mountaineer and the man of the plains have very different habits of progression, and each wouldbe at a loss in the other's place; but the method of progression, by putting one leg before the other, is the same in each case. Every step of each is a combination of a lift and a push; but the mountaineer lifts more and the lowlander pushes more. And I think the case of two sciences resembles this.

1 Save for the pleasure of doing so, I need hardly point out my obligations to Mr. J. S. Mill's "System of Logic," in this view of scientific method.

I do not question for a moment that while the Mathematician is busy with deductions *from* general propositions, the Biologist is more especially occupied with observation, comparison, and those processes which lead *to* general propositions. All I wish to insist upon is that this difference depends not on any fundamental distinction in the sciences themselves, but on the accidents of their subject-matter, of their relative complexity, and consequent relative perfection.

The Mathematician deals with two properties of objects only, number and extension, and all the inductions he wants have been formed and finished ages ago. He is occupied now with nothing but deduction and verification.

The Biologist deals with a vast number of properties of objects, and his inductions will not be completed, I fear, for ages to come; but when they are, his science will be as deductive and as exact as the Mathematics themselves.

Such is the relation of Biology to those sciences which deal with objects having fewer properties than itself. But as the student, in reaching Biology, looks back upon sciences of a less complex and therefore more perfect nature; so, on the other hand, does he look forward to other more complex and less perfect branches of knowledge. Biology deals only with living beings as isolated things – treats only of the life of the individual. but there is a higher division of science still, which considers living beings as aggregates – which deals with the relation of living beings one to another – the science which *observes* men – whose *experiments* are made by nations one upon another, in battlefields – whose *general propositions* are embodied in history, morality, and religion – whose *deductions* lead to our happiness or our misery – and whose *verifications* so often come too late, and serve only

"To point a moral or adorn a tale" –

I mean the science of Society or *Sociology.*

I think it is one of the grandest features of Biology that it occupies this central position in human knowledge. There is no side of the human mind which physiological study leaves uncultivated. Connected by innumerable ties with abstract science, Physiology is yet in the most intimate relation with humanity; and by teaching us that law and order, and a definite scheme of development, regulate even the strangest and wildest manifestations of individual life, she prepares the student to look for a goal even amid the erratic wanderings of mankind, and to believe that history offers something more than an entertaining chaos – a journal of a toilsome, tragi-comic march nowhither.

The preceding considerations have, I hope, served to indicate the replies which befit the first two of the questions which 1 set before you at starting; viz., What is the range and position of Physiological Science as a branch of knowledge, and what is its value as a means of mental discipline ?

Its *subject-matter* is a large moiety of the universe – its

position is midway between the physico-chemical and the social sciences. Its *value* as a branch of discipline is partly that which it has in common with all sciences – the training and strengthening of common-sense; partly that which is more peculiar to itself – the great exercise which it affords to the faculties of observation and comparison; and, I may add, the *exactness* of knowledge which it requires on the part of those among its votaries who desire to extend its boundaries.

If what has been said as to the position and scope of Biology be correct, our third question – What is the practical value of physiological instruction? – might, one would think, be left to answer itself.

On other grounds even, were mankind deserving of the title "rational," which they arrogate to themselves, there can be no question that they would consider, as the most necessary of all branches of instruction for themselves and for their children, that which professes to acquaint them with the conditions of the existence they prize so highly – which teaches them how to avoid disease and to cherish health, in themselves and those who are dear to them.

I am addressing, I imagine, an audience of educated persons; and yet I dare venture to assert that, with the exception of those of my hearers who may chance to have received a medical education, there is not one who could tell me what is the meaning and use of an act which he performs a score of times every minute, and. whose suspension would involve his immediate death; – I mean the act of breathing – or who could state in precise terms why it is that a confined atmosphere is injurious to health.

The *practical value* of Physiological knowledge/ Why is it that educated men can be found to maintain that a slaughter-house in the midst of a great city is rather a good thing than otherwise ? – that mothers persist in exposing the largest possible amount of surface of their children to the cold, by the absurd style of dress they adopt, and then marvel at the peculiar dispensation of Providence, which removes their infants by bronchitis and gastric fever? Why is it that quackery rides rampant over the land; and that not long ago one of the largest public rooms in this great city could be filled by an audience gravely listening to the reverend expositor of the doctrine – that the simple physiological phenomena known as spirit-rapping, table-turning, phreno-magnetism, and I know not what other absurd and inappropriate names, are due to the direct and personal agency of Satan ?

Why is all this, except from the utter ignorance as to the simplest laws of their own animal life, which prevails among even the most highly educated persons in this country ?

But there are other branches of Biological Science, besides Physiology proper, whose practical influence, though less obvious, is not, as I believe, less certain. I have heard educated men speak with an ill-disguised contempt of the studies of the naturalist, and ask, not without a shrug, "What is the use of knowing all about these miserable animals – what bearing has it on human life?"

I will endeavor to answer that question. I take it that all will admit there is definite Government of this universe – that its pleasures and pains are not scattered atrandom, but are distributed in accordance with orderly and fixed laws, and that it is only in accordance with all we know of the rest of the world, that there should be an agreement between one portion of the sensitive creation and another in these matters.

Surely then it interests us to know the lot of other animal creatures – however far below us, they are still the sole created things which share with us the capability of pleasure and the susceptibility to pain.

I cannot but think that he who finds a certain proportion of pain and evil inseparably woven up in the life of the very worms, will bear his own share with more courage and submission; and will, at any rate, view with suspicion those weakly amiable theories of the Divine government, which would have us believe pain to be an oversight and a mistake – to be corrected by and by. On the other hand, the predominance of happiness among living things – their lavish beauty – the secret and wonderful harmony which pervades them all, from the highest to the lowest, are equally striking refutations of that modern Manichean doctrine, which exhibits the world as a slave-mill, worked with many tears, for mere utilitarian ends.

There is yet another way in which natural history may, I am convinced, take a profound hold upon practical life – and that is, by its influence over our finer feelings, as the greatest of all sources of that pleasure which is derivable from beauty. I do not pretend that natural- history knowledge, as such, can increase our sense of the beautiful in natnral objects. I do not suppose that the dead soul of Peter Bell, of whom the great poet of nature says –

"A primrose by the river's brim,
A yellow primrose waa to him –
And it waa nothing more – "

would have been *a* whit roused from its apathy by the information that the primrose is a Dicotyledonous Exo- gen, with amonopetalous corolla and central placentation. But I advocate natural-history knowledge from this point of view, because it would lead us to *seek* the beauties of natural objects, instead of trusting to chance to force them on our attention. To a person uninstructed in natural history, his country or seaside stroll is a walk through a gallery filled with wonderful works of art, nine-tenths of which have their faces turned to the wall. Teach him something of natural history, and you place in his hands a catalogue of those which are worth turning round. Surely our innocent pleasures are not so abundant in this life that we can afford to despise this or any other source of them. We should fear being banished for our neglect to that limbo, where the great Florentine tells us are those who, during this life, "wept when they might be joyful."

But I shall be trespassing unwarrantably on your kindness, if I do not proceed at once to my last point – the time at which Physiological Science should first form a part of the Curriculum of Education.

The distinction between the teaching of the facts of a science as instruction, and the teaching it systematically as knowledge, has already been placed before you in a previous lecture: and it appears to me that, as with other sciences, the *common facts* of Biology – the uses of parts of the body – the names and habits of the living creatures which surround us – may be taught with advantage to theyoungest child. Indeed, the avidity of children for this kind of knowledge, and the comparative ease with which they retain it, is something quite marvellous. I doubt whether any toy would be so acceptable to young children as a vivarium of the same kind as, but of course on a smaller scale than, those admirable devices in the Zoological Gardens.

On the other hand, systematic teaching in Biology cannot be attempted with success until the student has attained to a certain knowledge of physics and chemistry: for though the phenomena of life are dependent neither on physical nor on chemical, but on vital forces, yet they result in all sorts of physical and chemical changes, which can only be judged by their own laws.

And now to sum up in a few words the conclusions to which I hope you see reason to follow me.

Biology needs no apologist when she demands a place – and a prominent place – in any scheme of education worthy of the name. Leave out the Physiological sciences from your curriculum, and you launch the student into the world, undisciplined in that science whose subject- matter would best develop his powers of observation; ignorant of facts of the deepest importance for his own apd others' welfare; blind to the richest sources of beauty in God's creation; and unprovided with that belief in a living law, and an order manifesting itself in and through endless change and variety, which might serve to check and moderate that phase of despair through which, if he take an earnest interest in social problems, he will assuredly sooner or later pass.

Finally, one word for myself. I have not hesitated to speak strongly where I have felt strongly; and I am buttoo conscious that the indicative and imperative moods have too often taken the place of the more becoming subjunctive and conditional. 1 feel, therefore, how necessary it is to beg you to forget the personality of him who has thus ventured to address you, and to consider only the truth or error in what has been said.

4

SECTION 4

III

EMANCIPATION-BLACK AND WHITE

[1865]

QDASHIE'S plaintive inquiry, "Am I not a man and a brother?" seems at last to have received its final reply – the recent decision of the fierce trial by battle on the other side of the Atlantic fully concurring with that long since delivered here in a more peaceful way.

The question is settled; but even those who are most thoroughly convinced that the doom is just, must see good grounds for repudiating half the arguments which have been employed by the winning side; and for doubting whether its ultimate results will embody the hopes of the victors, though they may more than realize the fears of the vanquished. It may be quite true that some negroes are better than some white men; but no rational man, cognizant of the facts, believes that the average negro is the equal, still less the superior, of the average white man. And, if this be true, it is simply incredible that, when all his disabilities are removed, and our prognathous relative has a fair field and no favor, as well as no oppressor, he will be able to compete successfully with his bigger-brained and smaller-jawed rival, in a contest which is to be carried on by thoughts and not by bites. The highest places in the hierarchy of civilization will assuredly not be within the reach of our dusky cousins, though it is by no means necessary that they should be restricted to the lowest. But whatever the position of stable equilibrium into which the laws of social gravitation may bring the negro, all responsibility for the result will henceforward lie between Nature and him. The white man may wash his hands of it, and the Caucasian conscience be void of reproach for evermore. And this, if we look to the' bottom of the matter, is the real justification for the abolition policy.

The doctrine of equal natural rights may be an illogical delusion; emancipation may convert the slave from a well-fed animal into a pauperized man; mankind may even have to do without cotton shirts; but all these evila must be faced if the moral law, that no human being can arbitrarily dominate over another without grievous damage to his own nature, be, as many think, as readily demonstrable by experiment as any physical truth. If this be true, no slavery can be abolished without a double emancipation, and the master will benefit by freedom more than the freed-man.

The like considerations apply to all the other questions of emancipation which are at present stirring the world – the multifarious demands that classes of mankind shall be relieved from restrictions imposed by the artifice of man, and not by the necessities of Nature. One of the most important, if not the most important, of all these, is that which daily threatens to become the "irrepressible" woman question. What social and political rights have women ? What ought they to be allowed, or not allowed, to do, be, and suffer ? And, as involved in, and underlying all these questions, how ought they to be educated?

There are philogynists as fanatical as any "misogynists" who, reversing our anti-quated notions, bid the man look upon the woman as the higher type of humanity; who ask us to regard the female intellect as the clearer and the quicker, if not the stronger; who desire us to look up to the feminine moral sense as the purer and the nobler; and bid man abdicate his usurped sovereignty over Nature in favor of the female line. On the other hand, there are persons not to be outdone in all loyalty and just respect for womankind, but by nature hard of head and haters of delusion, however charming, who not only repudiate the new woman-worship which so many sentimentalists and some philosophers are desirous of setting up, but, carrying their audacity further, deny even the natural equality of the sexes. They assert, on the contrary, that in every excellent character, whether mental or physical, the average woman is inferior to the average man, in the sense of having that character less in quantity and lower in quality. Tell these persons of the rapid perceptions and the instinctive intellectual insight of women, and they reply that the feminine mental peculiarities, which pass under these names, are merely the outcome of a greater impressibility to the superficial aspects of things, and of the absence of that restraint upon expression which, in men, is imposed by reflection and a sense of responsibility. Talk of the passive endurance of the weaker sex, and opponents of this kind remind you that Job was a man, and that, until quite recent times, patience and long-suffering were not counted among the specially feminine virtues. Claim passionate tenderness as especially feminine, and the inquiry is made whether all the best love-poetry in existence(except, perhaps, the "Sonnets from the Portuguese") has not been written by men; whether the song which embodies the ideal of pure and tender passion – "Ade- laida" – was written by *Frau* Beethoven; whether it was the Fornarina, or Rafael, who painted the Sistine Madonna. Nay, we have known one such heretic go so far as to lay his hands upon the ark itself, so to speak, and to defend the startling paradox that, even in physical beauty, man is the superior. He admitted, indeed, that there was a brief period of early youth when it might be hard to say whether the prize should be awarded to the graceful undulations of the female figure, or the perfect balance and supple vigor of the male frame. But while our new Paris might hesitate between the youthful Bacchus and the Venus emerging from the foam, he averred that, when Venus and Bacchus had reached thirty, the point no longer admitted of a doubt; the male form having then attained its greatest nobility, while the female is far gone in decadence; and that, at this epoch, womanly beauty, so far as it is independent of grace or expression, is a question of drapery and accessories.

Supposing, however, that all these arguments have a certain foundation; admitting, for a moment, that they are comparable to those by which the inferiority of the negro to the white man may be demonstrated, are they of any value as against woman-emancipation ? Do they afford us the smallest ground for refusing to educate women as well as men – to give women the same civil and political rights as men ? No mistake is so commonly made by clever people as that of assuming a cause to be bad because the arguments of its supporters are, to a great extent, nonsensical. And we conceive that those who may laugh at the arguments of the extreme philogynists, may yet feel bound to work heart and soul toward the attainment of their practical ends.

As regards education, for example. Granting the alleged defects of women, is it not somewhat absurd to sanction and maintain a system of education which would seem to have been specially contrived to exaggerate all these defects?

Naturally not so firmly strung, nor so well balanced as boys, girls are in great measure debarred from the sports and physical exercises which are justly thought absolutely necessary for the full development of the vigor of the more favored sex. Women are, by nature, more excitable than men – prone to be swept by tides of emotion, proceeding from hidden and inward, as well as from obvious and external causes; and female education does its best to weaken every physical counterpoise to this nervous mobility – tends in all ways to stimulate the emotional part of the mind and stunt the rest. We find girls naturally timid, inclined to dependence, born conservatives; and we teach them that independence is unladylike; that blind faith is the right frame of mind; and that whatever we may be permitted, and indeed encouraged, to do to our brother, our sister is to be left to the tyranny of authority and tradition. With few insignificant exceptions, girls have been educated either to be drudges, or toys, beneath man; or a sort of angels above him; the highest ideal aimed at oscillating between Clarchen and Beatrice. The possibility that the ideal of womanhood lies neither in the fair saint, nor in the fair sinner; that the female type of character is neither better nor worse than the male, but only weaker; that women are meant neither to be men's guides nor their playthings, but their comrades, their fellows, and their equals, so far as Nature puts no bar to that equality, does not seem to have entered into the minds of those who have had the conduct of the education of girls.

If the present system of female education stands self- condemned, as inherently absurd; and if that which we have just indicated is the true position of woman, what is the first step toward a better state of things ? We reply, emancipate girls. Recognize the fact that they share the senses, perceptions, feelings, reasoning powers, emotions, of boys, and that the mind of the average girl is less different from that of the average boy, than the mind of one boy is from that of another; so that whatever argument justifies a given education for all boys, justifies its application to girls as well. So far from imposing artificial restrictions upon the acquirement of knowledge by women, throw every facility in their way. Let our Faustinas, if they will, toil through the whole round of

"Juristerei und Medizin,
Und leider 1 auch Philosophic."

Let us have "sweet girl graduates" by all means. They will be none the less sweet for a little wisdom; and the "golden hair" will not curl less gracefully outside the head by reason of there being brains within. Nay, if obvious practical difficulties can be overcome, let those women who feel inclined to do so descend into the gladiatorial arena of life, not merely in the guise of *retiurice,* as heretofore, but as bold *sicarice,* breasting the openfray. Let them, if they so please, become merchants, barristers, politicians. Let them have a fair field, but let them understand, as the necessary' correlative, that they are to have no favor. Let Nature alone sit high above the lists, "rain influence and judge the prize."

And the result? For our part, though loth to prophesy, we believe it will be that of other emancipations. Women will find their place, and it will neither be that in which they have been held, nor that to which some of them aspire. Nature's old salic law will not be repealed, and no change of dynasty will be effected. The big chests, the massive brains, the vigorous muscles and stout frames of the best men will carry the day, whenever it is worth their while to contest the prizes of life with the best women. And the hardship of it is, that the very improvement of the women will lessen their chances. Better mothers will bring forth better sons, and the impetus gained by the one sex will be transmitted, in the next generation, to the other. The most Darwinian of theorists will not venture to propound the doctrine, that the physical disabilities under which women have hitherto labored in the struggle for existence with men are likely to be removed by even the most skilfully conducted process of educational selection.

We are, indeed, fully prepared to believe that the bearing of children may, and ought, to become as free from danger and long disability to the civilized woman as it is to the savage; nor is it improbable that, as society advances toward its right organization, motherhood will occupy a less space of woman's life than it has hitherto done. But still, unless the human species is tocome to an end altogether – a consummation which can hardly be desired by even the most ardent advocate of "women's rights" – somebody must be good enough to take the trouble and responsibility of annually adding to the world exactly as many people as die out of it. In consequence of some domestic difficulties, Sydney Smith is said to have suggested that it would have been good for the human race had the model offered by the hive been followed, and had all the working part of the female community been neuters. Failing any thorough-going reform of this kind, we see nothing for it but the old division of humanity into men potentially, or actually, fathers, and women potentially, if not actually, mothers. And we fear that so long as this potential motherhood is her lot, woman will be found to be fearfully weighted in the race of life.

The duty of man is to see that not a grain is piled upon that load beyond what Nature imposes; that injustice is not added to inequality.

A LIBERAL EDUCATION; AND WHERE TO FIND IT
[1868]

THE business which the South London Working Men's College has undertaken is a great work; indeed, I might say, that Education, with which that college proposes to grapple, is the greatest work of all those which lie ready to a man's hand just at present. And, at length, this fact is becoming generally recognized. You cannot go anywhere without hearing a buzz of more or less confused and contradictory talk on this subject – nor can you fail to notice that, in one point at any rate, there is a very decided advance upon like discussions in former days. Nobody outside the agricultural interest now dares to say that education is a bad thing. If any representative of the once large and powerful party, which, in former days, proclaimed this opinion, still exists in a semi-fossil state, he keeps his thoughts to himself. In fact, there is a chorus of voices, almost distressing in their harmony, raised in favor of the doctrine that education is the great panacea for human troubles, and that, if the country is not shortly to go to the dogs, everybody must be educated.

The politicians tell us, "You must educate the masses because they are going to be masters." The clergy join in the cry for education, for they affirm that the people are drifting away from church and chapel into the broadest infidelity. The manufacturers and the capitalists swell the chorus lustily. They declare that ignorance makes bad workmen; that England will soon be unable to turn out cotton goods, or steam engines, cheaper than other peopls; and then, Ichabod! Ichabod! the glory will be departed from us. And a few voices are lifted up in favor of the doctrine that the masses should be educated because they are men and women with unlimited capacities of being, doing, and suffering, and that it is as true now, as ever it was, that the people perish for lack of knowledge.

These members of the minority, with whom I confess I have a good deal of sympathy, are doubtful whether any of the other reasons urged in favor of the education of the people are of much value – whether, indeed, some of them are based upon either wise or noble grounds of action. They question if it be wise to tell people that you will do for them, out of fear of their power, what you have left undone, so long as your only motive was compassion for their weakness and their sorrows. And, if ignorance of everything which it is needful a ruler should know is likely to do so much harm in the governing classes of the future, why is it, they ask reasonably enough, that such ignorance in the governing classes of the past has not been viewed with equal horror?

Compare the average artisan and the average country squire, and it may be doubted if you will find a pin to choose between the two in point of ignorance, class feeling, or prejudice. It is true that the ignorance is of a different sort – that the class feeling is in favor of a different class – and that the prejudice has a distinct savor of wrong-headedness in each case – but it is questionable if

– SCIBNOB – 4

the one is either a bit better, or a bit worse, than the other. The old protectionist theory is the doctrine of trades unions as applied by the squires, and the modern trades unionism is the doctrine of the squires applied by the artisans. Why should we be worse off under one *regime* than under the other?

Again, this sceptical minority asks the clergy to think whether it is really want of education which keeps the masses away from their ministrations – whether the most completely educated men are not as open to reproach on this score as the workmen; and whether, perchance, this may not indicate that it is not education which lies at the bottom of the matter?

Once more, these people, whom there is no pleasing, venture to doubt whether the glory, which rests upon being able to undersell all the rest of the world, is a very safe kind of glory – whether we may not purchase it too dear; especially if we allow education, which ought to be directed to the making of men, to be diverted into a process of manufacturing human tools, wonderfully adroit in the exercise of some technical industry, but good for nothing else.

And, finally, these people inquire whether it is the masses alone who need a reformed and improved education. They ask whether the richest of our public schools might not well be made to supply knowledge, as well as gentlemanly habits, a strong class feeling, and eminent proficiency in cricket. They seem to think that the noble foundations of our old universities are hardly fulfilling their functions in their present posture of half- clerical seminaries, half racecourses, where men are trained to win a senior wranglership, or a double-first, as horses are trained to win a cup, with as little reference to the needs of after-life in the case of the man as in that of the racer. And, while as zealous for education as the rest, they affirm that, if the education of the richer classes were such as to fit them to be the leaders and the governors of the poorer, and if the education of the poorer classes were such as to enable them to appreciate really wise guidance and good governance, the politicians need not fear mob-law, nor the clergy lament their want of flocks, nor the capitalists prognosticate the annihilation of the prosperity of the country.

Such is the diversity of opinion upon the why and the wherefore of education. And my hearers will be prepared to expect that the practical recommendations which are put forward are not less discordant. There is a loud cry for compulsory education. We English, in spite of constant experience to the contrary, preserve a touching faith in the efficacy of acts of Parliament; and I believe we should have compulsory education in the course of next session, if there were the least probability that half a dozen leading statesmen of different parties would agree what that education should be.

Some hold that education without theology is worse than none. Others maintain, quite as strongly, that education with theology is in the same predicament. Bat this is certain, that those who hold the first opinion can by no means agree what theology should be taught; and that those who maintain the second are in a small minority.

At any rate "make people learn to read, write, and cipher," say a great many; and the advice is undoubtedly sensible as far as it goes. But, as has happened to mein former days, those who, in despair of getting anything better, advocate this measure, are met with the objection that it is very like making a child practice the use of a knife, fork, and spoon, without giving it a particle of meat. I really don't know what reply is to be made to such an objection.

But it would be unprofitable to spend more time in disentangling, or rather in showing up the knots in, the ravelled skeins of our neighbors. Much more to the purpose is it to ask if we possess any clew of our own which may guide us among these entanglements. And by way of a beginning, let us ask ourselves – What is education ? Above all things, what is our ideal of a thoroughly liberal education ? – of that education which, if we could begin life again, we would give ourselves – of that education which, if we could mold the fates to our own will, we would give our children ? Well, I know not what may be your conceptions upon this' matter, but I will tell you mine, and I hope I shall find that our views are not very discrepant.

Suppose it were perfectly certain that the life and fortune of every one of us would, one day or other, depend upon his winning or losing a game at chess. Don't you think that we should all consider it to be a primary duty to learn at least the names and the moves of the pieces; to have a notion of a gambit, and a keen eye for all the means of giving and getting out of check ? Do you not think that we should look with a disapprobation amounting to scorn upon the father who allowed his son, or the state which allowed its members, to grow up without knowing a pawn from a knight?

Yet it is a very plain and elementary truth that the life, the fortune and the happiness of every one of us, and, more or less, of those who are connected with us, do depend upon our knowing something of the rules of a game infinitely more difficult and complicated than chess. It is a game which has been played for untold ages, every man and woman of us being one of the two players in a game of his or her own. The chess-board is the world, the pieces are the phenomena of the universe, the rules of the game are what we call the laws of Nature. The player on the other side is hidden from us. We know that his play is always fair, just and patient. But also we know, to our cost, that he never overlooks a mistake, or makes the smallest allowance for ignorance. To the man who plays well, the highest stakes are paid, with that sort of overflowing generosity with which the strong shows delight in strength. And one who plays ill is checkmated without haste, but without remorse.

My metaphor will remind some of you of the famous picture in which Eetzsch has depicted Satan playing at chess with man for his soul. Substitute for the mocking fiend in that picture a calm, strong angel who is playing for love, as we say, and would rather lose than win – and I should accept it as an image of human life.

Well, what I mean by Education is learning the rules of this mighty game. In other words, education is the instruction of the intellect in the laws of Nature, under which name I include not merely things and their forces, but men and their ways; and the fashioning of the affections and of the will into an earnest and loving desire to move in harmony with those laws. For me, education means neither more nor less than this. Anything whichprofesses to call itself education must be tried by this standard, and if it fails to stand the test, I will not call it [education, whatever' may be the force of authority, or of numbers, upon the other side.

It is important to remember that, in strictness, there is no such thing as an uneducated man. Take an extreme case. Suppose that an adult man, in the full vigor of his faculties, could be suddenly placed in the world, as Adam is said to have been, and then left to do as he best might. How long would he be left uneducated? Not five minutes. Nature would begin to teach him, through the eye, the ear, the touch, the properties of objects. Pain and pleasure would be at his elbow telling him to do this and avoid that; and by slow degrees the man would receive an education which, if narrow, would be thorough, real, and adequate to his circumstances, though there would be no extras and very few accomplishments.

And if to this solitary man entered a second Adam, or, better still, an Eve, a new and greater world, that of social and moral phenomena, would be revealed. Joys and woes, compared with which all others might seem but faint shadows, would spring from the new relations. Happiness and sorrow would take the place of the coarser monitors, pleasure and pain; but conduct would still be shaped by the observation of the natural consequences of actions; or, in other words, by the laws of the nature of man.

To every one of us the world was once as fresh and new as to Adam. And then, long before we were susceptible of any other mode of instruction, Nature took us in hand, and every minute of waking life brought itseducational influence, shaping our actions into rough accordance with Nature's' laws, so that we might not be ended untimely by too gross disobedience. Nor should I speak of this process of education as past for any one, be he as old as he may. For every man the world is as fresh as it was at the first day, and as full of untold novelties for him who has the eyes to see them. And Nature is still continuing her patient education of us in that great university, the universe, of which we are all members – . Nature having no Test-Acts.

Those who take honors in Nature's university, who learn the laws which govern men and things and obey them, are the really great and successful men in this world. The great mass of mankind are the "Poll," who *'tick* up just enough to get through without much discredit. Those who won't learn at all are plucked; and then you can't come up again. Nature's pluck means extermination.

Thus the question of compulsory education is settled so far as Nature is concerned. Her bill on that question was framed and passed long ago. But, like all compulsory legislation, that of Nature is harsh and wasteful in its operation. Ignorance is visited as sharply as wilful disobedience – incapacity meets with the same punishment as crime. Nature's discipline is not even a word and a blow, and the blow first; but the blow without the word. It is left to you to find out why your ears are boxed.

The object of what we commonly call education – that education in which man intervenes and which I shall distinguish as artificial education – is to make good these defects in Nature's methods; to prepare the child to receive Nature's education, neither incapably nor ignorantly, nor with wilful disobedience; and to understand the preliminary symptoms of hev pleasure, without waiting for the box on the ear. In short, all artificial education ought to be an anticipation of natural education. And a liberal education is an artificial education which has not only prepared a man to escape the great evils of disobedience to natural laws, but has trained him to appreciate and to seize upon the rewards, which Nature scatters with as free a hand as her penalties.

That man, I think, has had a liberal education who has been so trained in youth that his body is the ready servant of his will, and does with ease and pleasure all the work that, as a mechanism, it is capable of; whose intellect is a clear, cold, logic engine, with all its parts of equal strength, and in smooth working order; ready, like a steam engine, to be turned to any kind of work, and spin the gossamers as well as forge the anchors of the mind; whose mind is stored with a knowledge of the great and fundamental truths of Nature and of the laws of her operations; one who, no stunted ascetic, is full of life and fire, but whose passions are trained to come to heel by a vigorous will, the servant of a tender conscience; who has learned to love all beauty, whether of Nature or of art, to hate all vileness, and to respect others as himself.

Such a one and no other, I conceive, has had a liberal education; for he is, as completely as a man can be, in harmony with Nature. He will make the best of her, and she of him. They will get on together rarely: she as his ever beneficent mother; he as her mouthpiece, her conscious self, her minister and interpreter.

Where is such an education as this to be had? Where is there any approximation to it? Has any one tried to found such an education? Looking over the length and breadth of these islands, I am afraid that all these questions must receive a negative answer. Consider our primary schools and what is taught in them. A child learns:

1. To read, write, and cipher, more or less well; but in a very large proportion of cases not so well as to take pleasure in reading, or to be able to write the commonest letter properly.

2. A quantity of dogmatic theology, of which the child, nine times out of ten, understands next to nothing.

3. Mixed up with this, so as to seem to stand or fall with it, a few of the broadest and simplest principles of morality. This, to my mind, is much as if a man of science should make the story of the fall of the apple in Newton's garden an integral part of the doctrine of gravitation, and teach it as of equal authority with the law of the inverse squares.

4. A good deal of Jewish history and Syrian geography, and perhaps a little something about English history and the geography of the child's own country. But I doubt if there is a primary school in England in which hangs a map of the hundred in which the village lies, so that the children may be practically taught by it what a map means.

6. A certain amount of regularity, attentive obedience, respect for others: obtained by fear, if the master be incompetent or foolish; by love and reverence, if he be wise.

So far as this school course embraces a training in the theory and practice of obedience to the moral lawsof Nature, I gladly admit, not only that it contains a valuable educational element, but that, so far, it deals with the most valuable and important part of all education. Yet, contrast what is done in this direction with what might be done; with the time given to matters of comparatively no importance; with the absence of any attention to things of the highest moment; and one is tempted to think of Falstaff s bill and "the halfpenny worth of bread to all that quantity of sack."

Let us consider what a child thus "educated" knows, and what it does not know. Begin with the most important topic of all – morality, as the guide of conduct. The child knows well enough that some acts meet with approbation and some with disapprobation. But it has never heard that there lies in the nature of things a reason for every moral law, as cogent and as well defined as that which underlies every physical law; that stealing and lying are just as certain to be followed by evil consequences, as putting your hand in the fire, or jumping out of a garret window. Again, though the scholar may have been made acquainted, in dogmatic fashion, with the broad laws of morality, he has had no training in the application of those laws to the difficult problems which result from the complex conditions of modern civilization. Would it not be very hard to expect any one to solve a problem in conic sections who had merely been taught the axioms and definitions of mathematical science ?

A workman has to bear hard labor, and perhaps privation, while he sees others rolling in wealth, and feeding their dogs with what would keep his children from starvation. Would it not be well to have helped that man to calm the natural promptings of discontent by showing him, in his youth, the necessary connection of the moral law which prohibits stealing with the stability of society – by proving to him, once for all, that it is better for his own people, better for himself, better for future generations, that he should starve than steal ? If you have no foundation of knowledge, or habit of thought, to work upon, what chance have you of persuading a hungry man that a capitalist is not a thief "with a circumbendibus"? And if he honestly believes that, of what avail is it to quote the commandment against stealing, when he proposes to make the capitalist disgorge ?

Again, the child learns absolutely nothing of the history or the political organization of his own country. His general impression is, that everything of much importance happened a very long while ago; and that the Queen and the gentlefolk govern the country much after the fashion of King David and the elders and nobles of Israel – his sole models. Will you give a man with this much information a vote? In easy times he sells it for a pot of beer. Why should he not? It is of about as much use to him as a chignon, and he knows as much what to do with it, for any other purpose. In bad times, on the contrary, he applies his simple theory of government, and believes that his rulers are the cause of his sufferings – a belief which sometimes bears remarkable practical fruits.

Least of all, does the child gather from this primary "education" of ours a conception of the laws of the physical world, or of the relations of cause and effect therein. And this is the more to be lamented, as the poor are especially exposed to physical evils, and are more interested in removing them than any other class of the community. If any one is concerned in knowing the ordinary laws of mechanics one would think it is the hand-laborer, whose daily toil lies among levers and pulleys; or among the other implements of artisan work. And if any one is interested in the laws of health, it is the poor workman, whose strength is wasted by ill- prepared food, whose health is sapped by bad ventilation and bad drainage, and half whose children are massacred by disorders which might be prevented. Not only does our present primary education carefully abstain from hinting to the workman that some of his greatest evils are traceable to mere physical agencies, which could be removed by energy, patience, and frugality; but it does worse – it renders him, so far as it can, deaf to those who could help him, and tries to substitute an Oriental Bubmission to what is falsely declared to be the will of God, for his natural tendency to strive after a better condition.

"What wonder, then, if very recently an appeal has been made to statistics for the profoundly foolish purpose of showing that education is of no good – that it diminishes neither misery nor crime among the masses of mankind? I reply, why should the thing which has been called education do either the one or the other? If I am a knave or a fool, teaching me to read and write won't make me less of either one or the other – unless somebody shows me how to put my reading and writing to wise and good purposes.

Suppose any one were to argue that medicine is of no use, because it could be proved statistically that thepercentage of deaths was just the same among people who had been taught how to open a medicine chest, and among those who did not so much as know the key by sight. The argument is absurd; but it is not more preposterous than that against which I am contending. The only medicine for suffering, crime, and all the other woes of mankind, is wisdom. Teach a man to read and write, and you have put into his hands the great keys of the wisdom box. But it is quite another matter whether he ever opens the box or not. And he is as likely to poison as to cure himself, if, without guidance, he swallows the first drug that comes to hand. In these times a man may as well be purblind, as unable to read – lame, as unable to write. But I protest that, if I thought the alternative were a necessary one, I would rather that the children of the poor should grow up ignorant of both these mighty arts, than that they should remain ignorant of that knowledge to which these arts are means.

It may be said that all these animadversions may apply to primary schools, but that the higher schools, at any rate, must be allowed to give a liberal education. In fact they professedly sacrifice everything else to this object.

Let us inquire into this matter. What do the higher schools, those to which the great middle class of the country sends its children, teach, over and above the instruction given in the primary schools? There is a little more reading and writing of English. But, for all that, every one knows that it is a rare thing to find a boy of the middle or upper classes who can read aloud decently, or who can put his thoughts on paper in clearand grammatical (to say nothing of good or elegant) language. The "ciphering" of the lower schools expands into elementary mathematics in the higher; into arithmetic, with a little algebra, a little Euclid. But I doubt if one boy in five hundred has ever heard the explanation of a rule of arithmetic, or knows his Euclid otherwise than by rote.

Of theology, the middle-class schoolboy gets rather less than poorer children, less absolutely and less relatively, because there are so many other claims upon his attention. I venture to say that, in the great majority of cases, his ideas on this subject when he leaves school are of the most shadowy and vague description, and associated with painful impressions of the weary hours spent in learning collects and catechism by heart.

Modern geography, modern history, modern literature; the English language as a language; the whole circle of the sciences, physical, moral and social, are even more completely ignored in the higher than in the lower schools. Up till within a few years back, a boy might have passed through any one of the great public schools with the greatest distinction and credit, and might never so much as have heard of one of the subjects I have just mentioned. He might never have heard that the earth goes round the sun; that England underwent a great revolution in 1688, and France another in 1789; that there once lived certain notable men called Chaucer, Shakespeare, Milton, Voltaire, Goethe, Schiller. The first might be a German and the last an Englishman for anything he could tell you to the contrary. And as for Science, the only idea the word would suggest to his mind would be dexterity in boxing.

I have said that this was the state of things a few years back, for the sake of the few righteous who are to be found among the educational cities of the plain. But I would not have you too sanguine about the result, if you sound the minds of the existing generation of public schoolboys, on such topics as those I have mentioned.

Now let us pause to consider this wonderful state of affairs; for the time will come when Englishmen will quote it as the stock example of the stolid stupidity of their ancestors in the nineteenth century. The most thoroughly commercial people, the greatest voluntary wanderers and colonists the world has ever seen, are precisely the middle classes of this country. If there be a people which has been busy making history on the great scale for the last three hundred years – and the most profoundly interesting history – history which, if it happened to be that of Greece or Rome, we should study with avidity – it is the English. If there be a people which, during the same period, has developed a remarkable literature, it is our own. If there be a nation whose prosperity depends absolutely and wholly upon their mastery over the forces of Nature, upon their intelligent apprehension of, and obedience to, the laws of the creation and distribution of wealth, and of the stable equilibrium of the forces of society, it is precisely this nation. And yet this is what these wonderful people tell their sons: "At the cost of from one to two thousand pounds of our hard-earned money, we devote twelve of the most precious years of your lives to school. There you shall toil, or be supposed to toil; but there you shall not learn one single thing of all those you will most want to know directly you leave school and enter upon the practical business of life. You will in all probability go into business, but you shall not know where, or how, any article of commerce is produced, or the difference between an export or an import, or the meaning of the word 'capital.' You will very likely settle in a colony, but you shall not know whether Tasmania is part of New South Wales, or *vice versd.*

"Very probably you may become a manufacturer, but you shall not be provided with the means of understanding the working of one of your own steam-engines, or the nature of the raw products you employ; and, when you are asked to buy a patent, you shall not have the slightest means of judging whether the inventor is an impostor who is contravening the elementary principles of science, or a man who will make you as rich as Croesus.

"You will very likely get into the House of Commons. You will have to take your share in making laws which may prove a blessing or a curse to millions of men. But you shall not hear one word respecting the political organization of your country; the meaning of the controversy between free-traders and protectionists shall never have been mentioned to you; you shall not so much as know that there are such things as economical laws.

"The mental power which will be of most importance in your daily life will be the power of seeing things as they are without regard to authority; and of drawing accurate general conclusions from particular facts. But at school and at college you shall know of no source of truth but authority; nor exercise your reasoning faculty upon anything but deduction from that which is laid down by authority.

"You will have to weary your soul with work, and many a time eat your bread in sorrow and in bitterness, and you shall not have learned to take refuge in the great source of pleasure without alloy, the serene resting- place for worn human nature – the world of art."

Said I not rightly that we are a wonderful people? I am quite prepared to allow that education entirely devoted to these omitted subjects might not be a completely liberal education. But is an education which ignores them all a liberal education? Nay, is it too much to say that the education which should embrace these subjects and no others would be a real education, though an incomplete one; while an education which omits them is really not an education at all, but a more or less useful course of intellectual gymnastics?

For what does the middle-class school put in the place of all these things which are left out? It substitutes what is usually comprised under the compendious title of the "classics" – that is to say, the languages, the literature, and the history of the ancient Greeks and . Romans, and the geography of so much of the world as was known to these two great nations of antiquity. Now, do not expect me to depreciate the earnest and enlightened pursuit of classical learning. I have not the least desire to speak ill of such occupations, nor any sympathy with those who run them down. On the contrary, if my opportunities had lain in that direction, there is no investigation into which I could have thrown myself with greater delight than that of antiquity.

What science can present greater attractions than philology? How can a lover of literary excellence fail to rejoice in the ancient masterpieces? And with whatconsistency could I, whose business lies so much in the attempt to decipher the past, and to build up intelligible forms out of the scattered fragments of long-extinct beings, fail to take a sympathetic, though an unlearned, interest in the labors of a Niebuhr, a Gibbon, or a Grote? Classical history is a great section of the paleontology of man; and I have the same double respect for it as for other kinds of paleontology – that is to say, a respect for the facts which it establishes as for all facts, and a still greater respect for it as a preparation for the discovery of a law of progress.

But if the classics were taught as they might be taught – if boys and girls were instructed in Greek and Latin, not merely as languages, but as illustrations of philological science; if a vivid picture of life on the shores of the Mediterranean two thousand years ago were imprinted on the minds of scholars; if ancient history were taught, not as a weary series of feuds and fights, but traced to its causes in such men placed under such conditions; if, lastly, the study of the classical books were followed in such a manner as to impress boys with their beauties, and with the grand simplicity of their statement of the everlasting problems of human life, instead of with their verbal and grammatical peculiarities; I still think it as little proper that they should form the basis of a liberal education for our contemporaries, as I should think it fitting to make that sort of paleontology with which I am familiar the backbone of modern education.

It is wonderful how close a parallel to classical training could be made out of that paleontology to which I refer. In the first place I could get up an osteological primer so arid, so pedantic in its terminology, so altogether distasteful to the youthful mind, as to beat the recent famous production of the head-masters out of the field in all these excellences. Next, I could exercise my boys upon easy fossils, and bring out all their powers of memory and all their ingenuity in the application of my osteo-grammatical rules to the interpretation, or construing, of those fragments. To those who had reached the higher classes, I might supply odd bones to be built up into animals, giving great honor and reward to him -who succeeded in fabricating monsters most entirely in accordance with the rules. That would answer to verse- making and essay-writing in the dead languages.

To be sure, if a great comparative anatomist were to look at these fabrications he might shake his head, or laugh. But what then ? Would such a catastrophe destroy the parallel ? What, think you, would Cicero, or Horace, say to the production of the best sixth form going? And would not Terence stop his ears and run out if he could be present at an English performance of his own plays? Would "Hamlet," in the mouths of a set of French actors, who should insist on pronouncing English after the fashion of their own tongue, be more hideously ridiculous?

But it will be said that I am forgetting the beauty, and the human interest, which appertain to classical studies. To this I reply that it is only a very strong man who can appreciate the charms of a landscape as he is toiling up a steep hill, along a bad road. What with short-windedness, stones, ruts, and a pervading sense of the wisdom of rest and be thankful, most of us have little enough sense of the beautiful under these circumstances. The ordinary schoolboy is precisely in this case. He finds Parnassus uncommonly steep, and there is no chance of his having much time or inclination to look about him till he gets to the top. And nine times out of ten he does not get to the top.

But if this be a fair picture of the results of classical teaching at its best – and I gather from those who have authority to speak on such matters that it is so – what is to be said of classical teaching at its worst, or, in other words, of the classics of our ordinary middle-class schools ? ' I will tell you. It means getting up endless forms and rules by heart. It means turning Latin and Greek into English, for the mere sake of being able to do it, and without the smallest regard to the worth, or worthlessness, of the author read. It means the learning of innumerable, not always decent, fables in such a shape that the meaning they once had is dried up into utter trash; and the only impression left upon a boy's mind is that the people who believed such things must have been the greatest idiots the world ever saw. And it means, finally, that, after a dozen years spent at this kind of work, the sufferer shall be incompetent to interpret a passage in an author he has not already got up; that he shall loathe the sight of a Greek or Latin book; and that he shall never open, or think of, a classical writer again, until, wonderful to relate, he insists upon submitting his sons to the same process.

These be your gods, O Israel! For the sake of this net result (and respectability) the British father denies his children all the knowledge they might turn to account in life, not merely for the achievement of vulgarsuccess, but for guidance in the great crises of human existence. This is the stone he offers to those whom he is bound by the strongest and tenderest ties to feed with bread.

1 For a justification of what is here said about these schools, see that valuable book, "Essays on a Liberal Education, passim,"

If primary and secondary education are in this unsatisfactory state, what is to be said to the universities? This is an awful subject, and one I almost fear to touch with my unhallowed hands; but I can tell you what those say who have authority to speak.

The Kector of Lincoln College, in his lately published valuable "Suggestions for Academical Organization with especial reference to Oxford," tells us (page 127):

"The colleges were, in their origin, endowments, not for the elements of a general liberal education, but for the prolonged study of special and professional faculties by men of riper age. The universities embraced both these objects. The colleges, while they incidentally aided in elementary education, were specially devoted to the highest learning

"This was the theory of the middle-age university and the design of collegiate foundations in their origin. Time and circumstances have brought about a total change. The colleges no longer promote the researches of science, or direct professional study. Here and there college walls may shelter an occasional student, but not in larger proportions than may be found in private life. Elementary teaching of youths under twenty is now the only function performed by the university, and almost the only object of college endowments. Colleges were homes for the life- study of the highest and most abstruse parts of knowledge. They have become boarding schools in whichthe elements of the learned languages are taught to youths."

If Mr. Pattison's high position, and his obvious love and respect for his university, be insufficient to convince the outside world that language so severe is yet no more than just, the authority of the Commissioners who reported on the University of Oxford in 1850 is open to no challenge. Yet they write:

"It is generally acknowledged that both Oxford and the country at large suffer greatly from the absence of a body of learned men devoting their lives to the cultivation of science, and to the direction of academical education.

"The fact that so few books of profound research emanate from the University of Oxford materially impairs its character as a seat of learning, and consequent!; its hold on the respect of the nation."

Cambridge can claim no exemption from the reproaches addressed to Oxford. And thus there seems no escape from the admission that what we fondly call our great seats of learning are simply "boarding schools" for bigger boys; that learned men are not more numerous in them than out of them; that the advancement of knowledge is not the object of fellows of colleges; that, in the philosophic calm and meditative stillness of their greenswarded courts, philosophy does not thrive, and meditation bears few fruits.

It is my good fortune to reckon among my friends resident members of both universities, who are men of learning and research, zealous cultivators of science, keeping before their minds a noble ideal of a university, and doing their best to make that ideal a reality; and, tome, they would necessarily typify the universities, did not the authoritative statements I have quoted compel me to believe that they are exceptional, and not representative men. Indeed, upon calm consideration, several circumstances lead me to think that the Rector of Lincoln College and the Commissioners cannot be far wrong.

I believe there can be no doubt that the foreigner who should wish to become acquainted with the scientific, or the literary, activity of modern England, would simply lose his time and his pains if he visited our universities with that object.

And, as for works of profound research on any subject, and, above all, in that classical lore for which the universities profess to sacrifice almost everything else, why, a third-rate, poverty-stricken German university turns out more produce of that kind in one year than our vast and wealthy foundations elaborate in ten.

Ask the man who is investigating any question, profoundly and thoroughly – be it historical, philosophical, philological, physical, literary, or theological; who is trying to make himself master of any abstract subject (except, perhaps, political economy and geology, both of which are intensely Anglican sciences), whether he is not compelled to read half a dozen times as many German as English books? And whether, of these English books, more than one in ten is the work of a fellow of a college, or a professor of an English university ?

Is this from any lack of power in the English as compared with the German mind ? The countrymen of Grote and of Mill, of Faraday, of Robert Brown, of Lyell, and of Darwin, to go no further back than the contemporaries of men of middle age, can afford to smile at such a suggestion. England can show now, as she has been able to show in every generation since civilization spread over the West, individual men who hold their own against the world, and keep alive the old tradition of her intellectual eminence.

But, in the majority of cases, these men are what they are in virtue of their native intellectual force, and of a strength of character which will not recognize impediments. They are not trained in the courts of the Temple of Science, but storm the walls of that edifice in all eorts of irregular ways, and with much loss of time and power, in order to obtain their legitimate positions.

Our universities not only do not encourage snch men; do not offer them positions, in which it should be their highest duty to do, thoroughly, that which they are most capable of doing; but, as far as possible, university training shuts out of the minds of those among them, who are subjected to it, the prospect that there is anything in the world for which they are specially fitted. Imagine the success of the attempt to still the intellectual hunger of any of the men I have mentioned, by putting before him, as the object of existence, the successful mimicry of the measure of a Greek song, or the roll of Ciceronian prose! Imagine how much success would be likely to attend the attempt to persuade such men that the education which leads to perfection in such elegances is alone to be called culture; while the facts of history, the process of thought, the conditions of moral and social existence, and the laws of physical nature are left to be dealt with as they may by outside barbarians!

It is not thus that the German universities, from being beneath notice a century ago, have become whatthey are now – the most intensely cultivated and the most productive intellectual corporations the world has ever seen.

The student who repairs to them sees in the list of classes and of professors a fair picture of the world of knowledge. Whatever he needs to know there is some one ready to teach him, some one competent to discipline him in the way of learning; whatever his special bent, let him but be able and diligent, and in due time he shall find distinction and a career. Among his professors, he sees men whose names are known and revered throughout the civilized world; and their living example infects him with a noble ambition, and a love for the spirit of work.

The Germans dominate the intellectual world by virtue of the same simple secret as that which made Napoleon the master of old Europe. They have declared *la carri&re ouverte aux talents,* and every Bursch marches with a professor's gown in his knapsack. Let him become a great scholar, or man of science, and ministers will compete for his services. In Germany, they do not leave the chance of his holding the office he would render illustrious to the tender mercies of a hot canvass, and the final wisdom of a mob of country parsons.

In short, in Germany, the universities are exactly what the Rector of Lincoln and the Commissioners tell us the English 'universities are not; that is to say, corporations "of learned men devoting their lives to the cultivation of science, and the direction of academical education." They are not "boarding schools for youths," nor clerical seminaries; but institutions for the
higher culture of men, in which the theological faculty
– Science – 5
is of no more importance, or prominence, than the rest; and which are truly "universities," since they strive to represent and embody the totality of human knowledge, and to find room for all forms of intellectual activity.

May zealous and clear-headed reformers like Mr. Patti- son succeed in their noble endeavors to shape our universities toward some such ideal as this, without losing what is valuable and distinctive in their social tone I But until they have succeeded, a liberal education will be no more obtainable in our Oxford and Cambridge Universities than in our public schools.

If I am justified in my conception of the ideal of a liberal education; and if what I have said about the existing educational institutions of the country is also true, it is clear that the two have no sort of relation to one another; that the best of our schools and the most complete of our university trainings give but a narrow, onesided, and essentially illiberal education while the worst give what is really next to no education at all. The South London Working Men's College could not copy any of these institutions if it would; I am bold enough to express the conviction that it ought not if it could.

For what is wanted is the reality and not the mere name of a liberal education; and this College must steadily set before itself the ambition to be able to give that education sooner or later. At present we are but beginning, sharpening our educational tools, as it were, and, except a modicum of physical science, we are not able to offer much more than is to be found in an ordinary school.

Moral and social science – one of the greatest and most fruitful of our future classes, I hope – at present lacks only one thing in our programme, and that is a teacher. A considerable want, no doubt; but it must be recollected that it is much better to want a teacher than to want the desire to learn.

Further, we need what, for want of a better name, I must call Physical Geography. What I mean is that which the Germans call "*Erdkunde.*" It is a description of the earth, of its place and relation to other bodies; of its general structure, and of its great features – winds, tides, mountains, plains: of the chief forms of the vegetable and animal worlds, of the varieties of man. It is the peg upon which the greatest quantity of useful and entertaining scientific information can be suspended.

Literature is not upon the College programme; but I hope some day to see it there. For literature is the greatest of all sources of refined pleasure, and one of the great uses of a liberal education is to enable us to enjoy that pleasure. There is scope enough for the purposes of liberal education in the study of the rich treasures of our own language alone. All that is needed is direction, and the cultivation of a refined taste by attention to sound criticism. But there is no reason why French and German should not be mastered sufficiently to read what is worth reading in those languages with pleasure and with profit.

And finally, by and by, we must have History; treated not as a succession of battles and dynasties; not as a series of biographies; not as evidence that Providence has always been on the side of either Whigs or Tories; but as the development of manin times past, and in other conditions than our own. But, as it is one of the principles of our College to be self-supporting, the public must lead, and we must follow, in these matters. If my hearers take to heart what I have said about liberal education, they will desire these things, and I doubt not we shall be able to supply them. But we must wait till the demand is made.

5

SECTION 5

SCIENTIFIC EDUCATION: NOTES OF AN AFTER-DINNER
SPEECH
[1869]

[KB. Thackeray, talking of after-dinner speeches, has lamented that "one never can recollect the fine things one thought of in the cab," in going to the place of entertainment. I am not aware that there are any "fine things" in the following pages, I. v. t such as there are stand to a speech which really did get itself spoken, at the hospitable table of the Liverpool Philomathic Society, more or less in the position of what "one thought of in the cab."]

THE introduction of scientific training into the general education of the country is a topic upon which I could not have spoken, without some more or less apologetic introduction, a few years ago. But upon this, as upon other matters, public opinion has of late undergone a rapid modification. Committees of both Houses of the Legislature have agreed that something must be done in this direction, and have even thrown out timid and faltering suggestions as to what should be done; while at the opposite pole of society, committees of working men have expressed their conviction that scientific training is the one thing needful for their advancement, whether as men, or as workmen. Only the other day, it was my duty to take part in the reception of a deputation of

London working men, who desired to learn from Sir Eoderick Murchison, the Director of the Royal School of Mines, whether the organization of the Institution in Jermyn Street could be made available for the supply of that scientific instruction theneed of which could not have been apprehended, or stated, more clearly than it was by them.

The heads of colleges in our great universities (who have not the reputation of being the most mobile of persons) have, in several cases, thought it well that, out of the great number of honors and rewards at their disposal, a few should hereafter be given to the cultivators of the physical sciences. Nay, I hear that some colleges have even gone so far as to appoint one, or, maybe, two special tutors for the purpose of putting the facts and principles of physical science before the undergraduate mind. And I say it with gratitude and great respect for those eminent persons, that the head masters of our public schools, Eton, Harrow, Winchester, have addressed themselves to the problem of introducing instruction in physical science among the studies of those great educational bodies, with much honesty of purpose and enlightenment of understanding; and I live in hope that, before long, important changes in this direction will be carried into effect in those strongholds of ancient prescription. In fact, such changes have already been made, and physical science, even now, constitutes a recognized element of the school curriculum in Harrow and Rugby, while I understand that ample preparations for such studies are being made at Eton and elsewhere.

Looking at these facts, I might perhaps spare myself the trouble of giving any reasons for the introduction of physical science into elementary education; yet I cannot but think that it may be well if I place before you some considerations which, perhaps, have hardly received full attention.

At other times, and in other places, I have endeavoredto state the higher and more abstract arguments, by which the study of physical science may be shown to be indispensable to the complete training of the human mind; but I do not wish it to be supposed that, because I happen to be devoted to more or less abstract and "unpractical" pursuits, I am insensible to the weight which ought to be attached to that which has been said to be the English conception of Paradise; namely, "getting on." I look upon it that "getting on" is a very important matter indeed. I do not mean merely for the sake of the coarse and tangible results of success, but because humanity is so constituted that a vast number of us would never be impelled to those stretches of exertion which make us wiser and more capable men, if it were not for the absolute necessity of putting on our faculties all the strain they will bear, for the purpose of "getting on" in the most practical sense.

Now the value of a knowledge of physical science as a means of getting on is indubitable. There are hardly any of our trades, except the merely huckstering ones, in which some knowledge of science may not be directly profitable to the pursuer of that occupation. As industry attains higher stages of its development, as its processes become more complicated and refined, and competition more keen, the sciences are dragged in, one by one, to take their share in the fray; and he who can best avail himself of their help is the man who will come out uppermost in that struggle for existence, which goes on as fiercely beneath the smooth surface of modern society as among the wild inhabitants of the woods.

But in addition to the bearing of science on ordinary practical life, let me direct your attention to its immenseinfluence on several of the professions. I ask any one who has adopted the calling of an engineer, how much time he lost when he left school, because he had to devote himself to pursuits which were absolutely novel and strange, and of which he had not obtained the remotest conception from his instructors? He had to familiarize himself with ideas of the course and powers of Nature, to which his attention had never been directed during his school-life, and to learn, for the first time, that a world of facts lies outside and beyond the world of words. I appeal to those who know what engineering is, to say how far I am right in respect to that profession ; but with regard to another, of no less importance, I shall venture to speak of my own knowledge. There is no one of us who may not at any moment be thrown, bound hand and foot by physical incapacity, into the hands of a medical practitioner. The chances of life and death for all and each of us may, at any moment, depend on the skill with which that practitioner is able to make out what is wrong in our bodily frames, and on his ability to apply the proper remedy to the defect.

The necessities of modern life are such, and the class from which the medical profession is chiefly recruited is so situated, that few medical men can hope to spend more than three or four, or it may be five, years in the pursuit of those studies which are immediately germane to physic. How is that all too brief period spent at present ? I speak as an old examiner, having served some eleven or twelve years in that capacity in the University of London, and therefore having a practical acquaintance with the subject; but I might fortify myself by the authority of the President of the College of Surgeons, Mr. Quain, whom I heard the other day in an admirable address (the Hunterian Oration) deal fully and wisely with this very topic.1

A young man commencing the study of medicine ia at once required to endeavor to make an acquaintance with a number of sciences, such as Physics, as Chemistry, as Botany, as Physiology, which are absolutely and entirely strange to him, however excellent his so-called education at school may have been. Not only is he devoid of all apprehension of scientific conceptions, not only does he fail to attach any meaning to the words "matter," "force," or "law" in their scientific senses, but, worse still, he has no notion of what it is to come into contact with Nature, or to lay his mind alongside of a physical fact, and try to conquer it, in the way our great naval hero told his captains to master their enemies. His whole mind has been given to books, and I amhardly exaggerating if I say that they are more real to him than Nature. He imagines that all knowledge can be got out of books, and rests upon the authority of some master or other; nor does he entertain any misgiving that the method of learning which led to proficiency in the rules of grammar will suffice to lead him to a mastery of the laws of Nature. The youngster, thus unprepared for serious study, is turned loose among his medical studies, with the result, in nine cases out of ten, that the first year of his curriculum is spent in learning how to learn. Indeed, he is lucky if, at the end of the first year, by the exertions of his teachers and his own industry, he has acquired even that art of arts. After which there remain not more than three, or perhaps four, years for the profitable study of such vast sciences as Anatomy, Physiology, Therapeutics, Medicine, Surgery, Obstetrics, and the like, upon his knowledge or ignorance of which it depends whether the practitioner shall diminish, or increase, the bills of mortality. Now what is it but the preposterous condition of ordinary school education which prevents a young man of seventeen, destined for the practice of medicine, from being fully prepared for the study of Nature; and from coming to the medical school, equipped with that preliminary knowledge of the principles of Physics, of Chemistry and of Biology, upon which he has now to waste one of the precious years, every moment of which ought to be given to those studies which bear directly upon the knowledge of his profession?

1 Mr. Quain'a words ("Medical Times and Gazette," February 20) are: "A few words as to our special Medical course of instruction and the influence upon it of such changes in the elementary schools as I have mentioned. The student now enters at once upon several sciences – physics, chemistry, anatomy, physiology, botany, pharmacy, therapeutics – all these, the facts and the language and the laws of each, to be mastered in eighteen months. Up to the beginning of the Medical course many have learned little. We cannot claim anything better than the Examiner of the University of London and the Cambridge Lecturer have reported for their Universities. Supposing that at school young people had acquired some exact elementary knowledge in physics, chemistry, and a branch of natural history – say botany – with the physiology connected with it, they would then have gained necessary knowledge, with some practice in inductive reasoning. The whole studies are processes of observation and induction – the best discipline of the mind for the purposes of life – for our purposes not less than any. 'By such study (says Dr. Wnewell) of one or more departments of inductive science the mind may escape from the thraldom of mere words.' By that plan the burden of the early Medical course would be much lightened, and more time devoted to practical studies, including Sir Thomas Watson's 'final and supreme stage' of the knowledge of Medicine."

There is another profession, to the members of which, I think, a certain preliminary knowledge of physical science might be quite as valuable as to the medicalman. The practitioner of medicine sets before himself the noble object of taking care of man's bodily welfare; but the members of this other profession undertake to "minister to minds diseased," and, so far as may be, to diminish sin and soften sorrow. Like the medical profession, the clerical, of which I now speak, rests its power to heal upon its knowledge of the order of the universe – upon certain theories of man's relation to that which lies outside him. It is not my business to express any opinion about these theories. I merely wish to point out that, like all other theories, they are professedly based upon matters of fact. Thus the clerical profession has to deal with the facts of Nature from a certain point of view; and hence it comes into contact with that of the man of science, who has to treat the same facts from another point of view. You know how often that contact is to be described as collision, or violent friction; and how great the heat, how little the light, which commonly results from it.

In the interests of fair play, to say nothing of those of mankind, I ask, Why do not the clergy as a body acquire, as a part of their preliminary education, some such tincture of physical science as will put them in a position to understand the difficulties in the way of accepting their theories, which are forced upon the mind of every thoughtful and intelligent man, who has taken the trouble to instruct himself in the elements of natural knowledge ?

Some time ago I attended a large meeting of the clergy, for the purpose of delivering an address which I had been invited to give. I spoke of some of the most elementary facts in physical science, and of the manner in which they directly contradict certain of the ordinary teachings of the clergy. The result was that, after I had finished, one section of the assembled ecclesiastics attacked me with all the intemperance of pious zeal, for stating facts and conclusions which no competent judge doubts; while, after the first speakers had subsided, amid the cheers of the great majority of their colleagues, the more rational minority rose to tell me that I had taken wholly superfluous pains, that they already knew all about what I had told them, and perfectly agreed with me. A hard-headed friend of mine, who was present, put the not unnatural question, "Then why don't you say so in your pulpits?" to which inquiry I heard no reply.

In fact the clergy are at present divisible into three sections: an immense body who are ignorant and speak out; a small proportion who know and are silent; and a minute minority who know and speak according to their knowledge. By the clergy, I mean especially the Protea- tant clergy. Our great antagonist – I speak as a man of science – the Roman Catholic Church, the one great spiritual organization which is able to resist, and must, as a matter of life and death, resist, the progress of science and modern civilization, manages her affairs much better.

It was my fortune some time ago to pay a visit to one of the most important of the institutions in which the clergy of the Roman Catholic Church in these islands are trained; and it seemed to me that the difference between these men and the comfortable champions of Anglicanism and of Dissent was comparable to the difference between our gallant Volunteers and the trained veterans of Napoleon's Old Guard.

The Catholic priest is trained to know his business, and do it effectually. The professors of the college in question, learned, zealous, and determined men, permitted me to speak frankly with them. We talked like outposts of opposed armies during a truce – as friendly enemies; and when I ventured to point out the difficulties their students would have to encounter from scientific thought, they replied: "Our Church has lasted many ages, and has passed safely through many storms. The present is but a new gust of the old tempest, and we do not turn out our young men less fitted to weather it, than they have been, in former times, to cope with the difficulties of those times. The heresies of the day are explained to them by their professors of philosophy and science, and they are taught how those heresies are to be met."

I heartily respect an organization which faces its enemies in this way; and I wish that all ecclesiastical organizations were in as effective a condition. I think it would be better, not only for them, but for us. The army of liberal thought is, at present, in very loose order; and many a spirited free-thinker makes use of his freedom mainly to vent nonsense. We should be the better for a vigorous and watchful enemy to hammer us into cohesion and discipline; and I, for one, lament that the bench of Bishops cannot show a man of the calibre of Butler of the "Analogy," who, if he were alive, would make short work of much of the current *d priori* "infidelity."

I hope you will consider that the arguments I have now stated, even if there were no better ones, constitute a sufficient apology for urging the introduction of science into schools. The next question to which I have to ad dress myself is, What sciences ought to be thus taught? And this is one of the most important of questions, because my side (I am afraid I am a terribly candid friend) sometimes spoils its cause by going in for too much. There are other forms of culture besides physical science; and I should be profoundly sorry to see the fact forgotten, or even to observe a tendency to starve, or cripple, literary, or a3sthetic, culture for the sake of science. Such a narrow view of the nature of education has nothing to do with my firm conviction that a complete and thorough scientific culture ought to be introduced into all schools. By this, however, I do not mean that every schoolboy should be taught everything in science. That would be a very absurd thing to conceive, and a very mischievous thing to attempt. What I mean is, that no boy nor girl should leave school without possessing a grasp of the general character of science, and without having been disciplined, more or less, in the methods of all sciences; so that, when turned into the world to make their own way, they shall be prepared to face scientific problems, not by knowing at once the conditions of every problem, or by being able at once to solve it; but by being familiar with the general current of scientific thought, and by being able to apply the methods of science in the proper way, when they have acquainted themselves with the conditions of the special problem.

That is what I understand by scientific education. To furnish a boy with such an education, it is by no means necessary that he should devote his whole school existence to physical science: in fact no one would lament so one-sided a proceeding more than I. Nay more, it is not necessary for him to give up more than a moderate shareof hifl time to such studies, if they be properly selected and arranged, and if he be trained in them in a fitting manner.

I conceive the proper course to be somewhat as follows. To begin with, let every child be instructed in those general views of the phenomena of Nature, for which we have no exact English name. The nearest approximation to a name for what I mean, which we possess, is "physical geography." The Germans have a better, "Erdkunde" ("earth knowledge" or "geology" in its etymological sense), that is to say, a general knowledge of the earth, and what is on it, in it, and about it. If any one who has had experience of the ways of young children will call to mind their questions, he will find that so far as they can be pat into any scientific category, they come under this head of "Erdkunde." The child asks, "What is the moon, and why does it shine?" "What is this water, and where does it run?" "What is the wind?" "What makes the waves in the sea?" "Where does this animal live, and what is the use of that plant?" And if not snubbed and stunted by being told not to ask foolish questions, there is no limit to the intellectual craving of a young child; nor any bounds to the slow, but solid, accretion of knowledge and development of the thinking faculty in this way. To all such questions, answers which are necessarily incomplete, though true as far as they go, may be given by any teacher whose ideas represent real knowledge and not mere book learning; and a panoramic view of Nature, accompanied by a strong infusion of the scientific habit of mind, may thus be placed within the reach of every child of nine or ten.

After this preliminary opening of the eyes to the greatspectacle of the daily progress of Nature, as the reasoning faculties of the child grow, and he becomes familiar with the use of the tools of knowledge – reading, writing, and elementary mathematics –

he should pass on to what is, in the more strict sense, physical science. Now there are two kinds of physical science: the one regards form and the relation of forms to one another; the other deals with causes and effects. In many of what we term sciences, these two kinds are mixed up together; but systematic botany is a pure example of the former kind, and physics of the latter kind, of science. Every educational advantage which training in physical science can give is obtainable from the proper study of these two; and I should be contented, for the present, if they, added to our "Erd- kunde," furnished the whole of the scientific curriculum of school. Indeed, I conceive it would be one of the greatest boons which could be conferred upon England, if henceforward every child in the country were instructed in the general knowledge of the things about it, in the elements of physics, and of botany. But I should be still better pleased if there could be added somewhat of chemistry, and an elementary acquaintance with human physiology.

So far as school education is concerned, I want to go no further just now; and I believe that such instruction would make an excellent introduction to that preparatory scientific training which, as I have indicated, is so essential for the successful pursuit of our most important professions. But this modicum of instruction must be so given as to insure real knowledge and practical discipline. If scientific education is to be dealt with as mere bookwork, it will be better not to attempt it, but to stickto the Latin Grammar which makes no pretence to be anything but bookwork.

If the great benefits of scientific training are sought, it is essential that such training should be real: that is to say, that the mind of the scholar should be brought into direct relation with fact, that he should not merely be told a thing, but made to see by the use of his own intellect and ability that the thing is so and no otherwise. The great peculiarity of scientific training, that in virtue of which it cannot be replaced by any other discipline whatsoever, is this bringing of the mind directly into contact with fact, and practicing the intellect in the completest form of induction; that is to say, in drawing conclusions from particular facts made known by immediate observation of Nature.

The other studies which enter into ordinary education do not discipline the mind in this way. Mathematical training is almost purely deductive. The mathematician starts with a few simple propositions, the proof of which is so obvious that they are called self-evident, and the rest of his work consists of subtle deductions from them. The teaching of languages, at any rate as ordinarily practiced, is of the same general nature – authority and tradition furnish the data, and the mental operations of the scholar are deductive.

Again: if history be the subject of study, the facts are still taken upon the evidence of tradition and authority. You cannot make a boy see the battle of Thermopylae for himself, or know, of his own knowledge, that Cromwell once ruled England. There is no getting into direct contact with natural fact by this road; there is no dispensing with authority, but rather a resting upon it.

In all these respects, science differs from other educational discipline, and prepares the scholar for common life. What have we to do in every-day life ? Most of the business which demands our attention is matter of fact, which needs, in the first place, to be accurately observed or apprehended; in the second, to be interpreted by inductive and deductive reasonings, which are altogether similar in their nature to those employed in science. In the one case, as in the other, whatever is taken for granted is so taken at one's own peril; fact and reason are the ultimate arbiters, and patience and honesty are the great helpers out of difficulty.

But if scientific training is to yield its most eminent results, it must, I repeat, be made practical. That is to say, in explaining to a child the general phenomena of Nature, you must, as far as possible, give reality to your teaching by object-lessons; in teaching him botany, he must handle the plants and dissect the flowers for himself; in teaching him physics and chemistry, you must not be solicitous to fill him with information, but you must be careful that what he learns he knows of his own knowledge. Don't be satisfied with telling him that a magnet attracts iron. Let him see that it does; let him feel the pull of the one upon the other for himself. And, especially, tell him that it is his duty to doubt until he is compelled, by the absolute authority of Nature, to believe that which is written in books. Pursue this discipline carefully and conscientiously, and you may make sure that, however scanty may be the measure of information which you have poured into the boy's mind, you have created an intellectual habit of priceless value in practical life.

One is constantly asked, When should this scientific education be commenced? I should say with the dawn of intelligence. As I have already said, a child seeks for information about matters of physical science as soon as it begins to talk. The first teaching it wants is an object- lesson of one sort or another; and as soon as it is fit for systematic instruction of any kind, it is fit for a modicum of science.

People talk of the difficulty of teaching young children such matters, and in the same breath insist upon their learning their Catechism, which contains propositions far harder to comprehend than anything in the educational course I have proposed. Again: I am incessantly told that we, who advocate the introduction of science in schools, make no allowance for the stupidity of the average boy or girl; but, in my belief, tht stupidity, in nine cases out of ten, *"Jit, non nascitur,"* and is developed by a long process of parental and pedagogic reprsssion of the natural intellectual appetites, accompanied by a persistent attempt to create artificial ones for food which is not onlj tasteless, but essentially indigestible.

Those who urge the difficulty of instructing young people in science are apt to forget another very important condition of success – important in all kinds of teaching, but most essential, I am disposed to think, when the scholars are very young. This condition is, that the teacher should himself really and practically know his subject. If he does, he will be able to speak of it in the easy language, and with the completeness of conviction, with which he talks of any ordinary every-day matter. If he does not, he will be afraid to wander beyond the limits of the technical phraseology which he has got up; and a dead dogmatism, which oppresses, or raises opposition, will take the place of the lively confidence, born of personal conviction, which cheers and encourages the eminently sympathetic mind of childhood.

I have already hinted that such scientific training as we seek for may be given without making any extravagant claim upon the time now devoted to education. We ask only for "a most favored nation" clause in our treaty with the schoolmaster; we demand no more than that science shall have as much time given to it as any other single subject – say four hours a week in each class of an ordinary school.

For the present, I think men of science would be well content with such an arrangement as this; but speaking for myself, I do not pretend to believe that such an arrangement can be, or will be, permanent. In these times the educational tree seems to me to have its roots in the air, its leaves and flowers in the ground; and, I confess, I should very much like to turn it upside down, so that its roots might be solidly imbedded among the facts of Nature, and draw thence a sound nutriment for the foliage and fruit of literature and of art. No educational system can have a claim to permanence, unless it recognizes the truth that education has two great ends to which everything else must be subordinated. The one of these is to increase knowledge; the other is to develop the love of right and the hatred of wrong.

With wisdom and uprightness a nation can make its way worthily, and beauty will follow in the footsteps of the two, even if she be not specially invited; while there is perhaps no sight in the whole world more saddening and revolting than is offered by men sunk in ignorance of everything but what other men have written; seemingly devoid of moral belief or guidance; but with the sense of beauty so keen, and the power of expression so cultivated, that their sensual caterwauling may be almost mistaken for the music of the spheres.

At present, education is almost entirely devoted to the cultivation of the power of expression, and of the sense of literary beauty. The matter of having anything to say, beyond a hash of other people's opinions, or of possessing any criterion of beauty, so that we may distinguish between the Godlike and the devilish, is left aside as of no moment. I think I do not err in saying that if science were made a foundation of education, instead of being, at most, stuck on as cornice to the edifice, this state of things could not exist.

In advocating the introduction of physical science as a leading element in education, I by no means refer only to the higher schools. On the contrary, I believe that such a change is even more imperatively called for in those primary schools in which the children of the poor are expected to turn to the best account the little time they can devote to the acquisition of knowledge. A great step in this direction has already been made by the establishment of science-classes under the Department of Science and Art – a measure which came into existence unnoticed, but which will, I believe, turn out to be of more importance to the welfare of the people than many political changes over which the noise of battle has rent the air.

Under the regulations to which I refer, a schoolmaster can set up a class in one or more branches of science,: his pupils will be examined, and the State will pay him, at a certain rate, for all who succeed in passing. I have acted as an examiner under this system from the beginning of its establishment, and this year I expect to have not fewer than a couple of thousand sets of answers to questions in Physiology, mainly from young people of the artisan class, who have been taught in the schools which are now scattered all over Great Britain and Ireland. Some of my colleagues, who have to deal with subjects such as Geometry, for which the present teaching power is better organized, I understand are likely to have three or four times as many papers. So far as my own subjects are concerned, I can undertake to say that a great deal of the teaching, the results of which are before me in these examinations, is very sound and good; and I think it is in the power of the examiners, not only to keep up the present standard, but to cause an almost unlimited improvement. Now what does this mean ? It means that, by holding out a very moderate inducement, the masters of primary schools in many parts of the country have been led to convert them into little foci of scientific instruction; and that they and their pupils have contrived to find, or to make, time enough to carry out this object with a very considerable degree of efficiency. That efficiency will, I doubt not, be very much increased as the system becomes known and perfected, even with the very limited leisure left to masters and teachers on week-days. And this leads me to ask, Why should scientific teaching be limited to week-days ?

Ecclesiastically-minded persons are in the habit of calling things they do not like by very hard names, and I should not wonder if they brand the propositionI am about to make as blasphemous, and worse. But, not minding this, I venture to ask, Would there really be anything wrong in using part of Sunday for the purpose of instructing those who have no other leisure, in a knowledge of the phenomena of Nature, and of man's relation to Nature ?

I should like to see a scientific Sunday-school in every parish, not for the purpose of superseding any existing means of teaching the people the things that are for their good, but side by side with them. I cannot but think that there is room for all of us to work in helping to bridge over the great abyss of ignorance which lies at our feet.

And if any of the ecclesiastical persons to whom I have referred object that they find it derogatory to the honor of the God whom they worship, to awaken the minds of the young to the infinite wonder and majesty of the works which they proclaim His, and to teach them those laws which must needs be His laws, and therefore of all things needful for man to know – I can only recommend them to be let blood and put on low diet. There must be something very wrong going on in the instrument of logic if it turns out such conclusions from such premises.

SCIENCE AND CULTURE

[1880]

SIX years ago, as some of my present hearers may remember, I had the privilege of addressing a large assemblage of the inhabitants of this city, who had gathered together to do honor to the memory of their famous townsman, Joseph Priestley;1 and, if any satisfaction attaches to posthumous glory, we may hope that the manes of the burned-out philosopher were then finally appeased.

No man, however, who is endowed with a fair share of common-sense, and not more than a fair share of vanity, will identify either contemporary or posthumous fame with the highest good; and Priestley's life leaves no doubt that he, at any rate, set a much higher value upon the advancement of knowledge, and the promotion of that freedom of thought which is at once the cause and the consequence of intellectual progress.

Hence I am disposed to think that, if Priestley could be among us to-day, the occasion of our meeting would afford him even greater pleasure than the proceedings which celebrated the centenary of his chief discovery. The kindly heart would be moved, the high sense of social duty would be satisfied, by the spectacle of well- earned wealth, neither squandered in tawdry luxury andvainglorious show, nor scattered with the careless charity which blesses neither him that gives nor him that takes, but expended in the execution of a well-considered plan for the aid of present and future generations of those who are willing to help themselves.

1 See the first essay in this volume.

We shall all be of one mind thus far. But it is needful to share Priestley's keen interest in physical science; and to have learned, as he had learned, the value of scientific training in fields of inquiry apparently far remote from physical science; in order to appreciate, as he would have appreciated, the value of the noble gift which Sir Josiah Mason has bestowed upon the inhabitants of the Midland district.

For us children of the nineteenth century, however, the establishment of a college under the conditions of Sir Josiah Mason's Trust, has a significance apart from any which it could have possessed a hundred years ago. It appears to be an indication that we are reaching the crisis of the battle, or rather of the long series of battles, which have been fought over education in a campaign which began long before Priestley's time, and will probably not be finished just yet.

In the last century, the combatants were the champions of ancient literature on the one side, and those of modern literature on the other; but, some thirty years1 ago, the contest became complicated by the appearance of a third army, ranged round the banner of Physical Science.

I am not aware that any one has authority to speakin the name of this new host. For it must be admitted to be somewhat of a guerilla force, composed largely of irregulars, each of whom fights pretty much for his own hand. But the impressions of a full private, who has seen a good deal of service in the ranks, respecting the present position of affairs and the conditions of a permanent peace, may not be devoid of interest; and I do not know that I could make a better use of the present opportunity than by laying them before you.

1 The advocacy of the introduction of physical science into general education by George Combe and others commenced a good deal earlier; but the movement had acquired hardly any practical force before the time to which I refer.

VIII – Science – 6

From the time that the first suggestion to introduce physical science into ordinary education was timidly whispered, until now, the advocates of scientific education have met with opposition of two kinds. On the one hand, they have been pooh-poohed' by the men of business who pride themselves on being the representatives of practicality; while, on the other hand, they have been excommunicated by the classical scholars, in their capacity of Levites in charge of the ark of culture and monopolists of liberal education.

The practical men believed that the idol whom they worship – rule of thumb – has been the source of the past prosperity, and will suffice for the future welfare of the arts and manufactures. They were of opinion that science is speculative rubbish; that theory and practice have nothing to do with one another; and that the scientific habit of mind is an impediment, rather than an aid, in the conduct of ordinary affairs.

I have used the past tense in speaking of the practical men – for although they were very formidable thirty years ago, I am not sure that the pure species has not been extirpated. In fact, so far as mere argument goes, theyhave been subjected to such a *feu d'enfer* that it is a miracle if any have escaped. But I have remarked that your typical practical man has an unexpected resemblance to one of Milton's angels. His spiritual wounds, such as are inflicted by logical weapons, may be as deep as a well and as wide as a . church door, but beyond shedding a few drops of ichor, celestial or otherwise, he is no whit the worse. So, if any of these opponents be left, I will not waste time in vain repetition of the demonstrative evidence of the practical value of science; but knowing that a parable will sometimes penetrate where syllogisms fail to effect an entrance, I will offer a story for their consideration.

Once upon a time, a boy, with nothing to depend upon but his own vigorous nature, was thrown into the thick of the struggle for existence in the midst of a great manufacturing population. He seems to have had a hard fight, inasmuch as, by the time he was thirty years . of age, his total disposable funds amounted to twenty pounds. Nevertheless, middle life found him giving proof of his comprehension of the practical problems he had been roughly called upon to solve, by a career of remarkable prosperity.

Finally, having reached old age with its . well- earned surroundings of "honor, troops of friends," the hero of my story bethought himself of those who were making a like start in life, and how he could stretch out a helping hand to them.

After long and anxious reflection, this successful practical man of business could devise nothing better than to provide them with the means of obtaining "sound, extensive, and practical scientific knowledge."And he devoted a large part of his wealth and five years of incessant work to this end.

I need not point the moral of a tale which, as the solid and spacious fabric of the Scientific College assures us, is no fable, nor can anything which I could say intensify the force of this practical answer to practical objections.

We may take it for granted then that, in the opinion of those best qualified to judge, the diffusion of thorough scientific education is an absolutely essential condition of industrial progress; and that the College which has been opened to-day will confer an inestimable boon upon those whose livelihood is to be gained by the practice of the arts and manufactures of the district.

The only question worth discussion is, whether the conditions, under which the work of the College is to be carried out, are such as to give it the best possible chance of achieving permanent success.

Sir Josiah Mason, without doubt most wisely, has left very large freedom of action to the trustees, to whom he proposes ultimately to commit the administration of the College, so that they may be able to adjust its arrangements in accordance with the changing conditions of the future. But, with respect to three points he has laid most explicit injunctions upon both administrators and teachers.

Party politics are forbidden to enter into the minds of either, so far as the work of the College is concerned; theology is as sternly banished from its precincts; and finally, it is especially declared that the College shall make no provision for "mere literary instruction and education."

It does not concern me at present to dwell upon the first two injunctions any longer than may be needful to express my full conviction of their wisdom. But the third prohibition brings us face to face with those other opponents of scientific education, who are by no means in the moribund condition of the practical man, but alive, alert, and formidable.

It is not impossible that we shall hear this express exclusion of "literary instruction and education" from a College which, nevertheless, professes to give a high and efficient education, sharply criticised. Certainly the time was that the Levites of culture would have sounded their trumpets against its walls as against an educational Jericho.

How often have we not been told that the study of physical science is incompetent to confer culture; that it touches none of the higher problems of life; and, what is worse, that the continual devotion to scientific studies tends to generate a narrow and bigoted belief in the applicability of scientific methods to the search after truth of all kinds? How frequently one has reason to observe that no reply to a troublesome argument tells so well as calling its author a "mere scientific specialist." And, as I am afraid it is not permissible to speak of this form of opposition to scientific education in the past tense, may we not expect to be told that this, not only omission, but prohibition, of "mere literary instruction and education" is a patent example of scientific narrow-mindedness ?

I am not acquainted with Sir Josiah Mason's reasons for the action which he has taken; but if, as I apprehend is the case, he refers to the ordinary classical course of our schools and universities by the name of "mere literary instruction and education," I venture to offer sundry reasons of my own in support of that action.

For I hold very strongly by two ' convictions – The first is, that neither the discipline nor the subject-matter of classical education is of such direct, value to the student of physical science as to justify the expenditure of valuable time upon either; and the second is, that for the purpose of attaining real culture, an exclusively scientific education is at least as effectual as an exclusively literary education.

I need hardly point out to you that these opinions, especially the latter, are diametrically opposed to those of the great majority of educated Englishmen, influenced as they are by school and university traditions. In their belief, culture is obtainable only by a liberal education; and a liberal education is synonymous, not merely with education and instruction in literature, but in one particular form of literature, namely, that of Greek and Boman antiquity. They hold that the man who has learned Latin and Greek, however little, is educated; while he who is versed in other branches of knowledge, however deeply, is a more or less respectable specialist, not admissible into the cultured caste. The stamp of the educated man, the University degree, is not for him.

I am too well acquainted with the generous catholicity of spirit, the true sympathy with scientific thought, which pervades the writings of our chief apostle of culture to identify him with these opinions; and yet one may coll from one and another of those epistles to the Pailissines, which so much delight all who do not answer to that name, sentences which lend them some support.

Mr. Arnold tells us that the meaning of culture is "to know the best that has been thought and said in the 'world." It is the criticism of life contained in literature. That criticism regards "Europe as being, for intellectual and spiritual purposes, one great confederation, bound to a joint action and working to a common result; and whose members have, for their common outfit, a knowledge of Greek, Roman, and Eastern antiquity, and of one another. Special, local, and temporary advantages being put out of account, that modern nation will in the intellectual and spiritual sphere make most progress which most thoroughly carries out this programme. And what is that but saying that we too, all of us, as individuals, the more thoroughly we carry it out, shall make the more progress?" '

We have here to deal with two distinct propositions. The first, that a criticism of life is the essence of culture; the second, that literature contains the materials which suffice for the construction of such a criticism.

I think that we must all assent to the first proposition. For culture certainly means something quite different from learning or technical skill. It implies the possession of an ideal, and the habit of critically estimating the value of things by comparison with a theoretic standard. Perfect culture should supply a complete theory of life, based upon a clear knowledge alike of its possibilities and of its limitations.

But we may agree to all this, and yet strongly dissent from the assumption that literature alone is competent to supply this knowledge. After having learned all thatGreek, Roman, and Eastern antiquity have thought and said, and all that modern literatures have to tell us, it is not self-evident that we have laid a sufficiently broad and deep foundation for that criticism of life, which constitutes culture.

1 "Essays in Criticism," page 37.

Indeed, to any one acquainted with the scope of physical science, it is not at all evident. Considering progress only in the "intellectual and spiritual sphere," I find myself wholly unable to admit that either nations or individuals will really advance, if their common outfit draws nothing from the stores of physical science. I should say that an army, without weapons of precision and with no particular base of operations, might more hopefully enter upon a campaign on the Rhine, than a man, devoid of a knowledge of what physical science has done in the last century, upon a criticism of life.

When a biologist meets with an anomaly, he instinctively turns to the study of development to clear it up. The rationale of contradictory opinions may with equal confidence be sought in history.

It is, happily, no new thing that Englishmen should employ their wealth in building and endowing institutions for educational purposes. But, five or six hundred years ago, deeds of foundation expressed or implied conditions as nearly as possible contrary to those which have been thought expedient by Sir Josiah Mason. That is to say, physical science was practically ignored, while a certain literary training was enjoined as a means to the acquirement of knowledge which was essentially theological.

The reason of this singular contradiction between theactions of men alike animated by a strong and disinterested desire to promote the welfare of their fellows, is easily discovered.

At that time, in fact, if any one desired knowledge beyond such as could be obtained by his own observation, or by common conversation, his first necessity was to learn the Latin language, inasmuch as all the higher knowledge of the western world was contained in works written in that language. Hence, Latin grammar, with logic and rhetoric, studied through Latin, were the fundamentals of education. With respect to the substance of the knowledge imparted through this channel, the Jewish and Christian Scriptures, as interpreted and supplemented by the Eomish Church, were held to contain a complete and infallibly true body of information.

Theological dicta were, to the thinkers of those days, that which the axioms and definitions of Euclid are to the geometers of these. The business of the philosophers of the Middle Ages was to deduce, from the data furnished by the theologians, conclusions in accordance with ecclesiastical decrees. They were allowed the high privilege of showing, by logical process, how and why that which the Church said was true, must be true. And if their demonstrations fell short of or exceeded this limit, the Church was maternally ready to check their aberrations; if need were by the help of the secular arm.

Between the two, our ancestors were furnished with a compact and complete criticism of life. They were told how the world began and how it would end; they learned that all material existence was but a base and insignificant blot upon the fair face of the spiritual world, and that nature was, to all intents and purposes, the playground of the devil; they learned that the earth is the centre of the visible universe, and that man is the cynosure of things terrestrial; and more especially was it inculcated that the course of nature had no fixed order, but that it could be, and constantly was, altered by the agency of innumerable spiritual beings, good and bad, according as they were moved by the deeds and prayers of men. The sum and substance of the whole doctrine was to produce the conviction that the only thing really worth knowing in this world was how to secure that place in a better which, under certain conditions, the Church promised.

Our ancestors had a living belief in this theory of life, and acted upon it in their dealings with education, as in all other matters. Culture meant saintliness – after the fashion of the saints of those days; the education that led to it was, of necessity, theological; and the way to theology lay through Latin.

That the study of nature – further than was requisite for the satisfaction of every-day wants – should have any bearing on human life was far from the thoughts of men thus trained. Indeed, as nature had been cursed for man's sake, it was an obvious conclusion that those who meddled with nature were likely to come into pretty close contact with Satan. And, if any born scientific investigator followed his instincts, he might safely reckon upon earning the reputation, and probably upon suffering the fate, of a sorcerer.

Had the western world been left to itself in Chinese isolation, there is no saying how long this state of things might have endured. But, happily, it was not left to itself. Even earlier than. the thirteenth century, the de

velopment of Moorish civilization in Spain and the great movement of the Crusades had introduced the leaven which, from that day to this, has never ceased to work. At first, through the intermediation of Arabic translations, afterward by the study of the originals, the western nations of Europe became acquainted with the writings of the ancient philosophers and poets, and, in time, with the whole of the vast literature of antiquity.

Whatever there was of high intellectual aspiration or dominant capacity in Italy, France, Germany and England, spent itself for centuries in taking possession of the rich inheritance left by the dead civilizations of Greece and Home. Marvellously aided by the invention of printing, classical learning spread and nourished. Those who possessed it prided themselves on having attained the highest culture then within the reach of mankind.

And justly. For, saving Dante on his solitary pinnacle, there was no figure in modern literature at the time of the Renascence to compare with the men of antiquity; there was no art to compete with their sculpture; there was no physical science but that which Greece had created. Above all, there was no other example of perfect intellectual freedom – of the unhesitating acceptance of reason as the sole guide to truth and the supreme arbiter of conduct.

The new learning necessarily soon exerted a profound influence upon education. The language of the monks and schoolmen seemed little better than gibberish to scholars fresh from Virgil and Cicero, and the study of Latin was placed upon a new foundation. Moreover, Latin itself ceased to afford the sole key to knowledge. The student who sought the highest thought of antiquity found only a second-hand reflection of it in Eoman literature, and turned his face to the full light of the Greeks. And after a battle, not altogether dissimilar to that which is at present being fought over the teaching of physical science, the study of Greek was recognized as an essential element of all higher education.

Thus the Humanists, as they were called, won the day; and the great reform which they effected was of incalculable service to mankind. But the Nemesis of all reformers is finality; and the reformers of education, like those of religion, fell into the profound, however common, error of mistaking the beginning for the end of the work of reformation.

The representatives of the Humanists, in the nineteenth century, take their stand upon classical education as the sole avenue to culture, as firmly as if we were still in the age of Eenascence. Yet, surely, the present intellectual relations of the modern and the ancient worlds are profoundly different from those which obtained three centuries ago. Leaving aside the existence of a great and characteristically modern literature, of modern painting, and, especially, of modern music, there is one feature of the present state of the civilized world which separates it more widely from the Renascence, than the Renascence was separated from the Middle Ages.

This distinctive character of our own times lies in the vast and constantly increasing part which is played by natural knowledge. Not only is our daily life shaped by it, not only does the prosperity of millions of men depend upon it, but our whole theory of life has long been influenced, consciously or unconsciously, by the general conceptions of the universe, which have been forced upon us by physical science.

In fact, the most elementary acquaintance with the results of scientific investigation shows us that they offer a broad and striking contradiction to the opinion so implicitly credited and taught in the Middle Ages.

The notions of the beginning and the end of the world entertained by our forefathers are no longer credible. It is very certain that the earth is not the chief body in the material universe, and that the world is not subordinated to man's use. It is even more certain that nature is the expression of a definite order with which nothing interferes, and that the chief business of mankind is to learn that order and govern themselves accordingly. Moreover, this scientific "criticism of life" presents itself to us with different credentials from any other. It appeals not to authority, nor to what anybody may have thought or said, but to Nature. It admits that all our interpretations of natural fact are more or less imperfect and symbolic, and bids the learner seek for truth not among words but among things. It warns us that the assertion which outstrips evidence is not only a blunder but a crime.

The purely classical education advocated by the representatives of the Humanists in our day, gives no inkling of all this. A man may be a better scholar than Erasmus, and know no more of the chief causes of the present intellectual fermentation than Erasmus did. Scholarly and pious persons, worthy of all respect, favor us with allocutions upon the sadness of the antagonism of science to their medieval way of thinking, which betray an ignorance of the first principles of scientific investigation, an incapacity for understanding what a man of sciencemeans by veracity, and an unconsciousness of the weight of established scientific truths, which is almost comical.

There is no great force in the *tu quoque* argument, or else the advocates of scientific education might fairly enough retort upon the modern Humanists that they may be learned specialists, but that they possess no such sound foundation for a criticism of life as deserves the name of culture. And, indeed, if we were disposed to be cruel, we might urge that the Humanists have brought this reproach upon themselves, not because they are too full of the spirit of the ancient Greek, but because they lack it.

The period of the Renascence is commonly called that of the "Kevival of Letters," as if the influences then brought to bear upon the mind of Western Europe had been wholly exhausted in the field of literature. I think it is very commonly forgotten that the revival of science, effected by the same agency, although less conspicuous, was not less momentous.

In fact, the few and scattered students of nature of that day picked up the clew to her secrets exactly as it fell from the hands of the Greeks a thousand years before. The foundations of mathematics were so well laid by them that our children learn their geometry from a book written for the schools of Alexandria two thousand years ago. Modern astronomy is the natural continuation and development of the work of Hipparchus and of Ptolemy; modern physics of that of Democritus and of Archimedes.; it was long before modern biological science outgrew the knowledge bequeathed to us by Aristotle, by Theophrastus, and by Galen.

We cannot know all the best thoughts and sayingsof the Greeks unless we know what they thought about natural phenomena. We cannot fully apprehend their criticism of life unless we understand the extent to which that criticism was affected by scientific conceptions. We falsely pretend to be the inheritors of their culture, unless we are penetrated, as the best minds among them were, with an unhesitating faith that the free employment of reason, in accordance with scientific method, is the sole method of reaching truth.

Thus I venture to think that the pretensions of our modern Humanists to the possession of the monopoly of culture and to the exclusive inheritance of the spirit of antiquity must be abated, if not abandoned. But I should be very sorry that anything I have said should be taken to imply a desire on my part to depreciate the value . of classical education, as it might be and as it sometimes is. The native capacities of mankind vary no less than their opportunities; and while culture is one, the road by which one man may best reach it is widely different from that which is most advantageous to another. Again, while scientific education is yet inchoate and tentative, classical education is thoroughly well organized upon the practical experience of generations of teachers. So that, given ample time for learning and destination for ordinary life, or for a literary career, I do not think that a young Englishman in search of culture can do better than follow the course usually marked out for him, supplementing its deficiencies by his own efforts.

But for those who mean to make science their serious occupation; or who intend to follow the profession of medicine; or who have to enter early upon the business of life; for all these, in my opinion, classical educationis a mistake; and it is for this reason that I am glad to see "mere literary education and instruction" shut out from the curriculum of Sir Josiah Mason's College, seeing that its inclusion would probably lead to the introduction of the ordinary smattering of Latin and Greek.

Nevertheless, I am the last person to question the importance of genuine literary education, or to suppose that intellectual culture can be complete without it. An exclusively scientific training will bring about a mental twist as surely as an exclusively literary training. The value of the cargo does not compensate for a ship's being out of trim; and I should be very sorry to think that the Scientific College would turn out none but lopsided men.

There is no need, however, that such a catastrophe should happen. Instruction in English, French and German is provided, and thus the three greatest literatures of the modern world are made accessible to the student.

French and German, and especially the latter language, are absolutely indispensable to those who desire full knowledge in any department of science. But even supposing that the knowledge of these languages acquired is not more than sufficient for purely scientific purposes, every Englishman has, in his native tongue, an almost perfect instrument of literary expression; and, in his own literature, models of every kind of literary excellence. If an Englishman 'cannot get literary culture out of his Bible, his Shakespeare, his Milton, neither, in my belief, will the profoundest study of Homer and Sophocles, Virgil and Horace, give it to him.

Thus, since the constitution of the College makes sufficient provision for literary as §well as for scientificeducation, and since artistic instruction is also contemplated, it seems to me that a fairly complete culture is offered to all who are willing to take advantage of it.

But I am not sure that at this point the "practical" man, scotched but not slain, may ask what all this talk about culture has to do with an Institution, the object of which is defined to be "to promote the prosperity of the manufactures and the industry of the country." He may suggest that what is wanted for this end is not culture, nor even a purely scientific discipline, but simply a knowledge of applied science.

I often wish that this phrase, "applied science," had never been invented. For it suggests that there is a sort of scientific knowledge of direct practical use, which can be studied apart from another sort of scientific knowledge, which is of no practical utility, and which is termed "pure science." But there is no more complete fallacy than this. What people call applied science is nothing but the application of pure science to particular classes of problems. It consists of deductions from those general principles, established by reasoning and observation, which constitute pure science. No one can safely make these deductions until he has a firm grasp of the principles; and he can obtain that grasp only by personal experience of the operations of observation and of reasoning on which they are founded.

Almost all the processes employed in the arts and manufactures fall within the range either of physics or of chemistry. In order to improve them, one must thoroughly understand them; and no one has a chance of really understanding them, unless he has obtained that mastery of principles and that habit of dealing with factswhich is given by long-continued and well-directed purely scientific training in the physical and the chemical laboratory. So that there really is no question as to the necessity of purely scientific discipline, even if the work of the College were limited by the narrowest interpretation of its stated aims.

And, as to the desirableness of a wider culture than that yielded by science alone, it is to be recollected that the improvement of manufacturing processes is only one of the conditions which contribute to the prosperity of industry. Industry is a means and not an end; and mankind work only to get something which they want. What that something is depends partly on their innate, and partly on their acquired, desires.

If the wealth resulting from prosperous industry is to be spent upon the gratification of unworthy desires, if the increasing perfection of manufacturing processes is to be accompanied by an increasing debasement of those who carry them on, I do not see the good of industry and prosperity.

Now it is perfectly true that men's views of what is desirable depend upon their characters; and that the innate proclivities to which we give that name are not touched by any amount of instruction. But it does not follow that even mere intellectual education may not, to an indefinite extent, modify the practical manifestation of the characters of men in their actions, by supplying them with motives unknown to the ignorant. A pleasure loving character will have pleasure of some sort; but, if you give him the choice, he may prefer pleasures which do not degrade him to those which do. And this choice is offered to every man who possesses in. literary or artistic culture a never-failing source of pleasures, which are neither withered by age, nor staled by custom, nor imbittered in the recollection by the pangs of self-reproach.

If the Institution opened to-day fulfils the intention of its founder, the picked intelligences among all classes of the population of this district will pass through it. No child born in Birmingham, henceforward, if he have the capacity to profit by the opportunities offered to him, first in the primary and other schools, and afterward in the Scientific College, need fail to obtain, not merely the instruction, but the culture most appropriate to the conditions of his life.

Within these walls, the future employer and the future artisan may sojourn together for a while, and carry, through all their lives, the stamp of the influences then brought to bear upon them. Hence, it is not beside the mark to remind you that the prosperity of industry depends not merely upon the improvement of manufacturing processes, not merely upon the ennobling of the individual character, but upon a third condition, namely, a clear understanding of the conditions of social life, on the part of both the capitalist and the operative, and their agreement upon common principles of social action. They must learn that social phenomena are as much the expression of natural laws as any others; that no social arrangements can be permanent unless they harmonize with the requirements of social statics and dynamics; and that, in the nature of things, there is an arbiter whose decisions execute themselves.

But this knowledge is only to be obtained by the application of the methods of investigation adopted inphysical researches to the investigation of the phenomena of society. Hence, I confess, I should like to see one addition made to the excellent scheme of education propounded for the College, in the shape of provision for the teaching of Sociology. For though we are all agreed that party politics are to have no place in the instruction . of the College; yet in this country, practically governed as it is now by universal suffrage, every man who does his duty must exercise political functions. And, if the evils which are inseparable from the good of political liberty are to be checked, if the- perpetual oscillation of nations between anarchy and despotism is to be replaced by the steady march of self-restraining freedom; it will be because men will gradually bring themselves to deal with political, as they now deal with scientific questions; to be as ashamed of undue haste and partisan prejudice in the one case as in the other; and to believe that the machinery of society is at least as delicate as that of a spinning-jenny, and as little likely to be improved by the meddling of those who have not taken the trouble to master the principles of its action.

In conclusion, I am sure that I make myself the mouthpiece of all present in offering to the venerable founder of the Institution, which now commences its beneficent career, our congratulations on the completion of his work; and in expressing the conviction that the remotest posterity will point to it as a crucial instance of the wisdom which natural piety leads all men to ascribe to their ancestors.

6

SECTION 6

711

ON SCIENCE AND ART IN RELATION TO EDUCATION
[1882]

WHEN a man is honored by such a request as that which reached me from the authorities of your institution some time ago, I think the first thing that occurs to him is that which occurred to those who were bidden to the feast in the Gospel – to begin to make an excuse; and probably all the excuses suggested on that famous occasion crop up in his mind one after the other, including his "having married a wife," as reasons for not doing what he is asked to do. But, in my own case, and on this particular occasion, there were other difficulties of a sort peculiar to the time, and more or less personal to myself; because I felt that, if I came among you, I should be expected, and, indeed, morally compelled, to speak upon the subject of Scientific Education. And then there arose in my mind the recollection of a fact, which probably no one here but myself remembers; namely, that some fourteen years ago I was the guest of a citizen of yours, who bears the honored name of Rathbone, at a very charming and pleasant dinner given by the Philomathic Society; and I there and then, and in this very city, made a speech upon the topic of Scientific Education. Under these circumstances, you see, one runs two dangers – the first, of repeating one's self, although I may fairly hope that everybody has forgotten the fact I have just now mentioned, except myself; and the second, and even greater difficulty, is the danger of saying something different from what one said before, because then, however forgotten your previous speech may be, somebody finds out its existence, and there goes on that process so hateful to members of Parliament, which may be denoted by the term "Hansardiza- tion." Under these circumstances, I came to the conclusion that the best thing I could do was to take the bull by the horns, and to "Hansardize" myself – to put before you, in the briefest possible way, the three- or four propositions which I endeavored to support on the occasion of the speech to which I have referred; and then to ask myself, supposing you were asking me, whether I had anything to retract, or to modify, in them, in virtue of the increased experience, and, let us charitably hope, the increased wisdom of an added fourteen years.

Now, the points to which I directed particular attention on that occasion were these: in the first place, that instruction in physical science supplies information of a character of especial value, both in a practical and a speculative point of view – information which cannot be obtained otherwise; and, in the second place, that, as educational discipline, it supplies, in a better form than any other study can supply, exercise in a special form of logic, and a peculiar method of testing the validity of our processes of inquiry. I said further, that, even at that time, a great and increasing attention was being paid to physical science in our schools and colleges, and that, most assuredly, such attention must go on growing andincreasing, until education in these matters occupied a very much larger share of the time which is given to teaching and training than had been the case heretofore. And I threw all the strength of argumentation of which I was possessed into the support of these propositions. But I venture to remind you, also, of some other words I used at that time, and which I ask permission to read to you. They were these: "There are other forms of culture besides physical science, and I should be profoundly sorry to see the fact forgotten, or even to observe a tendency to starve or cripple literary or aesthetic culture for the sake of science. Such a narrow view of the nature of education has nothing to do with my firm conviction that a complete and thorough scientific culture ought to be introduced into all schools."

I say I desire, in commenting upon these various points, and judging them as fairly as I can by the light of increased experience, to particularly emphasize this last, because I am told, although I assuredly do not know it of my own knowledge – though I think if the fact were so I ought to know it, being tolerably well acquainted with that which goes on in the scientific world, and which has gone on there for the last thirty years – that there is a kind of sect, or horde, of scientific Goths and Vandals, who think it would be proper and desirable to sweep away all other forms of culture and instruction, except those in physical science, and to make them the universal and exclusive, or, at any rate, the dominant training of the human mind of the future generation. This is not my view – I do not believe that it is anybody's view – but it is attributed to those who, like myself, advocate scientific education. I therefore dwellstrongly upon *the* point, and I beg you to believe that the words I have just now read were by no means intended by me as a sop to the Cerberus of culture. I have not been in the habit of offering sops to any kind of Cerberus; but it was an expression of profound conviction on my own part – a conviction forced upon me not only by my mental constitution, but by the lessons of what is now becoming a somewhat long experience of varied conditions of life.

I am not about to trouble you with my autobiography; the omens are hardly favorable, at present, for work of that kind. But I should like, if I may do so without appearing, what I earnestly desire not to be, egotistical – I should like to make it clear to you that such notions as these, which are sometimes attributed to me, are, as I have said, inconsistent with my mental constitution, and still more inconsistent with the upshot of the teaching of my experience. For I can certainly claim for myself that sort of mental temperament which can say that nothing human comes amiss to it. I have never yet met with any branch of human knowledge which I have found unattractive – which it would not have been pleasant to me to follow, so far as I could go; and I have yet to meet with any form of art in which it has not been possible for me to take as acute a pleasure as, I believe, it is possible for men to take.

And with respect to the circumstances of life, it so happens that it has been my fate to know many lands and many climates, and to be familiar, by personal experience, with almost every form of society, from the uncivilized savage of Papua and Australia and the civilized savages of the slums and dens of the povertystricken parts of great cities, to those who perhaps are occasionally the somewhat over-civilized members of our upper ten thousand. And I have never found, in any of these conditions of life, a deficiency of something which was attractive. Savagery has its pleasures, I assure you, as well as civilization, and I may even venture to confess – if you will not let a whisper of the matter get back to London, where I am known – I am even fain to confess that sometimes in the din and throng of what is called "a brilliant reception" the vision crosses my mind of waking up from the soft plank which had afforded me satisfactory sleep during the hours of the night, in the bright dawn of a tropical morning, when my comrades were yet asleep, when every sound was hushed, except the little lap-lap of the ripples against the sides of the boat, and the distant twitter of the sea-bird on the reef. And when that vision crosses my mind, I am free to confess I desire to be back in the boat again. So that, if I share with those strange persons to whose asserted, but still hypothetical existence I have referred, the want of appreciation of forms of culture other than the pursuit of physical science, all I can say is, that it is in spite of my constitution, and in spite of my experience, that such should be my fate.

But now let me turn to another point, or rather to . two other points, with which I propose to occupy myself. How far does the experience of the last fourteen years justify the estimate which I ventured to put forward of the value of scientific culture, and of the share – the increasing share – which it must take in ordinary education? Happily, in respect to that matter, you need not

rely upon my testimony. In the last half-dozen numbers

– Science – 7

of the "Journal of Education," you will find a series of very interesting and remark-able papers, by gentlemen who are practically engaged in the business of education in our great public and other schools, telling us what is doing in these schools, and what is their experience of the results of scientific education there, so far as it has *gone.* I am not going to trouble you with an abstract of those papers, which are well worth your study in their fulness and completeness, but I have copied out one remarkable passage, because it seems to me so entirely to bear out what I have formerly ventured to say about the value of science, both as to its subject-matter and as to the discipline which the learning of science involves. It is from a paper by Mr. Worthington – one of the masters at Clifton, the reputation of which school you know well, and at the head of which is an old friend of mine, the Kev. Mr. Wilson – to whom much credit is due for being one of the first, as I can say from my own knowledge, to take up this question and work it into practical shape. What Mr. Worthington says is this:

"It is not easy to exaggerate the importance of the information imparted by certain branches of science; it modifies the whole criticism of life made in maturer years. The study has often, on a mass of boys, a certain influence which, I think, was hardly anticipated, and to which a good deal of value must be attached – an influence as much moral as intellectual, which is shown in the increased and increasing respect for precision of statement, and for that form of veracity which consists in the acknowledgment of difficulties. It produces a real effect to find that Nature cannot be imposed upon, and the attention given to experimental lectures, at first superficial and curious only, soon becomes minute, serious, and practical."

Ladies and gentlemen, I could not have chosen better words to express – in fact, I have, in other words, expressed the same conviction in former days – what the influence of scientific teaching, if properly carried out, must be.

But now comes the question of properly carrying it out, because, when I hear the value of school teaching in physical science disputed, my first impulse is to ask, the disputer, "What have you known about it?" and he generally tells me some lamentable case of failure. Then I ask, "What are the circumstances of the case, and how was the teaching carried out?" I remember, some few years ago, hearing of the head master of a large school, who had expressed great dissatisfaction with the adoption of the teaching of physical science – and that after experiment. But the experiment consisted in this – in asking one of the junior masters in the school to get up science, in order to teach it; and the young gentleman went away for a year and got up science and taught it. Well, I have no doubt that the result was as disappointing as the head master said it was, and I have no doubt that it ought to have been as disappointing, and far more disappointing too; for, if this kind of instruction is to be of any good at all, if it is not to be less than no good, if it is to take the place of that which is already of some good, then there are several points which must be attended to.

And the first of these is the proper selection of topics, the second is practical teaching, the third is practical teachers, and the fourth is sufficiency of time. If these four points are not carefully attended to by anybody who undertakes the teaching of physical science inschools, my advice to him is to let it alone. I will not dwell at any length upon the first point, because there ia a general consensus of opinion as to the nature of the topics which should be chosen. The second point – practical teaching – is one of great importance, because it requires more capital to set it agoing, demands more time, and, last, but by no means least, it requires much more personal exertion and trouble on the part of those professing to teach, than is the case with other kinds of instruction.

When I accepted the invitation to be here this evening, your secretary was good enough to send me the addresses which have been given by distinguished persons who have previously occupied this chair. I don't know whether he had a malicious desire to alarm me; but, however that may be, I read the addresses, and derived the greatest pleasure and profit from some of them, and from none more than from the one given by the great historian, Mr. Freeman, which delighted me most of all; and, if I had not been ashamed of plagiarizing, and if I had not been sure of being found out, I should have been glad *to* have copied very much of what Mr. Freeman said, simply putting in the word science for history. There was one notable passage – "The difference between good and bad teaching mainly consists in this, whether the words used are really clothed with a meaning or not." And Mr. Freeman gives a remarkable example of this. He says, when a little girl was asked where Turkey was, she answered that it was in the yard with the other fowls, and that showed she had a definite idea connected with the word Turkey, and was, so far, worthy of praise. I quite agree with that commendation; butwhat a curious thing it is that one should now find it necessary to urge that this is the be-all and end-all of scientific instruction – the *sine qua non,* the absolutely necessary condition – and yet that it was insisted upon more than two hundred years ago by one of the greatest men science ever possessed in this country, William Harvey. Harvey wrote, or at least published, only two small books, one of which is the well-known treatise on the circulation of the blood. The other, the "Exercita- tiones de Generatione," is less known, but not less remarkable. And not the least valuable part of it is the preface, in which there occurs this passage: "Those who, reading the words of authors, do not form sensible images of the things referred to, obtain no true ideas, but conceive false imaginations and inane phantasms." You see, William Harvey's words are just the same in substance as those of Mr. Freeman, only they happen to be rather more than two centuries older. So that what I am now saying has its application elsewhere than in science; but assuredly in science the condition of knowing, of your own knowledge, things which you talk about, is absolutely imperative.

I remember, in my youth, there were detestable books which ought to have been burned by the hands of the common hangman, for they contained questions and answers to be learned by heart, of this sort, "What is a horse? The horse is termed *Equus caballus;* belongs to the class Mammalia; order, Pachydermata; family, Soli- dungula." Was any human being wiser for learning that magic formula? Was he not more foolish, inasmuch as he was deluded into taking words for knowledge ? It is that kind of teaching that one wants to get rid of, andbanished out of science. Make it as little as you like, but, unless that which is taught is based on actual observation and familiarity with facts, it is better left alone.

There are a great many people who imagine that elementary teaching might be properly carried out by teachers provided with only elementary knowledge. Let me assure you that that is the profoundest mistake in the world. There is nothing so difficult to do as to write a good elementary book, and there is nobody so hard to teach properly and well as people who know nothing about a subject, and I will tell you why. If I address an audience of persons who are occupied in the same line of work as myself, I can assume that they know a vast deal, and that they can find out the blunders I make. If they don't, it is their fault and not mine; but when I appear before a body of people who know nothing about the matter, who take for gospel whatever I say, surely it becomes needful that I consider what I say, make sure that it will bear examination, and that I do not impose upon the credulity of those who have faith in me. In the second place, it involves that difficult process of knowing what you know so well that you can talk about it as you can talk about your ordinary business. A man can always talk about his own business. He can always make it plain; but, if his knowledge is hearsay, he ia afraid to go beyond what he has recollected, and put it before those that are ignorant in such a shape that they shall comprehend it. That is why, to be a good elementary teacher, to teach the elements of any subject, requires most careful consideration, if you are a master of the subject; and, if you are not a master of it, it is needful you should familiarize yourself with so much as you arecalled upon to teach – soak yourself in it, so to speak – until you know it as part of your daily life and daily knowledge, and then you will be able to teach anybody. That is what I mean by practical teachers, and, although the deficiency of such teachers is being remedied to a large extent, I think it is one which has long existed, and which has existed from no fault of those who undertook to teach, but because, until the last score of years, it absolutely was not possible for any one in a great many branches of science, whatever his desire might be, to get instruction which would enable him to be a good teacher of elementary things. All that is being rapidly altered, and I hope it will soon become a thing of the past.

The last point I have referred to is the question of the sufficiency of time. And here comes the rub. The teaching of science needs time, as any other subject; but it needs more time proportionally than other subjects, for the amount of work obviously done, if the teaching is to be, as I have said, practical. "Work done in a laboratory involves a good deal of expenditure of time without always an obvious result, because we do not see anything of that quiet process of soaking the facts into the mind which takes place through the organs of the senses. On this ground there must be ample time given to science teaching. What that amount of time should be is a point which I need not discuss now; in fact, it is a point which cannot be settled until one has made up one's mind about various other questions.

All, then, that I have to ask for, on behalf of the scientific people, if I may venture to speak for more than myself, is that you should put scientific teaching into what statesmen call the condition of "the most favorednation"; that is to say, that it shall have as large a share of the time given to education as any other principal subject. You may say that that is a very vague statement, because the value of the allotment of time, under those circumstances, depends upon the number of principal subjects. It is x the time, and an unknown quantity of principal subjects dividing that, and science taking shares with the rest. That shows that we cannot deal with this question fully until we have made up our minds as to what the principal subjects of education ought to be.

I know quite well that launching myself into this discussion is a very dangerous operation; that it is a very large subject and one which is difficult to deal with, however much I may trespass upon your patience, in the time allotted to me. But the discussion is so fundamental, it is so completely impossible to make up one's mind on these matters until one has settled the question, that I will even venture to make the experiment. A great lawyer-statesman and philosopher of a former age – I mean Francis Bacon – said that truth came out of error much more rapidly than it came out of confusion. There is a wonderful truth in that saying. Next to being right in this world, the best of all things is to be clearly and definitely wrong, because you will come out somewhere. If you go buzzing about between right and wrong, vibrating and fluctuating, you come out nowhere; but if you are absolutely and thoroughly and persistently wrong, you must, some of these days, have the extreme good fortune of knocking your head against a fact, and that sets you all straight again. So I will not trouble myself as to whether I may be right or wrong in what I am about to say, but at any rate I hope to be clear anddefinite; and then you will be able to judge for yourselves whether, in following out the train of thought I have to introduce, you knock your heads against facts or not.

I take it that the whole object of education is, in the first place, to train the faculties of the young in such a manner as to give their possessors the best chance of being happy and useful in their generation; and, in the second place, to furnish them with the most important portions of that immense capitalized experience of the human race which we call knowledge of various kinds. I am using the term knowledge in its widest possible sense; and the question is, what subjects to select by training and discipline, in which the object I have just defined may be best attained.

I must call your attention further to this fact, that all the subjects of our thoughts – all feelings and propositions (leaving aside our sensations as the mere materials and occasions of thinking and feeling), all our mental furniture – may be classified under one of two heads – as either within the province of the intellect, something that can be put into propositions and affirmed or denied; or as within the province of feeling, or that which, before the name was defiled, was called the aesthetic side of our nature, and which can neither be proved nor disproved, but only felt and known.

According to the classification which I have put before you, then, the subjects of all knowledge are divisible into the two groups, matters of science and matters of art; for all things with which the reasoning faculty alone is occupied come under the province of science; and in the broadest sense, and not in the narrow and technicalsense in which we are now accustomed to use the word art, all things feelable, all things which stir our emotions, come under the term of art, in the sense of the subject- matter of the aesthetic faculty. So that we are shut up to this – that the business of education is, in the first place, to provide the young with the means and the habit of observation; and, secondly, to supply the subject-matter of knowledge either in the shape of science or of art, or of both combined.

Now, it is a very remarkable fact – but it is true of most things in this world – that there is hardly anything one-sided, or of one nature; and it is not immediately obvious what 'of the things that interest us may be regarded as pure science, and what may be regarded as pure art. It may be that there are some peculiarly constituted persons who, before they have advanced far into the depths of geometry, find artistic beauty about it; but, taking the generality of mankind, I think it may be said that, when they begin to learn mathematics, their whole souls are absorbed in tracing the connection between the premises and the conclusion, and that to them geometry is pure science. So I think it may be said that mechanics and osteology are pure science. On the other hand, melody in music is pure art. You cannot reason about it; there is no proposition involved in it. So, again, in the pictorial art, an arabesque, or a "harmony in gray," touches none but the aesthetic faculty. But a great mathematician, and even many persons who are not great mathematicians, will tell you that they derive immense pleasure from geometrical reasonings. Everybody knows mathematicians speak of solutions and problems as "elegant," and they tell you that a certain massof mystic symbols is "beautiful, quite lovely." Well, you do not see it. They do see it, because the intellectual process, the process of comprehending the reasons symbolized by these figures and these signs, confers upon them a sort of pleasure, such as an artist has in visual symmetry. Take a science of which I may speak with more confidence, and which is the most attractive of those I am concerned with. It is what we call morphology, which consists in tracing out the unity in variety of the infinitely diversified structures of animals and plants. I cannot give you any example of a thorough aesthetic pleasure more intensely real than a pleasure of this kind – the pleasure which arises in one's mind when a whole mass of different structures run into one harmony as the expression of a central law. That is where the province of art overlays and embraces the province of intellect. And, if I may venture to express an opinion on such a subject, the great majority of forms of art are not in the sense what I just now defined them to be – pure art; but they derive much of their quality from simultaneous and even unconscious excitement of the intellect.

When I was a boy, I was very fond of music, and I am so now; and it so happened that I had the opportunity of hearingxmuch good music. Among other things, J had abundant opportunities of hearing that great old master, Sebastian Bach. I jemember perfectly well – though I knew nothing about music then, and, I may add, know nothing whatever about it now – the intense satisfaction and delight which I had in listening, by the hour together, to Bach's fugues. It is a pleasure which remains with me, I am glad to think; but, of late years, I have tried to find out the why and wherefore, and ithas often occurred to me that the pleasure derived from musical compositions of this kind is essentially of the same nature as that which is derived from pursuits which are commonly regarded as purely intellectual. I mean, that the source of pleasure is exactly the same as in most of my problems in morphology – that you have the theme in one of the old master's works followed out in all its endless variations, always appearing and always reminding you of unity in variety. So in painting; what is called "truth to nature" is the intellectual element coming in, and truth to nature depends entirely upon the intellectual culture of the person to whom art is addressed. If you are in Australia, you may get credit for being a good artist – I mean among the natives – if you can draw a kangaroo after a fashion. But, among men of higher civilization, the intellectual knowledge we possess brings its criticism into our appreciation of works of art, and we are obliged to satisfy it, as well as the mere sense of beauty in color and in outline. And so, the higher the culture and information of those whom art addresses, the more exact and precise must be what we call its "truth to nature."

If we turn to literature, the same thing is true, and you find works of literature which may be' said to be pure art. A little song of Shakespeare or of Goethe is pure art; it is exquisitely beautiful, although its intellectual content may be nothing. A series of pictures is made to pass before your mind by the meaning of words, and the effect is a melody of ideas. Nevertheless, the great mass of the literature we esteem is valued, not merely because of having artistic form, but because of its intellectual content; and the value is the higher themore precise, distinct, and true is that intellectual content. And, if you will let me for a moment speak of the very highest forms of literature, do we not regard them as highest simply because the more we know the truer they seem, and the more competent we are to appreciate beauty the more beautiful they are? No man ever understands Shakespeare until he is old, though the youngest may admire him, the reason being that he satisfies the artistic instinct of the youngest and harmonizes with the ripest and richest experience of the oldest.

I have said this much to draw your attention to what, to my mind, lies at the root of all this matter, and at the understanding of one another by the men of science on the one hand, and the men of literature, and history, and art, on the other. It is not a question whether one order of study or another should predominate. It is a question of what topics of education you shall select which will combine all the needful elements in such due proportion as to give the greatest amount of food, support, and encouragement to those faculties which enable us to appreciate truth, and to profit by those sources of innocent happiness which are open to us, and, at- the same time, to avoid that which is bad, and coarse, and ugly, and keep clear of the multitude of pitfalls and dangers which beset those who break through the natural or moral laws.

I address myself, in this spirit, to the consideration of the question of the value of purely literary education. Is it good and sufficient, or is it insufficient and bad ? Well, here I venture to say that there are literary educations and literary educations. If I am to understand by that term the education that was current in the. great majority of middle-class schools, and upper schools too, in this country when I was a boy, and which consisted absolutely and almost entirely in keeping boys for eight or ten years at learning the rules of Latin and Greek grammar, construing certain Latin and Greek authors, and possibly making verses which, had they been English verses, would have been condemned as abominable doggerel – if that is what you mean by liberal education, then I say it is scandalously insufficient and almost worthless. My reason for saying *so* is not from the point of view of science at all, but from the point of view of literature. I say the thing professes to be literary education that is not a literary education at all. It was not literature at all that was taught, but science in a very bad form. It is quite obvious that grammar is science and not literature. The analysis of a text by the help of the rules of grammar is just as much a scientific operation as the analysis of a chemical compound by the help of the rules of chemical analysis. There is nothing that appeals to the aesthetic faculty in that operation; and I ask multitudes of men of my own age, who went through this process, whether they ever had a conception of art or literature until they obtained it for themselves after leaving school? Then you may say, "If that is so, if the education was scientific, why cannot you be satisfied with it?" I say, because, although it is a scientific training, it is of the most inadequate and inappropriate kind. If there is any good at all in scientific education, it is that men should be trained, as I said before, to know things for themselves at first hand, and that they should understand every step of the reason of that which they do.

I desire to speak with the utmost respect of thatscience – philology – of which grammar is a part and parcel; yet everybody knows that grammar, as it is usually learned at school, affords no scientific training. It is taught just aa you would teach the rules of chess or draughts. On the other hand, if I am to understand by a literary education the study of the literatures of either ancient or modern nations – but especially those of antiquity, and more especially that of ancient Greece; if this literature is studied, not merely from the point of view of philological science, and its practical application to the interpretation of texts, but as an exemplification of and commentary upon the principles of art; if you look upon the literature of a people as a chapter in the development of the human mind, if you work out this in a broad spirit, and with such collateral references to morals and politics, and physical geography, and the like, as are needful to make you comprehend what the meaning of ancient literature and civilization is – then, assuredly, it affords a splendid and noble education. But I still think it is susceptible of improvement, and that no man will ever comprehend the real secret of the difference between the ancient world and our present time, unless he haa learned to see the difference which the late development of physical science has made between the thought of this day and the thought of that, and he will never see that difference, unless he has some practical insight into some branches of physical science; and you must remember that a literary education such as that which 1 have just referred to is out of the reach of those whose school life is cut short at sixteen or seventeen.

But, you will say, all this is fault-finding; let us hear what you have in the way of positive suggestion. ThenI am bound to tell you that, if I could make a clean sweep of ' everything – I am very glad I cannot, because I might, and probably should, make mistakes – but if I could make a clean sweep of everything and start afresh, I should, in the first place, secure that training of the young in reading and writing, and in the habit of attention and observation, both to that which is told them, and that which they see, which everybody agrees to. But in addition to that, I should make it absolutely necessary for everybody, for a longer or shorter period, to learn to draw. Now, you may say, there are some people who cannot draw, however much they may be taught. I deny that *in toto,* because I never yet met with anybody who could not learn to write. Writing is a form of drawing; therefore if you give the same attention and trouble to drawing as you do to writing, depend upon it, there is nobody who cannot be made to draw, more or less well. Do not misapprehend me. I do not say for one moment you would make an artistic draughtsman. Artists are not made; they grow. You may improve the natural faculty in that direction, but you cannot make it; but you can teach simple drawing, and you will find it an implement of learning of extreme value. I do not think its value can be exaggerated, because it gives you the means of training the young in attention and accuracy, which are the two things in which all mankind are more deficient than in any other mental quality whatever. The whole of my life has been spent in trying to give my proper attention to things and to be accurate, and I have not succeeded as well as I could wish; and other people, I am afraid, are not much more fortunate. You cannot begin this habit too early, and I considerthere is nothing of so great a value as the habit of drawing, to secure those two desirable ends.

Then we come to the subject-matter, whether scientific or aesthetic, of education, and I should naturally have no question at all about teaching the elements of physical science, of the kind I have sketched, in a practical manner; but among scientific topics, using the word scientific in the broadest sense, I would also include the elements of the theory of morals and of that of political and social life, which, strangely enough, it never seems to occur to anybody to teach a child. I would have the history of our own country, and of all the influences which have been brought to bear upon it, with incidental geography, not as a mere chronicle of reigns and battles, but as a chapter in the development of the race, and the history of civilization.

Then with respect to aesthetic knowledge and discipline, we have happily in the English language one of the most magnificent storehouses of artistic beauty and of models of literary excellence which exists in the world at the present time. I have said before, and I repeat it here, that if a man cannot get literary culture of the highest kind out of his Bible, and Chaucer, and Shakespeare, and Milton, and Hobbes, and Bishop Berkeley, to mention only a few of our illustrious writers – I say, if he cannot get it out of those writers, he cannot get it out of anything; and I would assuredly devote a very large portion of the time of every English child to the careful study of the models of English writing of such varied and wonderful kind as we possess, and, what is still more important and still more neglected, the habit of using that language with precision, with force, and with art. I fancy we are almost the only nation in the world who seem to think that composition comes by nature. The French attend to their own language, the Germans study theirs; but Englishmen do not seem to think it is worth their while. Nor would I fail to include, in the course of study I am sketching, translations of all the best works of antiquity, or of the modern world. It is a very desirable thing to read Homer in Greek; but if you don't happen to know Greek, the next best thing we can do is to read as good a translation of it as we have recently been furnished with in prose. You won't get all you would get from the original, but you may get a great deal; and to refuse to know this great deal because you cannot get all, seems to be as sensible as for a hungry man to refuse bread because he cannot get partridge. Finally, I would add instruction in either music or painting, or, if the child should be so unhappy, as sometimes happens, as to have no faculty for either of those, and no possibility of doing anything in any artistic sense with them, then I would see what could be done with literature alone; but I would provide, in the fullest sense, for the development of the' aesthetic side of the mind. In my judgment, those are all the essentials of education for an English child. With that outfit, such as it might be made in the time given to education which is within the reach of nine- tenths of the population – with that outfit, an Englishman, within the limits of English life, is fitted to go anywhere, to occupy the highest positions, to fill the highest offices of the State, and to become distinguished in practical pursuits, in science, or in art. For, if he have the opportunity to learn all those things, and have his mind disciplined in the various directions the teaching of those topics would have necessitated, then, assuredly, he will be able to pick up, on his road through life, all the rest of the intellectual baggage he wants.

If the educational time at our disposition were sufficient, there are one or two things I . would add to those I have just now called the essentials; and perhaps you will be surprised to hear, though I hope you will not, that I should add, not more science, but one, or, if possible, two languages. The knowledge of some other language than one's own is, in fact, of singular intellectual value. Many of the faults and mistakes of the ancient philosophers are traceable to the fact that they knew no language but their own, and were often led into confusing the symbol with the thought which it embodied. I think it is Locke who says that one-half of the mistakes "of philosophers have arisen from questions about words; and one of the safest ways of delivering yourself from the bondage of words is to know how ideas look in words to which you are not accustomed. That is one reason for the study of language; another reason is that it opens new fields in art and in science. Another is the practical value of such knowledge; and yet another is this, that if your languages are properly chosen, from the time of learning the additional languages you will know your own language better than ever you did. So, I say, if the time given to education permits, add Latin and German. Latin, because it is the key to nearly one-half of English and to all the Romance languages; and German, because it is the key to almost all the remainder of English, and helps you to understand a race from whom most of us have sprung, and who have a character and a literature of a fateful force in the history of the world, such as probably has been allotted to those of Do other people, except the Jews, the Greeks, and ourselves. Beyond these, the essential and the eminently desirable elements of all education, let each man take up his special line – the historian devote himself to his history, the man of science to his science, the man of letters to his culture of that kind, and the artist to his special pursuit.

Bacon has prefaced some of his works with no more than this: *Franciscus Bacon sic cogitavit;* let "sic cogi- tavi" be the epilogue to what I have ventured to address to you to-night.

7

SECTION 7

VIII

UNIVERSITIES: ACTUAL AND IDEAL

[1874]

ELECTED by the suffrages of your four Nations Rector of the ancient University of which you are scholars, I take the earliest opportunity which has presented itself since my restoration to health, of delivering the Address which, by long custom, is expected of the holder of my office.

My first duty, in opening that Address, is to offer you my most hearty thanks for the signal honor you have conferred upon me – an honor of which, as a man unconnected with you by personal or by national ties, devoid of political distinction, and a plebeian who stands by his order, I could not have dreamed. And it was the more surprising to me, as the five-and-twenty years which have passed over my head since I reached intellectual manhood have been largely spent in no half-hearted advocacy of doctrines which have not yet found favor in the eyes of Academic respectability; so that, when the proposal to nominate me for your Rector came, I was almost as much astonished as was Hal o' the Wynd, "who fought for his own hand," by the Black Douglas's proffer of knighthood. And I fear that my acceptance must be taken as evidence that, less wise than the Armorer of Perth, I have not yet done with soldiering.

In fact, if for a moment I imagined that your intention was simply, in the kindness of your hearts, to dome honor; and that the Rector of your University, like that of some other Universities, was one of those happy beings who sit in glory for three years, with nothing to do for it save the making of a speech, a conversation with my distinguished predecessor soon dispelled the dream. I found that, by the constitution of the University of Aberdeen, the incumbent of the Rectorate is, if not a power, at any rate a potential energy; and that, whatever may be his chances of success or failure, it is his duty to convert that potential energy into a living force, directed toward such ends as may seem to him conducive to the welfare of the corporation of which lie is the theoretical head.

I need not tell you that your late Lord Rector took this view of his position, and acted upon it with the comprehensive, farseeing insight into the actual condition and tendencies, not merely of his own, but of other countries, which is his honorable characteristic among statesmen. I have already done my best, and, as long as I hold my office, I shall continue my endeavors, to follow in the path which he trod; to do what in me lies to bring this University nearer to the ideal – alas, that I should be obliged to say ideal – of all Universities; which, as J conceive, should be places in which thought is free from all fetters; and in which all sources of knowledge, and all aids to learning, should be accessible to all comers, without distinction of creed or country, riches or poverty.

Do not suppose, however, that I am sanguine enough to expect much to come of any poor efforts of mine. If your annals take any notice of my incumbency, I shall probably go down to posterity as the Rector who wasalways beaten. But if they add, as I think they will, that my defeats became victories in the hands of my successors, I shall be well content.

The scenes are shifting in the great theatre of the world. The act which commenced with the Protestant Eeformation is nearly played out', and a wider and deeper change than that effected three centuries ago – a reformation, or rather a revolution of thought, the extremes of which are represented by the intellectual heirs of John of Leyden and of Ignatius Loyola, rather than by those of Luther and of Leo – is waiting to come on, nay, visible behind the scenes to those who have good eyes. Men are beginning, once more, to awake to the fact that matters of belief and of speculation are of absolutely infinite practical importance; and are drawing off from that sunny country "where it is always afternoon" – . the sleepy hollow of broad indifferentism – to range themselves under their natural banners. Change is in the air. It is whirling feather-heads into all sorts of eccentric orbits, and filling the steadiest with a sense of insecurity. It insists on reopening all questions and asking all institutions, however venerable, by what right they exist, and whether they are, or are not, in harmony with the real or supposed wants of mankind. And it is remarkable that these searching inquiries are not so much forced on institutions from without, as developed from within. Consummate scholars question the value of learning; priests contemn dogma; and women turn their backs upon man's ideal of perfect womanhood, and seek satisfaction in apocalyptic visions of some, as yet, unrealized epicene reality.

If there be a type of stability in this world, one would be inclined to look for it in the old Universities of England. But it has been my business of late to hear a good deal about what is going on in these famous corporations; and I have been filled with astonishment by the evidences of internal fermentation which they exhibit. If Gibbon could revisit the ancient seat of learning of which he has written so cavalierly, assuredly he would no longer speak of "the monks of Oxford sunk in prejudice and port." There, as elsewhere, port has gone out of fashion, and so has prejudice – at least that particular fine, old, crusted sort of prejudice to which the great historian alludes.

Indeed, things are moving so fast in Oxford and Cambridge that, for my part, I rejoiced when the Royal Commission, of which I am a member, had finished and presented the Report which related to these Universities; for we should have looked like mere plagiarists, if, in consequence of a little longer delay in issuing it, all the measures of reform we proposed had been anticipated by the spontaneous action of the Universities themselves.

A month ago I should have gone on to say that one might speedily expect changes of another kind in Oxford and Cambridge. A Commission has been inquiring into the revenues of the many wealthy societies, in more or less direct connection with the,. Universities, resident in those towns. It is said that the Commission has reported, and that, for the first time in recorded history, the nation, and perhaps the Colleges themselves, will know what they are worth. And it was announced that a statesman, who, whatever his other merits or defects, has aims above the level of mere party fighting, and aclear vision into the most complex practical problems, meant to deal with these revenues.

But, *Bos locutus est.* That mysterious independent variable of political calculation, Public Opinion – which some whisper is, in the present case, very much the same thing as publican's opinion – has willed otherwise. The Heads may return to their wonted slumbers – at any rate for a space.

Is the spirit of change, which is working thus vigorously in the South, likely to affect the Northern Universities, and if so, to what extent? The violence of fermentation depends not so much on the quantity of the yeast as on the composition of the wort and its richness in fermentable material; and, as a preliminary to the discussion of this question, I venture to call to your minds the essential and fundamental differences between the Scottish and the English type of University.

Do not charge me with anything worse than official egotism, if I say that these differences appear to be largely symbolized by my own existence. There is no Rector in an English University. Now, the organization of the members of a University into Nations, with their elective Rector, is the last relic of the primitive constitution of Universities. The Rectorate was the most important of all offices in that University of Paris, upon the model of which the University of Aberdeen was fashioned; and which was certainly a great and flourishing institution in the twelfth century.

Enthusiasts for the antiquity of one of the two acknowledged parents of all Universities, indeed, do not hesitate to trace the origin of the "Studium Parisiense" up to that wonderful king of the Franks and Lombards,

YIII – Science – 8

Karl, surnamed the Great, whom we all called Charlemagne, and believed to be a Frenchman, until a learned historian, by beneficent iteration, taught us better. Karl is said not to have been much of a scholar himself, but he had the wisdom of which knowledge is only the servitor. And that wisdom enabled him to see that ignorance is one of the roots of all evil.

In the Capitulary which enjoins the foundation of monasterial and cathedral schools, he says: "Right action is better than knowledge; but in order to do what is right, we must know what is right." ' An irrefragable truth, I fancy. Acting upon it, the king took pretty full compulsory powers, and carried into effect a really considerable and effectual scheme of elementary education through the length and breadth of his dominions.

No doubt the idolaters out by the Elbe, in what is now part of Prussia, objected to the Prankish king's measures; no doubt the priests, who had never hesitated about sacrificing all unbelievers in their fantastic deities and futile conjurations, were the loudest in chanting the virtues of toleration; no doubt they denounced as a cruel persecutor the man who would not allow them, however sincere they might be, to go on spreading delusions which debased the intellect, as much as they deadened the moral sense, and undermined the bonds of civil allegiance; no doubt, if they had lived in these times, they would have been able to show, with ease, that the king's proceedings were totally contrary to the best liberal principles. But it may be said, in justification of the Teutonic ruler, first, that he was born before those principles, and did not suspect that the best way of getting disorder into order was to let it alone; and, secondly, that his rough and questionable proceedings did more or less bring about the end he had in view. For, in a couple of centuries, the schools he sowed broadcast produced their crop of men, thirsting for knowledge and craving for culture. Such men gravitating toward Paris, as a light amid the darkness of evil days, from Germany, from Spain, from Britain, and from Scandinavia, came together by natural affinity. By degrees they banded themselves into a society, which, as its end was the knowledge of all things knowable, called itself a *"jStudium Generale";* and when it had grown into a recognized corporation, acquired the name of " *Universitas Studii Generalis,"* which, mark you, means not a "Useful Knowledge Society," but a "Knowledge-of-things-in-general Society."

1 "Quamvis enim melius sit bene facere quam noase, priua tamen est nosae quatn facere." – "Karoli Magni Regis Constitutio de Scholia per singula Episco- pia et Monasteria inalituendis," addressed to the Abbot of Fuldu. Baluziua, "Capitularia Regum Francorum," X. i. p. 202.

And thus the first "University," at any rate on this side of the Alps, came into being. Originally it had but one Faculty, that of Arts. Its aim was to be a centre of knowledge and culture; not to be, in any sense, a technical sdhool.

The scholars seem to have studied Grammar, Logic, and . Rhetoric; Arithmetic and Geometry; Astronomy; Theology; and Music. Thus, their work,- however imperfect and faulty, judged by modern lights, it may have been, brought them face to face with all the leading aspects of the many-sided mind of man. For these studies did really contain, at any rate in embryo – sometimes, it may be, in caricature – what we now call Philosophy, Mathematical and Physical Science, and Art. And I doubt if the curriculum of any modern University shows so clear and generous a comprehension of what is meant by culture as this old Trivium and Quadrivium does.

The students who had passed through the University course, and had proved themselves competent to teach, became masters and teachers of their younger brethren. Whence the distinction of Masters and Regents on the one hand, and Scholars on the other.

Rapid growth necessitated organization. The Masters nd Scholars of various tongues and countries grouped themselves into four Nations; and the Nations, by their own votes at first, and subsequently by those of their Procurators, or representatives, elected their supreme head and governor, the Rector – at that time the sole representative of the University, and a very real power, who could defy Provosts interfering from without, or could inflict even corporal punishment on disobedient members within the University.

Such was the primitive constitution of the University of Paris. It is in reference to this original state of things that I have spoken of the Rectorate, and all that appertains to it, as the sole relic of that constitution.

But this original organization did not last long. Society was not then, any more than it is now, patient of culture, as such. It says to everything, "Be useful to me, or away with you." And to the learned, the unlearned man said then, as he does now, "What is the use of all your learning, unless you can tell me what I want to know? I am here blindly groping about, and constantly damaging myself by collision with three mighty powers, the power of the invisible God, the power of my fellow Man, and the power of brute Natare. Let your learning be turned to the study of these powers, that I may know how I am to comport myself with regard to them." In answer to this demand, some of the Masters of the Faculty of Arts devoted themselves to the study of Theology, some to that of Law, and some to that of Medicine; and they became Doctors – men learned in those technical, or, as we now call them, professional, branches of knowledge. Like cleaving to like, the Doctors formed schools, or Faculties, of Theology, Law, and Medicine, which sometimes assumed airs of superiority over their parent, the Faculty of Arts, though the latter always asserted and maintained its fundamental supremacy.

The Faculties arose by process of natural differentiation out of the primitive University. Other constituents, foreign to its nature, were speedily, grafted upon it. One of these extraneous elements was forced into it by the Roman Church, which in those days asserted with effect, that which it now asserts, happily without any effect in these realms, its right of censorship and control over all teaching. The local habitation of the University lay partly in the lands attached to the monastery of S. Gen- evieve, partly in the diocese of the Bishop of Paris; and he who would teach must have the license of the Abbot, or of the Bishop, as the nearest representative of the Pope, so to do, which license was granted by the Chancellors of these Ecclesiastics.

Thus, if I am what archeologists call a " survival" of the primitive head and ruler of the University, your Chancellor stands in the same relation to the Papacy; and, with all respect for his Grace, I think I may say that we both look terribly shrunken when compared with our great originals.

Not so is it with a second foreign element, which silently dropped into the soil of Universities, like the grain of mustard-seed in the parable; and; like that grain, grew into a tree, in whose branches a whole aviary of fowls took shelter. That element is the element of Endowment. It differed from the preceding, in its original design to serve as a prop to the young plant, not to be a parasite upon it. The charitable and the humane, blessed with wealth, were very early penetrated by the misery of the poor student. And the wise saw that intellectual ability is not so common or so unimportant a gift that it should be allowed to run to waste upon mere handicrafts and chores. The man who was a blessing to his contemporaries, but who so often has been converted into a curse, by the blind adherence of his posterity to- the letter, rather than to the spirit, of his wishes – I mean the "pious founder" – gave money and lands, that the student, who was rich in brain and poor in all else, might be taken from the plow or from the stithy, and enabled to devote himself to the higher service of mankind; and built colleges and halls in which he might be not only housed and fed, but taught.

The Colleges were very generally placed in strict subordination to the University by their founders; but, in many cases, their endowment, consisting of land, has undergone an "unearned increment," which has given these societies a continually increasing weight and importance as against the unendowed, or fixedly endowed, University. In Pharaoh's dream, the seven lean kine eat up the seven fat ones. In the reality of historical fact, the fat Colleges have eaten up the lean Universities.

Even here in Aberdeen, though the causes at workmay have been somewhat differ- ent, the effects have been similar; and you see how much more substantial an entity is the Very Reverend the Principal, analogue, if not ho- mologue, of the Principals of King's College, than the Rector, lineal representative of the ancient monarchs of the University, though now little more than a "king of shreds and patches."

Do not suppose that, in thus briefly tracing the process of University metamorphosis, I have had any intention of quarrelling with its results. Practically, it seems to me that the broad changes effected in 1858 have given the Scottish Universities a very liberal constitution, with as much real approximation to the primitive state of things as is at all desirable. If your fat kine have eaten the lean, they have not lain down to chew the cud ever since. The Scottish Universities, like the English, have diverged widely enough from their primitive model; but I cannot help thinking that the northern form has remained more faithful to its original, not only in constitution, but, what is more to the purpose, in view of the cry for change, in the practical application of the endowments connected with it.

In Aberdeen, these endowments are numerous, but so small that, taken altogether, they are not equal to the revenue of a single third-rate English college. They are scholarships, not fellowships; aids to do work – not rewards for such work as it lies within the reach of an ordinary, or even an extraordinary, young man to do. You do not think that passing a respectable examination is a fair equivalent for an income such as many a gray- headed veteran or clergyman would envy; and which is larger than the endowment of many Regius chairs. Youdo not care to make your University a school of manners for the rich; of sports for the athletic; or a hot-bed of high-fed, hypercritical refinement, more destructive to vigor and originality than are starvation and oppression. No; your little Bursaries of ten and twenty (I believe even fifty) pounds a year enabled any boy who has shown ability in the course of his education in those remarkable primary schools, which have made Scotland the power she is, to obtain the highest culture the country can give him; and when he is armed and equipped, his Spartan Alma Mater tells him that, so far, he has had his wages for his work, and that he may go and earn the rest.

When I think of the host of pleasant, moneyed, well- bred young gentlemen, who do a little learning and much boating by Cam and Isis, the vision is a pleasant one; and, as a patriot, I rejoice that the youth of the upper and richer classes of the nation receive a wholesome and a manly training, however small may be the modicum of knowledge they gather, in the intervals of this, their serious lousiness. I admit, to the full, the social and political value of that training. But, when I proceed to consider that these young men may be said to represent the great bulk of what the Colleges have to show for their enormous wealth, plus, at least, a hundred and fifty pounds a year apiece which each undergraduate costs his parents or guardians, I feel inclined to ask, whether the rate-in-aid of the education of the wealthy and professional classes, thus levied on the resources of the community, is not, after all, a little heavy? And, still further, I am tempted to inquire what has become of the indigent scholars, the sons of the masses of the peoplewhose daily labor just suffices to meet their daily wants, for whose benefit these rich foundations were largely, if not mainly, instituted? It seems as if Pharaoh's dream had been rigorously carried out, and that even the fat scholar has eaten the lean one. And when I turn from this picture to the no less real vision of many a brave and frugal Scotch boy, spending his summer in hard manual labor, that he may have the privilege of wending his way in autumn to this University, with a bag of oatmeal, ten pounds in his pocket, and his own stout heart to depend upon through the northern winter; not bent on seeking

"The bubble reputation at the cannon's mouth,"

but determined to wring knowledge from the hard hands of penury; when I see him win through all such outward ' obstacles to positions of wide usefulness and well-earned fame"; I cannot but think that, in essence, Aberdeen has departed but little from the primitive intention of the founders of Universities, and that the spirit of reform has' so much to do on the other side of the Border that it may be long before he has leisure to look this way.

As compared with other actual Universities, then, Aberdeen may, perhaps, be well satisfied with itself. But do not think me an impracticable dreamer, if I ask you not to rest and be thankful in this state of satisfaction; if I ask you to consider a while how this actual good stands related to that ideal better, toward which both men and institutions must progress, if they would not retrograde.

In an ideal University, as I conceive it, a man should be able to obtain instruction in all forms of knowledge, and discipline in the use of all the methods by which knowledge is obtained. In such a University, the force of living example should fire the student with a noble ambition to emulate the learning of learned men, and to follow in the footsteps of the explorers of new fields of knowledge. And the very air he breathes should be charged with that enthusiasm for truth, that fanaticism of veracity, which is a greater possession than much learning; a nobler gift than the power of increasing knowledge; by so much greater and nobler than these, as the moral nature of man is greater than the intellectual; for veracity is the heart of morality.

But the man who is all morality and intellect, although he may be good and even great, is, after all, only half a man. There is beauty in the moral world and in the intellectual world; but there is also a beauty which is neither moral nor intellectual – the beauty of the world of Art. There are men who are devoid of the power of seeing it, as there are men who are born deaf and blind, and the loss of those, as of these, is simply infinite. There are others in whom it is an overpowering passion; happy men, born with the productive, or at lowest, the appreciative, genius of the Artist. But, in the mass of mankind, the Esthetic faculty, like the reasoning power and the moral sense, needs to be roused, directed, and cultivated; and I know not why the development of that side of his nature, through which man has access to a perennial spring of ennobling pleasure, should be omitted from any comprehensive scheme of University education.

All Universities recognize Literature in the sense of the old . Rhetoric, which is art incarnate in words. Some, to their credit, recognize Art in its narrower sense, to acertain extent, and confer degrees for proficiency in some of its branches. If there are Doctors of Music, why should there be no masters of Painting, of Sculpture, of Architecture? I should like to see Professors of the Fine Arts in every University; and instruction in some branch of their work made a part of the Arts curriculum.

I just now expressed the opinion that, in our ideal University, a man should be able to obtain instruction in all forms of knowledge. Now, by "forms of knowledge" I mean the great classes of things knowable; of which the first, in logical, though not in natural, order is knowledge relating to the scope and limits of the mental faculties of man, a form of knowledge which, in its positive aspect, answers pretty much to Logic and part of Psychology, while, on its negative and critical side, it corresponds with Metaphysics.

A second class comprehends all that knowledge which relates to man's welfare, so far as it is determined by his own acts, or what we call his conduct. It answers to Moral and Religious philosophy. Practically it is the most directly valuable of all forms of knowledge, but speculatively it is limited and criticised by that which precedes and by that which follows it in my order of enumeration.

A third class embraces knowledge of the phenomena of the Universe, as that which lies about the individual man; and of the rules which those phenomena are observed to follow in the order of their occurrence, which we term the laws of Nature.

This is what ought to be called Natural Science, or Physiology, though those terms are hopelessly diverted from such a meaning; and it includes all exact knowledgeof natural fact, whether Mathematical, Physical, Biological or Social.

Kant has said that the ultimate object of all knowledge is to give replies to these three questions: What can I do? What ought I to do? What may I hope for? The forms of knowledge which I have enumerated should furnish such replies as are within human reach to the first and second of these questions. While to the third, perhaps the wisest answer is, "Do what you can to do what you ought, and leave hoping and fearing alone."

If this be a just and an exhaustive classification of the forms of knowledge, no question as to their relative importance, or as to the superiority of one to the other, can be seriously raised.

On the face of the matter, it is absurd to ask whether it is more important to know the limits of one's powers; or the ends for which they ought to be exerted; or the conditions under which they must be exerted. One may as well inquire which of the terms of a Rule of Three sum one ought to know, in order to get a trustworthy result. Practical life is such a sum, in which your duty multiplied into your capacity, and divided by your circumstances, gives you the fourth term in the proportion, which is your deserts, with great accuracy. All agree, I take it, that men ought to have these three kinds of knowledge. The so-called "conflict of studies" turns upon the "question of how they may best be obtained.

The founders of Universities held the theory that the Scriptures and Aristotle taken together, the latter being limited by the former, contained all knowledge worth having, and that the business of philosophy was to interpret and co-ordinate these two. I imagine that in thetwelfth century this was a very fair conclusion from known facts. Nowhere in the world, in those days, was there such an encyclopedia of knowledge of all three classes as is to be found in those writings. The scholastic philosophy is a wonderful monument of the patience and ingenuity with which the human mind toiled to build up a logically consistent theory of the Universe out of such materials. And that philosophy is by no means dead and buried, as many vainly suppose. On the contrary, numbers of men of no mean learning and accomplishment, and sometimes of rare power and subtlety of thought, hold by it as the best theory of things which has yet been stated. And, what is still more remarkable, men who speak the language of modern philosophy nevertheless think the thoughts of the schoolmen. "The voice is the voice of Jacob, but the hands are the hands of Esau." Every day I hear "Cause," "Law," "Force," "Vitality," spoken of as entities, by people who can enjoy Swift's joke about the meat-roasting quality of the smoke-jack, and comfort themselves with the reflection that they are not even as those benighted schoolmen.

"Well, this great system had its day, and then it was sapped and mined by two influences. The first was the study of classical literature, which familiarized men with methods of philosophizing; with conceptions of the highest Good; with ideas of the order of Nature; with notions of Literary and Historical Criticism; and, above all, with visions of Art, of a kind which not only would not fit into the scholastic scheme, but showed them a pre Christian, and indeed altogether un-Christian world, of such grandeur and beauty that they ceased to think of any other. They were as men who had kissed the FairyQueen, and wandering with her in the dim loveliness of the under-world, cared not to return to the familiar ways of home and fatherland, though they lay, at arm's length, overhead. Cardinals were more familiar with Virgil than with Isaiah; and Popes labored, with great success, to re-paganize Rome.

The second influence was the slow, but sure, growth of the physical sciences. It was discovered that some results of speculative thought, of immense practical and theoretical importance, can be verified by observation; and are always true, however severely they may be tested. Here, at any rate, was knowledge, to the certainty of which no authority could add, or take away, one jot or tittle, and to which the tradition of a thousand years was as insignificant as the hearsay of yesterday. To the scholastic system, the study of classical literature might be inconvenient and distracting, but it was possible to hope that it could be kept within bounds. Physical science, on the other hand, was an irreconcilable enemy, to be excluded at all hazards. The College of Cardinals has not distinguished itself in Physics or Physiology; and no Pope has, as yet, set up public laboratories in the Vatican.

People do not always formulate the beliefs on which, they act. The instinct of fear and dislike is quicker than the reasoning process; and I suspect that, taken in conjunction with some other causes, such instinctive aversion is at the bottom of the long exclusion of any serious discipline in the physical sciences from the general curriculum of Universities; while, on the other hand, classical literature has been gradually made the backbone of the Arts course.

I am ashamed to repeat here what I have said elsewhere, in season and out of season, respecting the value of Science as knowledge and discipline. But the other day I met with some passages in the Address to another Scottish University, of a great thinker, recently lost to us, which express so fully, and yet so tersely, the truth in this matter that I am fain to quote them:

"To question all things; – never to turn away from any difficulty; to accept no doctrine either from ourselves or from other people without a rigid scrutiny by negative criticism; letting no fallacy, or incoherence, or confusion of thought, step by unperceived; above all, to insist upon having the meaning of a word clearly understood before using it, and the meaning of a proposition before assenting to it; – these are the lessons we learn from" workers in Science. "With all this vigorous management of the negative element, they inspire no scepticism about the reality of truth or indifference to its pursuit. The noblest enthusiasm, both for the search after truth and for applying it to its highest uses, pervades those writers." "In cultivating, therefore," Science as an essential ingredient in education, "we are all the while laying an admirable foundation for ethical and philosophical culture." '

The passages I have quoted were uttered by John Stuart Mill; but you cannot hear inverted commas, and it is therefore right that I should add, without delay, that I have taken the liberty of substituting "workers in Science" for "ancient dialecticians," and "Science as an essential ingredient in education" for "the ancient languages as our best literary education." Mill did, in fact, deliver a noble panegyric upon classical studies. I do not doubt its justice, nor presume to question its wisdom. But I venture to maintain that no wise or just judge, who has a knowledge of the facts, will hesitate to say that it applies with equal force to scientific training.

1 Inaugural Address delivered to the University of St. Andrews, February 1, 1867, by J. S. Mill, Rector of the University (pp. 32, 33).

But it is only fair to the Scottish Universities to point out that they have long understood the value of Science as a branch of general education. I observe, with the greatest satisfaction, that candidates for the degree of Master of Arts in this University are required to have a knowledge, not only of Mental and Moral Philosophy, and of Mathematics and Natural Philosophy, but of Natural History, in addition to the ordinary Latin and Greek course; and that a candidate may take honors in these subjects and in Chemistry.

I do not know what the requirements of your examiners may be, but I sincerely trust they are not satisfied with a mere book knowledge of these matters. For my own part I would not raise a finger, if I could thereby introduce mere book work in science into every Arts curriculum in the country. Let those who want to study books devote themselves to Literature, in which we have the perfection of books, both as to substance and as to form. If I may paraphrase Hobbes's well-known aphorism, I would say that "books are the money of Literature, but only the counters of Science," Science (in the sense in which I now use the term) being the knowledge of fact, of which every verbal description is but an incomplete and symbolic expression. And be assured that no teaching of science is worth anything, as a mental discipline, which is not based upon direct perception of the facts, and practical exercise of the observing and logical faculties upon them. Even in such a simple matter as the mere comprehension of form, ask the most practiced and widely informed anatomist what is the difference between his knowledge of a structure which he has read about, and his knowledge of the same structure when he has seen it for himself; and he will tell you that the two things are not comparable – the difference is infinite. Thus I am very strongly inclined to agree with some learned schoolmasters who say that, in their experi- / ence, the teaching of science is all waste time. As they teach it, I have no doubt it is. But to teach it otherwise requires an amount of personal labor and a development of means and appliances which must strike horror and dismay into a man accustomed to mere book work; and who has been in the habit of teaching a class of fifty without much strain upon his energies. And this is one of the real difficulties in the way of the introduction of physical science into the ordinary University course, to which I have alluded. It is a difficulty which will not be overcome, until years of patient study have organized scientific teaching as well as, or I hope better than, classical teaching has been organized hitherto.

A little while ago, I ventured to hint a doubt as to the perfection of some of the arrangements in the ancient Universities of England; but, in their provision for giving instruction in Science as such, and without direct reference to any of its practical applications, they have set a brilliant example. Within the last twenty years, Oxford alone has sunk more than a hundred and twenty thousand pounds in building and furnishing Physical, Chemical, and Physiological Laboratories, and a magnificent Museum, arranged with an almost luxurious regard for the needs of the student. Cambridge, less rich, but aided by the munificence of her Chancellor, is taking the same course; and in a few years it will be for no lack of the means and appliances of sound teaching if the mass of English University men remain in their present state of barbarous ignorance of even the rudiments of scientific culture.

Yet another step needs to be made before Science can be said to have taken its proper place in the Universities. That is its recognition as a Faculty, or branch of study demanding recognition and special organization, on account of its bearing on the wants of mankind. The Faculties of Theology, Law, and Medicine, are technical schools, intended to equip men who have received general culture, with the special knowledge which is needed for the proper performance of the duties of clergymen, lawyers, and medical practitioners.

When the material well-being of the country depended upon rude pasture and agriculture, and still ruder mining; in the days when all the innumerable applications of the principles of physical science to practical purposes were non-existent even as dreams; days which men living may have heard their fathers speak of; what little physical science could be seen to bear directly upon human life, lay within the province of Medicine. Medicine was the foster-mother of Chemistry, because it has to do with the preparation of drugs and the detection of poisons; of Botany, because it enabled the physician to recognize medicinal herbs; of Comparative Anatomy and Physiology, because the man who studied Human Anatomy and Physiology for purely medical purposes was led to extend his studies to the rest of the animal world.

Within my recollection, the only way in which a student could obtain anything like a training in Physical Science was by attending the lectures of the Professors of Physical and Natural Science attached to the Medical Schools. But, in the course of the last thirty years, both foster-mother and child have grown so big that they threaten not only to crush one another, but to press the very life out of the unhappy student who enters the nursery; to the great detriment of all three.

I speak in the presence of those who know practically what medical education is; for I may assume that a large proportion of my hearers are more or less advanced students of medicine. I appeal to the most industrious and conscientious among you, to those who are most deeply penetrated with a sense of the extremely serious responsibilities which attach to the calling of a medical practitioner, when I ask whether, out of the four years which you devote to your studies, you ought to spare even so much as an hour for any work which does not tend directly to fit you for your duties?

Consider what that work is. Its foundation is a sound and practical acquaintance with the structure of the human organism, and with the modes and conditions of its action in health. I say a sound and practical acquaintance, to guard against the supposition that my intention is to suggest that you ought all to be minute anatomists and accomplished physiologists. The devotion of your whole four years to Anatomy and Physiology alone would be totally insufficient to attain that end. What I mean is, the sort of practical, familiar, finger-end knowledge which a watchmaker has of a watch, and which you expect that craftsman, as an honest man, to have, whenyou intrust to him a watch that goes badly. It is a kind of knowledge which is to be acquired, not in the lecture- room, nor in the library, but in the dissecting-room and the laboratory. It is to be had not by sharing your attention between these and sundry other subjects, but by concentrating your minds, week after week, and month after month, six or seven hours a day, upon all the complexities of organ and function, until each of the greater truths of anatomy and physiology has become an organic part of your minds – until you would know them if you were roused and questioned in the middle of the night, as a man knows the geography of his native place and the daily life of his home. That is the sort of knowledge which, once obtained, is a life-long possession. Other occupations may fill your minds – it may grow dim, and seem to be forgotten – but there it is, like the inscription on a battered and defaced coin, which comes out when you warm it.

If I had the power to remodel Medical Education, the first two years of the medical curriculum should be devoted to nothing but such thorough study of Anatomy and Physiology, with Physiological Chemistry and Physics; the student should then pass a real, practical examination in these subjects; and, having gone through that ordeal satisfactorily, he should be troubled no more with them. His whole mind should then be given with equal intentness to Therapeutics, in its broadest sense, to Practical Medicine and to Surgery, with instruction in Hygiene and in Medical Jurisprudence;

and of these subjects only – surely there are enough of them – should he be required to show a knowledge in his final examina

I cannot claim any special property in this theory of what the medical curriculum should be, for I find that views, more or less closely approximating these, are held by all who have seriously considered the very grave and pressing question of Medical Reform; and have, indeed, been carried into practice to some extent by the most enlightened Examining Boards. I have heard but two kinds of objections to them. There is, first, the objection of vested interests, which I will not deal with here, because I want to make myself as pleasant as I can, and no discussions are so unpleasant as those which turn on such points. And there is, secondly, the much more respectable objection, which takes the general form of the reproach that, in thus limiting the curriculum, we are seeking to narrow it. We are told that the medical man ought to be a person of good education and general information, if his profession is to hold its own among other professions; that he ought to know Botany, or else, if he goes abroad, he will not be able to tell poisonous fruits from edible ones; that he ought to know drugs, as a druggist knows them, or he will not be able to tell sham bark and senna from the real articles; that he ought to know Zoology, because – well, I really have never been able to learn exactly why he is to be expected to know zoology. There is, indeed, a popular superstition, that doctors know all about things that are queer or nasty to the general mind, and may, therefore, be reasonably expected to know the "barbarous binomials" applicable to snakes, snails, and slugs; an amount of information with which the general mind is usually completely satisfied. And there is a scientific superstition that Physiology is largely aided by Comparative Anatomy' – a superstition which, like most superstitions, once had a grain of truth at bottom; but the grain has become homeopathic, since Physiology took its modern experimental development, and became what it is now, the application of the principles of Physics and Chemistry to the elucidation of the phenomena of life.

I hold as strongly as any one can do that the medical practitioner ought to be a person of education and good general culture; but I also hold by the old theory of a Faculty, that a man should have his general culture before he devotes himself to the special studies of that Faculty; and I venture to maintain that, if the general culture obtained in the Faculty of Arts were what it ought to be, the student would have quite as much knowledge of the fundamental principles of Physics, of Chemistry, and of Biology, as he needs, before he commenced his special medical studies.

Moreover, I would urge that a thorough study of Human Physiology is, in itself, an education broader and more comprehensive than much that passes under that name. There is no side of the intellect which it does not call into play, no region of human knowledge into which either its roots, or its branches, do not extend; like the Atlantic between the Old and the New Worlds, its waves wash the shores of the two worlds of matter and of mind; its tributary streams flow from both; through its waters, as yet unfurrowed by the keel of any Columbus, lies the road, if such there be, from the one to the other; far away from that Northwest Passage of mere speculation, in which so many brave souls have been hopelessly frozen up.

But whether I am right or wrong about all this, thepatent fact of the limitation of time remains. As the

Bong runs:

"If a man could be sure

That his life would endure

For the space of a thousand long years – "

he might do a number of things not practicable under present conditions. Methuselah might, with much propriety, have taken half a century to get his doctor's degree; and might, very fairly, have been required to pass a practical examination upon the contents of the British Museum, before commencing practice as a promising young fellow of two hundred, or thereabout. But you have four years to do your work in, and are turned loose, to save or slay, at two or three and twenty.

Now, I put it to you, whether you think that, when you come down to the realities of life – when you stand by the sick-bed, racking your brains for the principles which shall furnish you with the means of interpreting symptoms, and forming a rational theory of the condition of your patient, it will be satisfactory for you to find that those principles are not there – although, to use the examination slang which is unfortunately too familiar to me, you can quite easily "give an account of the leading peculiarities of the *Marsupialia,*" or "enumerate the chief characters of the *Compositce,*" or "state the class and order of the animal from which Castoreum is obtained."

I really do not think that state of things will be satisfactory to you; I am very sure it will not be so to your patient. Indeed, I am so narrow-minded myself, that if I had to choose between two physicians – one who did not know whether a whale is a fish or not, and could not tell gentian from ginger, but did understand the applicationaof the institutes of medicine to his art; while the other, like Talleyrand's doctor, "knew everything, even a little physic" – with all my love for breadth of culture, I should assuredly consult the former.

It is not pleasant to incur the suspicion of an inclination to injure or depreciate particular branches of knowledge. But the fact that one of those which I should have no hesitation in excluding from the medical curriculum is that to which my own life has been specially devoted, should, at any rate, defend me from the suspicion of being urged to this course by any but the very gravest considerations of the public welfare.

And I should like, further, to call your attention to the important circumstance that, in thus proposing the exclusion of the study of such branches of knowledge aa Zoology and Botany, from those compulsory upon the medical student, I am not, for a moment, suggesting their exclusion from the University. I think that sound and practical instruction in the elementary facts and broad principles of Biology should form part of the Arts Curriculum: and here, happily, my theory is in entire accordance with your practice. Moreover, as I have already said, I have no sort of doubt that, in view of the relation of Physical Science to the practical life of the present day, it has the same right as Theology, Law, and Medicine, to a Faculty of its own in which men shall be trained to be professional men of science. It may be doubted whether Universities are the places for technical schools of Engineering or Applied Chemistry, or Agriculture. But there can surely be little question that instruction in the branches of Science which lie at the foundation of these Arts, of a far more advanced andspecial character than could, with any propriety, be included in the ordinary Arts Curriculum, ought to be obtainable by means of a duly organized Faculty of Science in every University.

The establishment of such a Faculty would have the additional advantage of providing, in some measure, for one of the greatest wants of our time and country. I mean the proper support and encouragement of original research.

The other day, an emphatic friend of mine committed himself to the opinion that, in England, it is better for a man's worldly prospects to be a drunkard than to be smitten with the divine dipsomania of the original investigator. I am inclined to think he was not far wrong. And, be it observed, that the question is not, whether such a man shall be able to make as much out of his abilities as his brother, of like ability, who goes into Law, or Engineering, or Commerce; it is not a question of "maintaining a due number of saddle horses," as George Eliot somewhere puts it – it is a question of living or starving.

If a student of my own subject shows power and originality, I dare not advise him to adopt a scientific career; for, supposing he is able to maintain himself until he has attained distinction, I cannot give him the assurance that any amount of proficiency in the Biological Sciences will be convertible into, even the most modest, bread and cheese. And I believe that the case is as bad, or perhaps worse, with other branches of Science. In this respect Britain, whose immense wealth and prosperity hang upon the thread of Applied Science, is far

behind France, and infinitely behind Germany.

– Science – 9

And the worst of it is, that it is very difficult to see one's way to any immediate remedy for this state of affairs which shall be free from a tendency to become worse than the disease.

Great schemes for the Endowment of Research have been proposed. It has been suggested that Laboratories for all branches of Physical Science, provided with every apparatus needed by the investigator, shall be established by the State: and shall be accessible, under due conditions and regulations, to all properly qualified persons. I see no objection to the principle of such a proposal. If it be legitimate to spend great sums of money on public Libraries and public collections of Painting and Sculpture, in aid of the Man of Letters, or the Artist, or for the mere sake of affording pleasure to the general public, I apprehend that it cannot be illegitimate to do as much for the promotion of scientific investigation. To take the lowest ground, as a mere investment of money, the latter is likely to be much more immediately profitable. To my mind, the difficulty in the way of such schemes is not theoretical, but practical. Given the laboratories, how are the investigators to be maintained ? What career is open to those who have been thus encouraged to leave bread- winning pursuits? If they are to be provided for by endowment, we come back to the College Fellowship system, the results of which, for Literature, have not been so brilliant that one would wish to see it extended to Science; unless some much better securities than at present exist can be taken that it will foster real work. You know that, among the Bees, it depends on the kind of cell in which the egg is deposited, and the quantity and quality of food which is supplied to the grub, whether itshall turn out a busy little worker or a big idle queen. And, in the human hive, the cells of the endowed larvas are always tending to enlarge, and their food to improve, until we get queens, beautiful to behold, but which gather no honey and build no comb.

I do not say that these difficulties may not be overcome, but their gravity is not to be lightly estimated.

In the meanwhile, there is one step in the direction of the endowment of research which is free from such objections. It is possible to place the scientific inquirer in a position in which he shall have ample leisure and opportunity for original work, and yet shall give a fair and tangible equivalent for those privileges. The establishment of a Faculty of Science in every University, implies that of a corresponding number of Professorial chairs, the incumbents of which need not be so burdened with teaching as to deprive them of ample leisure for original work. I do not think that it is any impediment to an original investigator to have to devote a moderate portion of his time to lecturing, or superintending practical instruction. On the contrary, I think it may be, and often is, a benefit to be obliged to take a comprehensive survey of your subject; or to bring your results to a point, and give them, as it were, a tangible objective existence. The besetting sins of the investigator are two: the one is the desire to put aside a subject, the general bearings of which he has mastered himself, and pass on to something which has the attraction of novelty; and the other, the desire for too much perfection, which leads him to

"Add and alter many times,

Till all be ripe and rotten ";

to spend the energies which should be reserved for action in whitening the decks and polishing the guns.

The obligation to produce results for the instruction of others seems to me to be a more effectual check on these tendencies than even the love of usefulness or the ambition for fame.

But supposing the Professorial forces of our University to be duly organized, there remains an important question, relating to the teaching power, to be considered. Is the Professorial system – the system, *I* mean, of teaching in the lecture-room alone, and leaving the student to find his own way when he is outside the lecture-room – adequate to the wants of learners? In answering this question, I confine myself to my own province, and I venture to reply for Physical Science, assuredly and undoubtedly, No. As I have already intimated, practical work in the Laboratory is absolutely indispensable, and that practical work must be guided and superintended by a sufficient staff of Demonstrators, who are for Science what Tutors are for other branches of study. And there must be a good supply of such Demonstrators. I doubt if the practical work of more than twenty students can be properly superintended by one Demonstrator. If we take the working day at six hours, that is less than twenty minutes apiece – not a very large allowance of time for helping a dull man, for correcting an inaccurate one, or even for making an intelligent student clearly apprehend what he is about. And, no doubt, the supplying of a proper amount of this tutorial, practical teaching is a difficulty in the way of giving proper instruction in Physical Science in such Universities as that of Aberdeen, which are devoid of endowments; and, unlike the English Universities, have no moral claim on the funds of richly endowed bodies to supply their wants.

Examination – thorough, searching examination – is an indispensable accompaniment of teaching; but I am almost inclined to commit myself to the very heterodox proposition that it is a necessary evil. I am a very old Examiner, having, for some twenty years past, been occupied with examinations on a considerable scale, of all sorts and conditions of men, and women too – from the boys and girls of elementary schools to the candidates for Honors and Fellowships in the Universities. I will not say that, in this case as in so many others, the adage, that familiarity breeds contempt, holds good; but my admiration for the existing system of examination and its products does not wax warmer as I see more of it. Examination, like fire, is a good servant, but a bad master; and there seems to me to be some danger of its becoming our master. I by no means stand alone in this opinion. Experienced friends of mine do not hesitate to say that students whose career they watch, appear to them to become deteriorated by the constant effort to pass this or that examination, just as we hear of men's brains becoming affected by the daily necessity of catching a train. They work to pass, not to know; and outraged Science takes her revenge. They do pass, and they don't know. I have passed sundry examinations in my time, not without credit, and I confess I am ashamed to think how very little real knowledge underlay the torrent of stuff which I was able to pour out on paper. In fact, that which examination, as ordinarily conducted, tests, is simply a man's power of work under stimulus, and his capacity for rapidly and clearly producing that which, for the time, he has got into his mind. Now, these faculties are by no means to be despised. They are of great value in practical life, and are the making of many an advocate, and of many a so-called statesman. But in the pursuit of truth, scientific or other, they count for very little, unless they are supplemented by that long-continued, patient "intending of the mind," as Newton phrased it, which makes very little show in Examinations. I imagine that an Examiner who knows his students personally must not infrequently have found himself in the position of finding A's paper better than B's, though his own judgment tells him, quite clearly, that B is the man who has the larger share of genuine capacity.

Again, there is a fallacy about Examiners. It is commonly supposed that any one who knows a subject is competent to teach it; and no one seems to doubt that any one who knows a subject is competent to examine in it. I believe both these opinions to be serious mistakes: the latter, perhaps, the more serious of the two. In the first place, I do not believe that any one who is not, or has not been, a teacher is really qualified to examine advanced students. And in the second place, Examination is an Art, and a difficult one, which has to be learned like all other arts.

Beginners always set too difficult questions – partly because they are afraid of being suspected of ignorance if they set easy ones, and partly from not understanding their business. Suppose that you want to test the relative physical strength of a score of young men. You do not put a hundredweight down before them, and tell each to swing it round. If you do, half of them won't be able to lift it at all, and only one or two will be able to perform the task. You must give them half a hundredweight, and see how they manoeuvre that, if you want to form any estimate of the muscular strength of each. So, a practiced Examiner will seek for information respecting the mental vigor and training of candidates from the way in which they deal with questions easy enough to let reason, memory, and method have free play.

No doubt, a great deal is to be done by the careful selection of Examiners, and by the copious introduction of practical work, to remove the evils inseparable from examination; but, under the best of circumstances, I believe that examination will remain but an imperfect test of knowledge, and a still more imperfect test of capacity, while it tells next to nothing about a man's power as an investigator.

There is much to be said in favor of restricting the highest degrees in each Faculty to those who have shown evidence of such original power, by prosecuting a research under the eye of the Professor in whose province it lies; or, at any rate, under conditions which shall afford satisfactory proof that the work is theirs. The notion may sound revolutionary, but it is really very old; for, I take it, that it lies at the bottom of that presentation of a thesis by the candidate for a doctorate, which has now, too often, become little better than a matter of form.

Thus far, I have endeavored to lay before you, in a too brief and imperfect manner, my views respecting the teaching half – the Magistri and Regentes – of the University of the Future. Now let me turn to the learning half – the Scholares.

If the Universities are to be sanctuaries of the highestculture of the country, those who would enter that sanctuary must not come with unwashed hands. If the good seed is to yield its hundredfold harvest, it must not be scattered amid the stones of ignorance, or the tares of undisciplined indolence and wantonness. On the contrary, the soil must have been carefully prepared, and the Professor should find that the operations of clod-crushing, draining and weeding, and even a good deal of planting, have been done by the Schoolmaster.

That is exactly what the Professor does not find in any University in the three Kingdoms that I can hear of – the reason of which state of things lies in the extremely faulty organization of the majority of secondary schools. Students come to the Universities ill-prepared in classics and mathematics, not at all prepared in anything else; and half their time is spent in learning that which they ought to have known when they came.

I sometimes hear it said that the Scottish Universities differ from the English, in being to a much greater extent places of comparatively elementary education for a younger class of students. But it would seem doubtful if any great difference of this kind really exists; for a high authority, himself Head of an English College, has solemnly affirmed that: "Elementary teaching of youths under twenty is now the only function performed by the University"; and that Colleges are "boarding-schools in which the elements of the learned languages are taught to youths." '

This is not the first time that I have quoted those remarkable assertions. I should like to engrave themin public view, for they have not been refuted; and I am convinced that if their import is once clearly apprehended they will play no mean part when the question of University reorganization, with a view to practical measures, comes on for discussion. You are not responsible for this anomalous state of affairs now; but, as you pass into active life and acquire the political influence to which your education and your position should entitle you, you will become responsible for it, unless each in his sphere does his best to alter it, by insisting on the improvement of secondary schools.

1 "Suggestions for Academical Organization, with Especial Reference to Oxford." By the Hector of Lincoln.

Your present responsibility is of another, though not less serious, kind. Institutions do not make men, any more than organization makes life; and even the ideal University we have been dreaming about will be but a superior piece of mechanism, unless each student strive after the ideal of the Scholar. And that ideal, it seems to me, has never been better embodied than by the great Poet, who, though lapped in luxury, the favorite of a Court, and the idol of his countrymen, remained through all the length of his honored years a Scholar in Art, in Science, and in Life.

"Wouldst shape a noble life ? Then cast
No backward glances toward the past:
And though somewhat be lost and gone,
Yet do thou act as one new-born.
What each day needs, that shall thou ask;
Each day will set its proper task.
Give others' work just share of praise;
Not of thine own the merits raise.
Beware no fellow man thou hate:
And so in God's hands leave thy fate." '

1 Goethe, "Zahme Xenien, Vierte Abtheilung." I should be glad to take credit for the close and vigorous English version; but it is my wife's, and not mine.

8

SECTION 8

IX

ADDRESS ON UNIVERSITY EDUCATION1

[1876]

THE actual work of the University founded in this city by the well-considered munificence of Johns Hopkins commences to-morrow, and among the many marks of confidence and goodwill which have been bestowed upon me in the United States, there is none which I value more highly than that conferred by the authorities of the University when they invited me to deliver an address on such an occasion.

For the event which has brought us together is, in many respects, unique. A vast property is handed over to an administrative body, hampered by no conditions save these: That the principal shall not be employed in building: that the funds shall be appropriated, in equal proportions, to the promotion of natural knowledge and to the alleviation of the bodily sufferings of mankind; and, finally, that neither political nor ecclesiastical sectarianism shall be permitted to disturb the impartial distribution of the testator's benefactions.

In my experience of life a truth which sounds verymuch like a paradox has often asserted itself; namely, that a man's worst difficulties begin when he is able to do as he likes. So long as a man is struggling with obstacles hc has an excuse for failure or shortcoming; but when fortune removes them all and gives him the power of doing as he thinks best, then comes the time of trial. There is but one right, and the possibilities of wrong are infinite. I doubt not that the trustees of the Johns Hopkins University felt the full force of this truth when they entered on the administration of their trust a year and a half ago; and I can but admire the activity and resolution which have enabled them, aided by the able president whom they have selected, to lay down the great outlines of their plan, and carry it thus far into execution. It is impossible to study that plan without perceiving that great care, forethought, and sagacity have been bestowed upon it, and that it demands the most respectful consideration. I have been endeavoring to ascertain how far the principles which underlie it are in accordance with those which have been established in my own mind by much and long-continued thought upon educational questions. Permit me to place before you the result of my reflections.

1 Delivered at the formal opening of the Johns Hopkins University at Baltimore, U. S., September 12. The total amount bequeathed by Johns Hopkins is more than 7,000,000 dollars. The sum of 3,600,000 dollars is appropriated to a university, a like sum to a hospital, and the rest to local institutions of education and charity.

Under one aspect a university is a particular kind of educational institution, and the views which we may take of the proper nature of a university are corollaries from those which we hold respecting education in general. I think it must be admitted that the school should prepare for the university, and that the university should crown the edifice, the foundations of which are laid in the school. University education should not be something distinct from elementary education, but should be the natural outgrowth and development of the latter. Now I have a very clear conviction as to what elementary education ought to be; what it really may be, when properly organized; and what I think it will be, before many years have passed over our heads, in England and in America. Such education should enable an average boy of fifteen or sixteen to read and write his own language with ease and accuracy, and with a sense of literary excellence derived from the study of our classic writers; to have a general acquaintance with the history of his own country and with the great laws of social existence; to have acquired the rudiments of the physical and psychological sciences, and a fair knowledge of elementary arithmetic and geometry. He should have obtained an acquaintance with logic rather by example than by precept; while the acquirement of the elements of music and drawing should have been pleasure rather than work.

It may sound strange to many ears if I venture to maintain the proposition that a young person, educated thus far, has had a liberal, though perhaps not a full, education. But it seems to me that such training as that to which I have referred may be termed liberal, in both the senses in which that word is employed, with perfect accuracy. In the first place, it is liberal in breadth. It extends over the whole ground of things to be known and of faculties to be trained, and it gives equal importance to the two great sides of human activity – art and science. In the second place, it is liberal in the sense of being an education fitted for free men; for men to whom every career is open, and from whom their country may demand that they should be fitted to perform the duties of any career. I cannot too strongly impress upon you the fact that, with such a primary education as this, and with no more than is to be obtained by building strictly upon its lines, a man of ability may become a great writer or speaker, a statesman, a lawyer, a man of science, painter, sculptor, architect, or musician. That even development of all a man's faculties, which is what properly constitutes culture, may be effected by such an education, while it opens the way for the indefinite strengthening of any special capabilities with which he may be gifted.

In a country like this, where most men have to carve out their own fortunes and devote themselves early to the practical affairs of life, comparatively few can hope to pursue their studies up to, still less beyond, the age of manhood. But it is of vital importance to the welfare of the community that those who are relieved from the need of making a livelihood, and, still more, those who are stirred by the divine impulses of intellectual thirst or artistic genius, should be enabled to devote themselves to the higher service of their kind, as centres of intelligence, interpreters of Nature, or creators of new forms of beauty. And it is the function of a university to furnish such men with the means of becoming that which it is their privilege and duty to be. To this end the university need cover no ground foreign to that occupied by the elementary school. Indeed it cannot; for the elementary instruction which I have referred to embraces all the kinds of real knowledge and mental activity possible to man. The university can add no new departments of knowledge, can offer no new fields of mental activity; bat what it can do is to intensify and specialize theinstruction in each department. Thus literature and philology, represented in the elementary school by English alone, in the university will extend over the ancient and modern languages. History, which, like charity, best begins at home, but, like charity, should not end there, will ramify into anthropology, archeology, political history, and geography, with the history of the growth of the human mind and of its products in the shape of philosophy, science, and art. And the university will present to the student libraries, museums of antiquities, collections of coins, and the like, which will efficiently subserve these studies. Instruction in the elements of social economy, a most essential, but hitherto sadly- neglected part of elementary education, will develop in the university into political economy, sociology, and law. Physical science will have its great divisions of physical geography, with geology and astronomy; physics; chemistry and biology; represented not merely by professors and their lectures, but by laboratories, in which the students, under guidance of demonstrators, will work out facts for themselves and come into that direct contact with reality which constitutes the fundamental distinction of scientific education. Mathematics will soar into its highest regions; while the high peaks of philosophy may be scaled by those whose aptitude for abstract thought has been awakened by elementary logic. Finally, schools of pictorial and plastic art, of architecture, and of music, will offer a thorough discipline in the principles and practice of art to those in whom lies nascent the rare faculty of aesthetic representation, or the still rarer powers of creative genius.

The primary school and the university are the alphaand omega of education. Whether institutions intermediate between these (so-called secondary schools) should exist, appears to me to be a question of practical convenience. If such schools are established, the important thing is that they should be true intermediaries between the primary school and the university, keeping on the wide track of general culture, and not sacrificing one branch of knowledge for another.

Such appear to me to be the broad outlines of the relations which the university, regarded as a place of education, ought to bear to the school, but a number of points of detail require some consideration, however briefly and imperfectly I can deal with them. In the first place, there is the important question of the limitations which should be fixed to the entrance into the university; or, what qualifications should be required of those who propose to take advantage of the higher training offered by the university. On the one hand, it is obviously desirable that the time and opportunities of the university should not be wasted in conferring such elementary instruction as can be obtained elsewhere; while, on the other hand, it is no less desirable that the higher instruction of the university should be made accessible to every one who can take advantage of it, although he may not have been able to go through any very extended course of education. My own feeling is distinctly against any absolute and defined preliminary examination, the passing of which shall be an essential condition of admission to the university. I would admit to the university any one who could be reasonably expected to profit by the instruction offered to him; and I should be inclined, on the whole, to test the fitnessof the student, not by examination before he enters the university, but at the end of his first term of study. If, on examination in the branches of knowledge to which he has devoted himself, he show himself deficient in industry or in capacity, it will be best for the university and best for himself to prevent him from pursuing a vocation for which he is obviously unfit. And I hardly know of any other method than this by which his fitness or unfitness can be safely ascertained, though no doubt a good deal may be done, not by formal cut and dried examination, but by judicious questioning, at the outset of his career.

Another very important and difficult practical question is, whether a definite course of study shall be laid down for those who enter the university; whether a curriculum shall be prescribed; or whether the student shall be allowed to range at will among the subjects which are open to him. And this question is inseparably connected with another, namely, the conferring of degrees. It is obviously impossible that any student should pass through the whole of the series of courses of instruction offered by a university. If a degree is to be conferred as a mark of proficiency in knowledge, it must be given on the ground that the candidate is proficient in a certain fraction of those studies; and then will arise the necessity of insuring an equivalency of degrees, so that the course by which a degree is obtained shall mark approximately an equal amount of labor and of acquirements in all cases. But this equivalency can hardly be secured in any other way than by prescribing a series of definite lines of study. This is a matter which will require grave consideration The important points to bear in mind, Ithink, are that there should not be too many subjects in the curriculum, and that the aim should be the attainment of thorough and sound knowledge of each.

One half of the Johns Hopkins bequest is devoted to the establishment of a hospital, and it was the desire of the testator that the university and the hospital should co-operate in the promotion of medical education. The trustees will unquestionably take the best advice that is to be had as to the construction and administration of the hospital. In respect to the former point, they will doubtless remember that a hospital may be so arranged as to kill more than it cures; and, in regard to the latter, that a hospital may spread the spirit of pauperism among the well-to-do, as well as relieve the sufferings of the destitute. It is not for me to speak on these topics – rather let me confine myself to the one matter on which my experience as a student of medicine, and an examiner of long standing, who has taken a great interest in the subject of medical education, may entitle me to a hearing. I mean the nature of medical education itself, and the co-operation of the university in its promotion.

What is the object of medical education? It is to enable the practitioner, on the one hand, to prevent disease by his knowledge of hygiene; on the other hand, to divine its nature, and to alleviate or cure it, by his knowledge of pathology, therapeutics, and practical medicine. That is his business in life, and if he has not a thorough and practical knowledge of the conditions of health, of the causes which tend to the establishment of disease, of the meaning of symptoms, and of the uses of medicines and operative appliances, he is incompetent, even if he were the best anatomist, or physiologist, orchemist, that ever took a gold medal or won a prize certificate. This is one great truth respecting medical education. Another is, that all practice in medicine is based upon theory of some sort or other; and, therefore, that it is desirable to have such theory in the closest possible accordance with fact. The veriest empiric who gives a drug in one case because he has seen it do good in another of apparently the same sort, acts upon the theory that similarity of superficial symptoms means similarity of lesions; which, by the way, is perhaps as wild a hypothesis as could be invented. To understand the nature of disease we must understand health, and the understanding of the healthy body means the having a knowledge of its structure and of the way in which its manifold actions are performed, which is what is technically termed human anatomy and human physiology. The physiologist again must needs possess an acquaintance with physics and chemistry, inasmuch as physiology is, to a great extent, applied physics and chemistry. For ordinary purposes a limited amount of such knowledge is all that is needful; but for the pursuit of the higher branches of physiology no knowledge of these branches of science can be too extensive, or too profound. Again, what we call therapeutics, which has to do with the action of drugs and medicines on the living organism, is, strictly speaking, a branch of experimental physiology, and is daily receiving a greater and greater experimental development.

The third great fact which is to be taken into consideration in dealing with medical education is that the practical necessities of life do not, as a rule, allow aspirants to medical practice to give more than three, or it may befour, years to their studies. Let us put it at four years, and then reflect that, in the course of this time, a young man fresh from school has to acquaint himself with, medicine, surgery, obstetrics, therapeutics, pathology, hygiene, as well as with the anatomy and the physiology of the human body; and that his knowledge should be of such a character that it can be relied upon in any emergency, and always ready for practical application. Consider, in addition, that the medical practitioner may be called upon, at any moment, to give evidence in a court of justice in a criminal case; and that it is therefore well that he should know something of the laws of evidence, and of what we call medical jurisprudence. On a medical certificate, a man may be taken from his home and from his business and confined in a lunatic asylum; surely, therefore, it is desirable that the medical practitioner should have some rational and clear conceptions as to the nature and symptoms of mental disease. Bearing in mind all these requirements of medical education, you will admit that the burden on the young aspirant for the medical profession is somewhat of the heaviest, and that it needs some care to prevent his intellectual back from being broken.

Those who are acquainted with the existing systems of medical education will observe that, long as is the catalogue of studies which I have enumerated, I have omitted to mention several that enter into the usual medical curriculum of the present day. I have said not a word about zoology, comparative anatomy, botany, or materia medica. Assuredly this is from no light estimate of the value or importance of such studies in themselves. It may be taken for granted that I should be the lastperson in the world to object to the teaching of zoology, or comparative anatomy, in themselves; but I have the strongest feeling that, considering the number and the gravity of those studies through which a medical man must pass, if he is to be competent to discharge the serious duties which devolve upon him, subjects which lie so remote as these do from his practical pursuits should be rigorously excluded. The young man, who has enough to do in order to acquire such familiarity with the structure of the human body as will enable him to perform the operations of surgery, ought not, in my judgment, to be occupied with investigations into the anatomy of crabs and starfishes. Undoubtedly the doctor should know the common poisonous plants of his own country when he sees them; but that knowledge may be obtained by a few hours devoted to the examination of specimens of such plants, and the desirableness of such knowledge is no justification, to my mind, for spending three months over the study of systematic botany. Again, materia medica, so far as it is a knowledge of drugs, is the business of the druggist. In all other callings the necessity of the division of labor is fully recognized, and it is absurd to require of the medical man that he should not avail himself of the special knowledge of those whose business it is to deal in the drugs which he uses. It is all very well that the physician should know that castor oil comes from a plant, and castoreum from an animal, and how they are to be prepared; but for all the practical purposes of his profession that knowledge is not of one whit more value, has no more relevancy, than the knowledge of how the steel of his scalpel is made.

All knowledge is good. It is impossible to say thatany fragment of knowledge, however insignificant or remote from one's ordinary pursuits, may not some day be turned to account. But in medical education, above all things, it is to be recollected that, in order to know a little well, one must be content to be ignorant of a great deal.

Let it not be supposed that I am proposing to narrow medical education, or, as the cry is, to lower the standard of the profession. Depend upon it there is only one way of really ennobling any calling, and that is to make those who pursue it real masters of their craft, men who can truly do that which they profess to be able to do, and which they are credited with being able to do by the public. And there is no position so ignoble as that of the so-called "liberally-educated practitioner," who may be able to read Galen in the original; who knows all the plants, from the cedar of Lebanon to the hyssop upon the wall; but who finds himself, with the issues of life and death in his hands, ignorant, blundering, and bewildered, because of his ignorance of the essential and fundamental truths upon which practice must be based. Moreover, I venture to say, that any man who has seriously studied all the essential branches of medical knowledge; who has the needful acquaintance with the elements of physical science; who has been brought by medical jurisprudence into contact with law; whose study of insanity has taken him into the fields of psychology; has *ipso facto* received a liberal education.

Having lightened the medical curriculum by culling out of it everything which is unessential, we may next consider whether something may not be done to aid the medical student toward the acquirement of real knowledge by modifying the system of examination. In England, within my recollection, it was the practice to require of the medical student attendance on lectures upon the most diverse topics during three years; so that it often happened that he would have to listen, in the course of the day, to four or five lectures upon totally different subjects, in addition to the hours given to dissection and to hospital practice: and he was required to keep all the knowledge he could pick up, in this distracting fashion, at examination point, until, at the end of three years, he was set down to a table and questioned pell-mell upon all the different matters with which he had been striving to make acquaintance. A worse system and one more calculated to obstruct the acquisition of sound knowledge and to give full play to the "crammer" and the "grinder" could hardly have been devised by human ingenuity. Of late years great reforms have taken place. Examinations have been divided so as to diminish the number of subjects among which the attention has to be distributed. Practical examination has been largely introduced; but there still remains, even under the present system, too much of the old evil inseparable from the contemporaneous pursuit of a multiplicity of diverse studies.

Proposals have recently been made to get rid of general examinations altogether, to permit the student to be examined in each subject at the end of his attendance on the class; and then, in case of the result being satisfactory, to allow him to have done with it; and I may say that this method has been pursued for many years in the Eoyal School of Mines in London, and has been found to work very well. It allows the student to concentrate his mind upon what he is about for the time being, and then to dismiss it. Those who are occupied in intellectual work will, I think, agree with me that it is important, not so much to know a thing, as to have known it, and known it thoroughly. If you have once known a thing in this way it is easy to renew your knowledge when you have forgotten it; and when you begin to take the subject up again, it slides back upon the familiar grooves with great facility.

Lastly comes the question as to how the university may co-operate in advancing medical education. A medical school is strictly a technical school – a school in which a practical profession is taught – while a university ought to be a place in which knowledge is obtained without direct reference to professional purposes. It is clear, therefore, that a university and its antecedent, the school, may best co-operate with the medical school by making due provision for the study of those branches of knowledge which lie at the foundation of medicine.

At present, young men come to the medical schools without a conception of even the elements of physical science; they learn, for the first time, that there are such sciences as physics, chemistry, and physiology, and are introduced to anatomy as a new thing. It may be safely said that, with a large proportion of medical students, much of the first session is wasted in learning how to learn – in familiarizing themselves with utterly strange conceptions, and in awakening their dormant and wholly untrained powers of observation and of manipulation. It is difficult to overestimate the magnitude of the obstacles which are thrown in the way of scientific training by the existing system of school education. Not only are mentrained in mere book-work, ignorant of what observation means, but the habit of learning from books alone begets a disgust of observation. The book-learned student will rather trust to what he sees in a book than to the witness of his own eyes.

There is not the least reason why this should be so, and, in fact, when elementary education becomes that which I have assumed it ought to be, this state of things will no longer exist. There is not the slightest difficulty in giving sound elementary instruction in physics, in chemistry, and in the elements of human physiology, in ordinary schools. In other words, there is no reason why the student should not come to the medical school provided with as much knowledge of these several sciences as he ordinarily picks up in the course of his first year of attendance at the medical school.

I am not saying this withont full practical justification for the statement. For the last eighteen years we have had in England a system of elementary science teaching carried out under the auspices of the Science and Art Department, by which elementary scientific instruction is made readily accessible to the scholars of all the elementary schools in the country. Commencing with small beginnings, carefully developed and improved, that system now brings up for examination as many as seven thousand scholars in the subject of human physiology alone. I can say that, out of that number, a large proportion have acquired a fair amount of substantial knowledge; and that no inconsiderable percentage show as good an acquaintance with human physiology as used to be exhibited by the average candidates for medical degrees in the University of London, when I was first an examinerthere twenty years ago; and quite as much knowledge as is possessed by the ordinary student of medicine at the present day. I am justified, therefore, in looking forward to the time when the student who proposes to devote himself to medicine will come, not absolutely raw and inexperienced as he is at present, but in a certain state of preparation for further study; and I look to the university to help him still further forward in that stage of preparation, through the organization of its biological department. Here the student will find means of acquainting himself with the phenomena of life in their broadest acceptation. He will study not botany and zoology, which, as I have said, would take him too far away from his ultimate goal; but, by duly arranged instruction, combined with work in the laboratory upon the leading types of animal and vegetable life, he will lay a broad, and at the same time solid, foundation of biological knowledge; he will come to his medical studies with a comprehension of the great truths of morphology and of physiology, with his hands trained to dissect and his eyes taught to see. I have no hesitation in saying that such preparation is worth a full year added on to the medical curriculum. In other words, it will set free that much time for attention to those studies which bear directly upon the student's most grave and serious duties as a medical practitioner.

Up to this point I have considered only the teaching aspect of your great foundation, that function of the university in virtue of which it plays the part of a reservoir of ascertained truth, so far as our symbols can ever interpret nature. All can learn; all can drink of this lake.

It is given to few to add to the store of knowledge, to

VIII – Science – 10

strike new springs of thought, or to shape new forms of beauty. But so sure as it is that men live not by bread, but by ideas, so sure is it that the future of the world lies in the hands of those who are able to carry the interpretation of nature a step further than their predecessors; so certain is it that the highest function of a university is to seek out those men, cherish them, and give their ability to serve their kind full play.

I rejoice to observe that the encouragement of research occupies so prominent a place in your official documents, and in the wise and liberal inaugural address of your president. This subject of the encouragement, or, as it is sometimes called, the endowment of research, has of late years greatly exercised the minds of men in England. It was one of the main topics of discussion by the members of the Royal Commission of whom I was one, and who not long since issued their report, after five years' labor. Many seem to think that this question is mainly one of money; that you can go into the market and buy research, and that supply will follow demand, as in the ordinary course of commerce. This view does not commend itself to my mind. I know of no more difficult practical problem than the discovery of a method of encouraging and supporting the original investigator without opening the door to nepotism and jobbery. My own conviction is admirably summed up in the passage of your president's address, "that the best investigators are usually those who have also the responsibilities of instruction, gaining thus the incitement of colleagues, the encouragement of pupils, and the observation of the public."

At the commencement of this address I ventured to assume that I might, if I thought fit, criticise the arrangements which have been made by the board of trustees, but I confess that I have little to do but to applaud them. Most wise and sagacious seems to me the determination not to build for the present. It has been my fate to see great educational funds fossilize into mere bricks and mortar, in the petrifying springs of architecture, with nothing left to work the institution they were intended to support. A great warrior is said to have made a desert and called it peace. Administrators of educational funds have sometimes made a palace and called it a university. If I may venture to give advice in a matter which lies out of my proper competency, I would say that whenever you do build, get an honest bricklayer, and make him build you just such rooms as you really want, leaving ample space for expansion. And a century hence, when the Baltimore and Ohio shares are at one thousand premium, and you have endowed all the professors you need, and built all the laboratories that are wanted, and have the best museum and the finest library that can be imagined; then, if you have a few hundred thousand dollars you don't know what to do with, send for an architect and tell him to put up a facade. If American is similar to English experience, any other course will probably lead you into having some stately structure, good for your architect's fame, but not in the least what you want.

It appears to me that what I have ventured to lay down as the principles which should govern the relations of a university to education in general are entirely in accordance with the measures you have adopted. You have set no restrictions upon access to the instruction you propose to give; you have provided that such instruction, either as given by the university or by associatedinstitutions, should cover the field of human intellectual activity. You have recognized the importance of encouraging research. You propose to provide means by which young men, who may be full of zeal for a literary or for a scientific career, but who also may have mistaken aspiration for inspiration, may bring their capacities to a test, and give their powers a fair trial. If such a one fail, his endowment terminates, and there is no harm done. If he succeed, you may give power of flight to the genius of a Davy or a Faraday, a Carlyle or a Locke, whose influence on the future of his fellowmen shall be absolutely incalculable. You have enunciated the principle that "the glory of the university should rest upon the character of the teachers and scholars, and not upon their numbers or buildings constructed for their use." And I look upon it as an essential and most important feature of your plan that the income of the professors and teachers shall be independent - of the number of students whom they can attract. In this way you provide against the danger, patent elsewhere, of finding attempts at improvement obstructed by vested interests; and, in the department of medical education especially, you are free of the temptation to set loose upon the world men utterly incompetent to perform the serious and responsible duties of their profession.

It is a delicate matter for a stranger to the practical working of your institutions, like myself, to pretend to give an opinion as to the organization of your governing power. I can conceive nothing better than that it should remain as it is, if you can secure a succession of wise, liberal, honest, and conscientious men to fill the vacancies that occur among you. I do not greatly believe in theefficacy of any kind of machinery for securing such a result; but I would venture to suggest that the exclusive adoption of the method of co-optation for filling the vacancies which must occur in your body appears to me to be somewhat like a tempting of Providence. Doubtless there are grave practical objections to the appointment of persons outside of your body and not directly interested in the welfare of the university; but might it not be well if there were an understanding that your academic staff should be officially represented on the board, perhaps even the heads of one or two independent learned bodies, so that academic opinion and the views of the outside world might have a certain influence in that most important matter, the appointment of your professors? I throw out these suggestions, as I have said, in ignorance of the practical "difficulties that may lie in the way of carrying them into effect, on the general ground that personal and local influences are very subtle, and often unconscious, while the future greatness and efficiency of the noble institution which now commences its work must largely depend upon its freedom from them.

I constantly hear Americans speak of the charm which our old mother country has for them, of the delight with which they wander through the streets of ancient towns or climb the battlements of medieval strongholds, the names of which are indissolubly associated with the great epochs of that noble literature which is our common inheritance; or with the blood-stained steps of that secular progress, by which the descendants of the savage Britons and of the wild pirates of the North Sea have become converted into warriors of order and champions of peaceful freedom, exhausting what still remains of the old Berserk spirit m subduing nature, and turning the wilderness into a garden. But anticipation has no less charm than retrospect, and to an Englishman landing upon your shores for the first time, travelling for hundreds of miles through strings of great and well-ordered cities, seeing your enormous actual, and almost infinite potential, wealth in all commodities, and in the energy and ability which turn wealth to account, there is something sublime in the vista of the future. Do not suppose that I am pandering to what is commonly understood by national pride. I cannot say that I am in the slightest degree impressed by your bigness, or your material resources, as such. Size is not grandeur, and territory does not make a nation. The great issue, about which hangs a true sublimity, and the terror of overhanging fate, is what are you going to do with all these things? What is to be the end to which these are to be the means? You are making a novel experiment in politics on the greatest scale which the world has yet seen. Forty millions at your first centenary, it is reasonably to be expected that, at the second, these States will be occupied by two hundred millions of English-speaking people, spread over an area as large as that of Europe, and with climates and interests as diverse as those of Spain and Scandinavia, England and Russia. You and your descendants have to ascertain whether this great mass will hold together under the forms of a republic, and the despotic reality of universal suffrage; whether State rights will hold out against centralization, without separation; whether centralization will get the better, without actual or disguised monarchy; whether shifting corruption is better than a permanent bureaucracy; and as population thickens in your great cities, and he pressure of want is felt, the gaunt spectre of pauperism will stalk among you, , and communism and socialism will claim to be heard. Truly America has a great future before her; great in toil, in care, and in responsibility; great in true glory if she be guided in wisdom and righteousness; great in shame if she fail. I cannot understand why other nations should envy you, or be blind to the fact that it is for the highest interest of mankind that you should succeed; but the one condition of success, your sole safeguard, is the moral worth and intellectual clearness of the individual citizen. Education cannot give these, but it may cherish them and bring them to the front in whatever station of society they are to be found; and the universities ought to be, and may be, the fortresses of the higher life of the nation.

May the university which commences its practical activity to-morrow abundantly fulfil its high purpose; may its renown as a seat of true learning, a centre of free inquiry, a focus of intellectual light, increase year by year, until men wander hither from all parts of the earth, as of old they sought Bologna, or Paris, or Oxford.

And it is pleasant to me to fancy that, among the English students who are drawn to you at that time, there may linger a dim tradition that a countryman of theirs was permitted to address you as he has done today, and to feel as if your hopes were his hopes and your success his joy.

9

SECTION 9

ON THE STUDY OF BIOLOGY
   [1876]

   IT IS my duty to-night to speak about the study of Biology, and while it may be that there are many of my audience who are quite familiar with that study, yet as a lecturer of some standing, it would, I know by experience, be very bad policy on my part to suppose such to be extensively the case. On the contrary, I must imagine that there are many of you who would like to know what Biology is; that there are others who have that amount of information, but would nevertheless gladly hear why it should be worth their while to study Biology; and yet others, again, to whom these two points are clear, but who desire to learn how they had best study it, and, finally, when they had best study it.

   I shall, therefore, address myself to the endeavor to give you some answer to these four questions – What Biology is; why it should be studied; how it should be studied; and when it should be studied.

   In the first place, in respect to what Biology is, there are, I believe, some persons who imagine that the term "Biology" is simply a new-fangled denomination, a neologism in short, for what used to be known under the title of "Natural History"; but I shall try to show you, on the contrary, that the word is the expression of the growth of science during the last 200 years, and came into existence half a century ago.

At the revival of learning, knowledge was divided into two kinds – the knowledge of nature and the knowledge of man; for it was the current idea then (and a great deal of that ancient conception still remains) that there was a sort of essential antithesis, not to say antagonism, between nature and man; and that the two had not very much to do with one another, except that the one was oftentimes exceedingly troublesome to the other. Though it is one of the salient merits of our great philosophers of the seventeenth century, that they recognized but one scientific method, applicable alike to man and to nature, we find this notion of the existence of a broad distinction between nature and man in the writings both of Bacon and of Hobbes of Malmesbury; and I have brought with me that famous work which is now so little known, greatly as it deserves to be studied, "The Leviathan," in order that I may put to you, in the wonderfully terse and clear language of Thomas Hobbes, what was his view of the matter. He says:

"The register of knowledge of fact is called history. Whereof there be two sorts, one called natural history; which is the history of such facts or effects of nature as have no dependence on man's will; such as are the histories of metals, plants, animals, regions, and the like. The other is civil history; which is the history of the voluntary actions of men in commonwealths."

So that all history of fact was divided into these two great groups of natural and of civil history. The . Royal Society was in course of foundation about the time that Hobbes was writing this book, which was published in 1651; and that Society was termed a "Society for the Improvement of Natural Knowledge," which was then nearly the same thing as a "Society for the Improvement of Natural History." As time went on, and the various branches of human knowledge became more distinctly developed and separated from one another, it was found that some were much more susceptible of precise mathematical treatment than others. The publication of the "Princi- pia" of Newton, which probably gave a greater stimulus to physical science than any work ever published before, or which is likely to be published hereafter, showed that precise mathematical methods were applicable to those branches of science such as astronomy, and what we now call physics, which occupy a very large portion of the domain of what the older writers understood by natural history. And inasmuch as the partly deductive and partly experimental methods of treatment to which Newton and others subjected these branches of human knowledge, showed that the phenomena of nature which belonged to them were susceptible of explanation, and thereby came within the reach of what was called "philosophy" in those days; so much of this kind of knowledge as was not included under astronomy came to be spoken of as "natural philosophy" – a term which Bacon had employed in a much wider sense. Time went on, and yet other branches of science developed themselves. Chemistry took a definite shape; and since ail these sciences, such as astronomy, natural philosophy, and chemistry, were susceptible either of mathematical treatment or of experimental treatment, or of both, a broad distinction was drawn between the experimental branches of what had previously been called natural history and the observational branches – those in which experiment was (or appeared to be) of doubtful use, and where, at that time, mathematical methods were inapplicable. Under these circumstances the old name of "Natural History" stuck by the residuum, by those phenomena which were not, at that time, susceptible of mathematical or experimental treatment; that is to say, those phenomena of nature which come now under the general heads of physical geography, geology, mineralogy, the history of plants, and the history of animals. It was in this sense that the term was understood by the great writers of the middle of the last century – Buffon and Linnaeus – by Buffon in his great work, the "Histoire Naturelle Gdne'rale," and by Linnaeus in his splendid achievement, the "Sys- tema Nature." The subjects they deal with are spoken of as "Natural History," and they called themselves and were called "Naturalists." But you will observe that this was not the original meaning of these terms; but that they had, by this time, acquired a signification widely different from that which they possessed primitively.

The sense in which "Natural History" was used at the time I am now speaking of has, to a certain extent, endured to the present day. There are now in existence, in some of our northern universities, chairs of "Civil and Natural History," in which "Natural History" is used to indicate exactly what Hobbes and Bacon meant by that term. The unhappy incumbent of the chair of Natural History is, or was, supposed to cover the whole ground of geology, mineralogy, and zoology, perhaps even botany, in his lectures.

But as science made the marvellous progress which itdid make at the latter end of the last and the beginning of the present century, thinking men began to discern that under this title of "Natural History" there were included very heterogeneous constituents – that, for example, geology and mineralogy were, in many respects, widely different from botany and zoology; that a man might obtain an extensive knowledge of the structure and functions of plants and animals, without having need to enter upon the study of geology or mineralogy, and *vice versd*; and, further as knowledge advanced, it became clear that there was a great analogy, a very close alliance, between those two sciences, of botany and zoology which deal with human beings, while they are much more widely separated from all other studies. It is due to Buffon to remark that he clearly recognized this great fact. He says: "Ces deux genres d'etres organises [les animaux et les ve'ge'taux] ont beaucoup plus de proprietes communes que de differences re'elles." Therefore, it is not wonderful that, at the beginning of the present century, in two different countries, and, so far as I know, without any intercommunication, two famous men clearly conceived the notion of uniting the sciences which deal with living matter into one whole, and of dealing with them as one discipline. In fact, I may say there were three men to whom this idea occurred contemporaneously, although there were but two who carried it into effect, and only one who worked it out completely. The persons to whom I refer were the eminent physiologist Bichat, and the great naturalist Lamarck, in France; and a distinguished German, Treviranus. Bichat' assumed the existence of a special group of "physiological" sciences. Lamarck, in a work published in 1801,' for the first time made use of the name "Biologic," from the two Greek words which signify a discourse upon life and living things. About the same time, it occurred to Treviranus that all those sciences which deal with living matter are essentially and fundamentally one, and ought to be treated as a whole; and, in the year 1802, he published the first volume of what he also called "Biologie." Treviranus's great merit lies in this, that he worked out his idea, and wrote the very remarkable book to which I refer. It consists of six volumes, and occupied its author for twenty years – from 1802 to 1822.

1 See the distinction between the "sciences physiques" and the "sciences physiologiques" in the "Anatomie Generate," 1801.

That is the origin of the term "Biology"; and that is how it has come about that all clear thinkers and lovers of consistent nomenclature have substituted for the old confusing name of "Natural History," which has conveyed so many meanings, the term "Biology," which denotes the whole of the sciences which deal with living things, whether they be animals or whether they be plants. Some little time ago – in the course of this year, I think – I was favored by a learned classic, Dr. Field of Norwich, with a disquisition, in which he endeavored to prove that, from a philological point of view, neither Treviranus nor Lamarck had any right to coin this new word "Biology" for their purpose; that, in fact, the Greek word "Bios" had relation only to human life and human affairs, and that a different word was employed by the Greeks when they wished to speak of the life of animals and plants. So Dr. Field tells us we are allwrong in using the term biology, and that we ought to employ another; only he is not sure about the propriety of that which he proposes as a substitute. It is a somewhat hard one – "zootocology." I am sorry we are wrong, because we are likely to continue so. In these matters we must have some sort of "Statute of Limitations." When a name has been employed for half a century, persons of authority' have been using it, and its sense has become well understood, I am afraid people will go on using it, whatever the weight of philological objection.

1 "Hydrogeologie," an. x. (1801).

Now that we have arrived at the origin of this word "Biology," the next point to consider is: What ground does it cover? I have said that in its strict technical sense it denotes all the phenomena which are exhibited by living things, as distinguished from those which are not living; but while that is all very well, so long as we confine ourselves to the lower animals and to plants, it lands us in considerable difficulties when we reach the higher forms of living things. For whatever view we may entertain about the nature of man, one thing is perfectly certain, that he is a living creature. Hence, if our definition is to be interpreted strictly, we must include man and all his ways and works under the head of Biology; in which case, we should find that psychology, politics, and political economy would be absorbed into the province of Biology. In fact, civil history would be merged in natural history. In strict logic it may behard to object to this course, because no one can doubt that the rudiments and outlines of our own mental phenomena are traceable among the lower animals. They have their economy and their polity, and if, as is always admitted, the polity of bees and the commonwealth of wolves fall within the purview of the biologist proper, it becomes hard to say why we should not include therein human affairs, which, in so many cases, resemble those of the bees in zealous getting, and are not without a certain parity in the proceedings of the wolves. The real fact is that we biologists are a self-sacrificing people; and inasmuch as, on a moderate estimate, there are about a quarter of a million different species of animals and plants to know about already, we feel that we have more than sufficient territory. There has been a sort of practical convention by which we give up to a different branch of science what Bacon and Hobbes would have called "Civil History." That branch of science has constituted itself under the head of Sociology. I may use phraseology which, at present, will be well understood, and say that we have allowed that province of Biology to become autonomous; but I should like you to recollect that that is a sacrifice, and that you should not be surprised if it occasionally happens that you see a biologist apparently trespassing in the region of philosophy or politics; or meddling with human education; because, after all, that is a part of his kingdom which he has only voluntarily forsaken.

1 "The term *Biology,* which means exactly what we wish to express, *the Science of Life,* has often been used, and has of late become not uncommon, among good writers." – Whewell, "Philosophy of the Inductive Sciences," vol. i. p. 544 (edition of 1847).

Having now defined the meaning of the word Biology, and having indicated the general scope of Biological Science, I turn to my second question, which is – Why should we study Biology? Possibly the time may comewhen that will seem a very odd question. That we, living creatures, should not feel a certain amount of interest in what it is that constitutes our life will eventually, under altered ideas of the fittest objects of human inquiry, appear to be a singular phenomenon; but at present, judging by the practice of teachers and educators, Biology would seem to be a topic that does not concern us at all. I propose to put before you a few considerations with which I dare say many will be familiar already, but which will suffice to show – not fully, because to demonstrate this point fully would take a great- many lectures – that there are some very good and substantial reasons why it may be advisable that we should know something about this branch of human learning.

I myself entirely agree with another sentiment of the philosopher of Malmesbury, "that the scope of all speculation is the performance of some action or thing to be done," and I have not any very great respect for, or interest in, mere knowing as such. I judge of the value of human pursuits by their bearing upon human interests; in other words, by their utility; but I should like that we should quite clearly understand what it is that we mean by this word "utility." In an Englishman's mouth. it generally means that by which we get pudding or praise, or both. I have no doubt that is one meaning of the word utility, but it by no means includes all I mean by utility. I think that knowledge of every kind is useful in proportion as it tends to give people right ideas, which are essential to the foundation of right practice, and to remove wrong ideas, which are the no less essential foundations and fertile mothers of every description of error in practice. And inasmuch as, whatever practicalpeople may say, this world is, after all, absolutely governed by ideas, and very often by the wildest and most hypothetical ideas, it is a matter of the very greatest importance that our theories of things, and even of things that seem a long way apart from our daily lives, should be as far as possible true, and as far as possible removed from error. It is not only in the coarser, practical sense of the word "utility," but in this higher and broader sense, that I measure the value of the study of biology by its utility; and I shall try to point out to you that you will feel the need of some knowledge of biology at a great many turns of this present nineteenth century life of ours. For example, most of us attach great importance to the conception which we entertain of the position of man in this universe and his relation to the rest of nature. We have almost all been told, and most of us hold by the tradition, that man occupies an isolated and peculiar position in nature; that though he is in the world he is not of the world; that his relations to things about him are of a remote character; that his origin is recent, his duration likely to be short, and that he is the great central figure round which other things in this world revolve. But this is not what the biologist tells us. At the present moment you will be kind enough to separate me from them, because it is in no way essential to my present argument that I should advocate their views. Don't suppose that I am saying this for the purpose of escaping the responsibility of their beliefs; indeed, at other times and in other places, I do not think that point has been left doubtful; but I want clearly to point out to you that for my present argument they may all be wrong; and, nevertheless,, my argument will holdgood. The biologists tell us that all this is an entire mistake. They turn to the physical organization of man. They examine his whole structure, his bony frame arid. all that clothes it. They resolve him into the finest particles into which the microscope will enable them to break him up. They consider the performance of his various functions and activities, and they look at the manner in which he occurs on the surface of the world. Then they turn to other animals, and taking the first handy domestic animal – say a dog – they profess to be able to demonstrate that the analysis of the dog leads them, in gross, to precisely the same results as the analysis of the man; that they find almost identically the same bones, having the same relations; that they can name the muscles of the dog by the names of the muscles of the man; and the nerves of the dog by those of the nerves of the man, and that, such structures and organs of sense as we find in the man such also we find in the dog; they analyze the brain and spinal cord and they find that the nomenclature which fits the one answers for the other. They carry their microscopic inquiries in the case of the dog as far as they can, and they find that his body is resolvable into the same elements as those of the man. Moreover, they trace back the dog's and the man's development, and they find that, at a certain stage of their existence, the two creatures are not distinguishable the one from the other; they find that the dog and his kind have a certain distribution over the surface of the world, comparable in its way to the distribution of the human species. What is true of the dog they tell us is true of all the higher animals; and they assert that they can lay down a common plan for the

whole of these creatures, and regard the man and the dog, the horse and the ox, as minor modifications of one great fundamental unity. Moreover, the investigations of the last three-quarters of a century have proved, they tell as, that similar inquiries, carried out through all the different kinds of animals which are met with in nature, will lead us, not in one straight series, but by many roads, step by step, gradation by gradation, from man, at the summit, to specks of animated jelly at the bottom of the series. So that the idea of Leibnitz, and of Bonnet, that animals form a great scale of being, in which there are a series of gradations from the most complicated form to the lowest and simplest; that idea, though not exactly in the form in which it was propounded by those philosophers, turns out to be substantially correct. More than this, when biologists pursue' their investigations into the vegetable world, they find that they can, in the same way, follow out the structure of the plant, from the most gigantic and complicated trees down through a similar series of gradations, until they arrive at specks of animated jelly, which they are puzzled to distinguish from those specks which they reached by the animal road.

Thus, biologists have arrived at the conclusion that a fundamental uniformity of structure pervades the animal and vegetable worlds, and that plants and animals differ from one another simply as diverse modifications of the same great general plan.

Again, they tell us the same story in regard to the study of function. They admit the large and important interval which, at the present time, separates the manifestations of the mental faculties observable in the higherforms of mankind, and even in the lower forms, such as we know them, from those exhibited by other animals; but, at the same time, they tell us that the foundations, or rudiments, of almost all the faculties of man are to be met with in the lower animals; that there is a unity of mental faculty as well as of bodily structure, and that, here also, the difference is a difference of degree and not of kind. I said "almost all," for a reason. Among the many distinctions which have been drawn between the lower creatures and ourselves, there is one which is hardly ever insisted on,1 but which may be very fitly spoken of in a place so largely devoted to Art as that in which we are assembled. It is this, that while, among various kinds of animals, it is possible to discover traces of all the other faculties of man, especially the faculty of mimicry, yet that particular form of mimicry which shows itself in the imitation of form, either by modelling or by drawing, is not to be met with. As far as I know, there is no sculpture or modelling, and decidedly no painting or drawing, of animal origin. I mention the fact, in order that such comfort may be derived therefrom as artists may feel inclined to take.

If what the biologists tell us is true, it will be needful to get rid of our erroneous conceptions of man, and of his place in nature, and to substitute right ones for them. But it is impossible to form any judgment as to whether the biologists are right or wrong, unless we are able to appreciate the nature of the arguments which they have to offer.

One would almost think this to be a self-evidentproposition. I wonder what a scholar would say to tEe man who should undertake to criticise a difficult passage in a Greek play, but who obviously had not acquainted himself with the rudiments of Greek grammar. And yet, before giving positive opinions about these high questions of Biology, people not only do not seem to think it necessary to be acquainted with the grammar of the subject, but they have not even mastered the alphabet. You find criticism and denunciation showered about by persons who not only have not attempted to go through the discipline necessary to enable them to be judges, but who have not even reached that stage of emergence from ignorance in which the knowledge that such a discipline is necessary dawns upon the mind. I have had to watch with some attention – in fact I have been favored with a good deal of it myself – the sort of criticism with which biologists and biological teachings are visited. I am told every now and then that there is a "brilliant article" ' in so-and-so, in which we are all demolished. I used to read these things once, but I am getting old now, and I have ceased to attend very much to this cry of "wolf." When one does read any of these productions, what one finds generally, on the face of it, is, that the brilliant critic is devoid of even the elements of biological knowledge, and that his brilliancy is like the light given out by the crackling of thorns under a pot of which Solomon speaks. So far as I recollect, Solomon makes use of the image for purposes of comparison; but I will not proceed further into that matter.

1 I think that my friend, Professor Allman, was the first to draw attention to it.

1 Galileo was troubled by a sort of people whom he called "paper philosophers," because they fancied that the true reading of nature was to be detected by the collation of texts. The race is not extinct, but, as of old, brings forth its "winds of doctrine" by which the weathercock heads among us are much exercised.

Two things must be obvious: in the first place, that every man who has the interests of truth at heart must earnestly desire that every well-founded and just criticism that can be made should be made; but that, in the second place, it is essential to anybody's being able to benefit by criticism that the critic should know what he is talking about, and be in a position to form a mental image of the facts symbolized by the words he uses. If not, it is as obvious in the case of a biological argument, as it is in that of a historical or philological discussion, that such criticism is a mere waste of time on the part of its author, and wholly undeserving of attention on the part of those who are criticised. Take it then as an illustration of the importance of biological study, that thereby alone are men able to form something like a rational conception of what constitutes valuable criticism of the teachings of biologists.1

1 Some critics do not even take the trouble to read. I have recently been adjured with much solemnity to state publicly why I have "changed my opinion" as to the value of the paleontological evidence of the occurrence of evolution.

To this my reply is, Why should I, when that statement was made seven years ago ? An address delivered from the Presidential Chair of the Geological Society, in 1870, may be said to be a public document, inasmuch as it not only appeared in the "Journal" of that learned body, but was republished, in 1873, in a volume of "Critiques and Addresses," to which my name is attached. Therein will be found a pretty full statement of my reasons for enunciating two propositions: (1) that "when we turn to the higher *Vertebrata*, the results of recent investigations, however we may sift and criticise them, seem to me to leave a clear balance in favor of the evolution of living forms one from another"; and (2) that the case of the horse is one which "will stand rigorous criticism."

Thus I do not see clearly in what way I can be said to have changed myopinion, except in the way of intensifying it, when, in consequence of the accumulation of similar evidence since 1870, I recently spoke of the denial of evolution as not worth serious consideration.

Next, I may mention another bearing of biological knowledge – a more practical one in the ordinary sense of the word. Consider the theory of infectious disease. Surely that is of interest to all of us. Now the theory of infectious disease is rapidly being elucidated by biological study. It is possible to produce, from among the lower animals, examples of devastating diseases which spread in the same manner as our infectious disorders, and which are certainly and unmistakably caused by living organisms. This fact renders it possible, at any rate, that that doctrine of the causation of infectious disease which is known under the name of "the germ theory" may be well-founded; and, if so, it must needs lead to the most important practical measures in dealing with those terrible visitations. It may be well that the general, as well as the professional, public should have a sufficient knowledge of biological truths to be able to take a rational interest in the discussion of such problems, and to see, what I think they may hope to see, that, to those who possess a sufficient elementary knowledge of Biology, they are not all quite open questions.

Let me mention another important practical illustration of the value of biological study. Within the last forty years the theory of agriculture has been revolutionized. The researches of Liebig, and those" of our own Lawes and Gilbert, have had a bearing upon that branch of industry the importance of which cannot be overestimated; but the whole of these new views have grown out of the better explanation of certain processes which go on inplants; and which, of course, form a part of the subject-matter of Biology.

I might go on multiplying these examples, but I see that the clock won't wait for me, and I must therefore pass to the third question to which I referred: Granted that Biology is something worth studying, what is the best way of studying it? Here I must point out that, since Biology is a physical science, the method of studying it must needs be analogous to that which is followed in the other physical sciences. It has now long been recognized that, if a man wishes to be a chemist, it is not only necessary that he should read chemical books and attend chemical lectures, but that he should actually perform the fundamental experiments in the laboratory for himself, and thus learn exactly what the words which he finds in his books and hears from his teachers mean. If he does not do so, he may read till the crack of doom, but he will never know much about chemistry. That is what every chemist will tell you, and the physicist will do the same for his branch of science. The great changes and improvements in physical and chemical scientific education which have taken place of late have all resulted from the combination of practical teaching with the reading of books and with the hearing of lectures. The same thing is true in Biology. Nobody will ever know anything about Biology, except in a dilettante "paper-philosopher'1 way, who contents himself with reading books on botany, zoology, and the like; and the reason of this is simple and easy to understand. It is that all language is merely symbolical of the things of which it treats; the more complicated the things, the more bare is the symbol, and the more its verbal definitionrequires to be supplemented by the information derived directly from the handling, and the seeing, and the touching of the thing symbolized: – that is really what is at the bottom of the whole matter. It is plain common-sense, as all truth, in the long run, is only common- sense clarified. If you want a man to be a tea merchant, you don't tell him to read books about China or about tea, but you put him into a tea-merchant's office, where he has the handling, the smelling, and the tasting of tea. Without the sort of knowledge which can be gained only in this practical way, his exploits as a tea merchant will soon come to a bankrupt termination. The "paper- philosophers" are under the delusion that physical science can be mastered as literary accomplishments are acquired, but unfortunately it is not so. You may read any quantity of books, and you may be almost as ignorant as you were at starting, if you don't have, at the back of your minds, the change for words in definite images which can only be acquired through the operation of your observing faculties on the phenomena of nature.

It may be said: "That is all very well, but you told us just now that there are probably something like a quarter of a million different kinds of living and extinct animals and plants, and a human life could not suffice for the examination of one-fiftieth part of all these." That is true, but then comes the great convenience of the way things are arranged; which is that, although there are these immense numbers of different kinds of living things in existence, yet they are built up, after all, upon marvellously few plans.

There are certainly more than 100,000 species of insects, and yet anybody who knows one insect – if a

Vill – Science – 11

properly chosen one – will be able to have a very fair conception of the structure of the whole. I do not mean to say he will know that structure thoroughly, or as well as it is desirable he should know it; but he will have enough real knowledge to enable him to understand what he reads, to have genuine images in his mind of those structures which become so variously modified in all the forms of insects he has not seen. In fact, there are such things as types of form among animals and vegetables, and for the purpose of getting a definite knowledge of what constitutes the leading modifications of animal and plant life, it is not needful to examine more than a comparatively small number of animals and plants.

Let me tell you what we do in the biological laboratory which is lodged in a building adjacent to this. There I lecture to a class of students daily for about four and a half months, and my class have, of course, their text-books; but the essential part of the whole teaching, and that which I regard as really the most important part of it, is a laboratory for practical work, which is simply a room with all the appliances needed for ordinary dissection. We have tables properly arranged in regard to light, microscopes, and dissecting instruments, and we work through the structure of a certain number of animals and plants. As, for example, among the plants, we take a yeast plant, a *Protococcus,* a common mould, a *Chara,* a fern, and some flowering plant; among animals we examine such things as an *Amoeba,* a *Vorticella,* and a fresh-water polype. We dissect a starfish, an earthworm, a snail, a squid, and a fresh-water mussel. We examine a lobster and a crayfish, and a black beetle. We go on to a common skate, a codfish, a frog, a tortoise, a pigeon, and a rabbit, and that takes us about all the time we have to give. The purpose of this course is not to make skilled dissectors, but to give every student a clear and definite conception, by means of sense-images, of the characteristic structure of each of the leading modifications of the animal kingdom; and that is perfectly possible by going no further than the length of that list of forms which I have enumerated. If a man knows the structure of the animals I have mentioned, he has a clear and exact, however limited, apprehension of the essential features of the organization of all those great divisions of the animal and vegetable kingdoms to which the forms I have mentioned severally belong. And it then becomes possible for him to read with profit; because every time he meets with the name of a structure, he has a definite image in his mind of what the name means in the particular creature he is reading about, and therefore the reading is not mere-reading. It is not mere repetition of words; but every term employed in the description, we will say, of a horse, or of an elephant, will call up the image of the things he had seen in the rabbit, and he is able to form a distinct conception of that which he has not seen, as a modification of that which he has seen.

I find this system to yield excellent results; and I have no hesitation whatever in saying that any one who has gone through such a course, attentively, is in a better position to form a conception of the great truths of biology, especially of morphology (which is what we chiefly deal with), than if he had merely read all the books on that topic put together.

The connection of this discourse with the Loan Collection of Scientific Apparatus arises out of the exhibition in that collection of certain aids to our laboratory work. Such of you as have visited that very interesting collection may have noticed a series of diagrams and of preparations illustrating the structure of a frog. Those diagrams and preparations have been made for the use of the students in the biological laboratory. Similar diagrams and preparations, illustrating the structure of all the other forms of life we examine, are either made or in course of preparation. Thus the student has before him, first, a picture of the structure he ought to see; secondly, the structure itself worked out; and if with these aids, and such needful explanations and practical hints as a demonstrator can supply, he cannot make out the facts for himself in the materials supplied to him, he had better take to some other pursuit than that of biological science.

I should have been glad to have said a few words about the use of museums in the study of Biology, but I see that my time is becoming short, and I have- yet another question to answer. Nevertheless, I must, at the risk of wearying you, say a word or two upon the important subject of museums. "Without doubt there are no helps to the study of Biology, or rather to some branches of it, which are, or may be, more important than natural history museums; but, in order to take this place in regard to Biology, they must be museums of the future. The museums of the present do not, by any means, do so much for us as they might do. I do not wish to particularize, but I dare say many of you, seeking knowledge, or in the laudable desire to employ a holiday usefully, have visited some great natural history museum. You have walked through a quarter of a mile of animals, more or less well stuffed, with their long names written out underneath them; and, unless your experience is very different from that of most people, the upshot of it all is that you leave that splendid pile with sore feet, a bad headache, and a general idea that the animal kingdom is a "mighty maze without a plan." I do not think that a museum which brings about this result does all that may be reasonably expected from such an institution. What is needed in a collection of natural history is that it should be made as accessible and as useful as possible, on the one hand to the general public, and on the other to scientific workers. That need is not met by constructing a sort of happy hunting-ground of miles of glass cases; and, under the pretence of exhibiting everything, putting the maximum amount of obstacle in the way of those who wish properly to see anything.

What the public want is easy and unhindered access to such a collection as they can understand and appreciate; and what the men of science want is similar access to the materials of science. To this end the vast mass of objects of natural history should be divided into two parts – one open to the public, the other to men of science, every day. The former division should exemplify all the more important and interesting forms of life. Explanatory tablets should be attached to them, and catalogues containing clearly-written popular expositions of the general significance of the objects exhibited should be provided. The latter should contain, packed into a comparatively small space, in rooms adapted for working purposes, the objects of purely scientific interest. For example, we will say *I* am an ornithologist. I go to examine a collection of birds. It is a positive nuisance to have them stuffed. It is not only sheer waste, but I have to reckon with the ideas of the bird-staffer, while, if I have the skin and nobody has interfered with it, I can form my own judgment as to what the bird was like. For ornithological purposes, what is needed is not glass cases full of stuffed birds on perches, but convenient drawers into each of which a great quantity of skins will go. They occupy no great space and do not require any expenditure beyond their original cost. But for the edification of the public, who want to learn indeed, but do not seek for minute and technical knowledge, the case is different. What one of the general public walking into a collection of birds desires to see is not all the birds that can be got together. He does not want to compare a hundred species of the sparrow tribe side by side; but he wishes to know what a bird is, and what are the great modifications of bird structure, and to be able to get at that knowledge easily. What will best serve his purpose is a comparatively small number of birds carefully selected, and artistically, as well as accurately, set up; with their different ages, their nests, their young, their eggs, and their skeletons side by side; and, in accordance with the admirable plan which is pursued in this museum, a tablet, telling the spectator in legible characters what they are and what they mean. For the instruction and recreation of the public such a typical collection would be of far greater value than any many-acred imitation of Noah's ark.

Lastly comes the question as to when biological study may best be pursued. I do not see any valid reason why it should not be made, to a certain extent, a part of ordinary school training. I have long advocated this view, and I am perfectly certain that it can be carried out with ease, and not only with ease, but with very considerable profit to those who are taught; but then such instruction must be adapted to the minds and needs of the scholars. They used to have a very odd way of teaching the classical languages when *I* was a boy. The first task set you was to learn the rules of the Latin grammar in the Latin language – that being the language you were going to learn I I thought then that this was an odd way of learning a language, but did not venture to rebel against the judgment of my superiors. Now, perhaps, I am not so modest as I was then, and I allow myself to think that it was a very absurd fashion. But it would be no less absurd, if we were to set about teaching biology by putting into the hands of boys a series of definitions of the classes and orders of the animal kingdom, and making them repeat them by heart. That is so very favorite a method of teaching that I sometimes fancy the spirit of the old classical system has entered into the new scientific system, in which case I would much rather that any pretence at scientific teaching were abolished altogether. What really has to be done is to get into the young mind some notion of what animal and vegetable life is. In this matter, you have to consider practical convenience as well as other things. There are difficulties in the way of a lot of boys making messes with slugs and snails; it might not work in practice. But there is a very convenient and handy animal which everybody has at hand, and that is himself; and it is a very easy and simple matter to obtain common plants.

Hence the general truths of anatomy and physiology can be taught to young people in a very real fashion by dealing with the broadfacts of human structure. Such viscera as they cannot very well examine in themselves, such as hearts, lungs and livers, may be obtained from the nearest butcher's shop. In respect to teaching something about the biology of plants, there is no practical difficulty, because almost any of the common plants will do, and plants do not make a mess – at least they do not make an unpleasant mess; so that, in my judgment, the best form of Biology for teaching to very young people is elementary human physiology on the one hand, and the elements of botany on the other; beyond that I do not think it will be feasible to advance for some time to come. But then I see no reason why, in secondary schools, and in the Science Classes which are under the control of the Science and Art Department – and which I may say, in passing, have in my judgment done so very much for the diffusion of a knowledge of science over the country – we should not hope to see instruction in the elements of Biology carried out, not perhaps to the same extent, but still upon somewhat the same principle as here. There is no difficulty, when you have to deal with students of the ages of fifteen or sixteen, in practicing a little dissection and in getting a notion of, at any rate, the four or five great modifications of the animal form; and the like is true in regard to the higher anatomy of plants.

"While, lastly, to all those who are studying biological science with a view to their own edification merely, or with the intention of becoming zoologists or botanists; to all those who intend to pursue physiology – and especially to those who propose to employ the working years of their lives in the practice of medicine – I say that there is no training so fitted, or which may be of such important service to them, as the discipline in practical biological work which I have sketched out as being pursued in the laboratory hard by.

I may add that, beyond all these different classes of persons who may profit by the study of Biology, there is yet one other. I remember, a number of years ago, that a gentleman who was a vehement opponent of Mr. Darwin's views, and had written some terrible articles against them, applied to me to know what was the best way in which he could acquaint himself with the strongest arguments in favor of evolution. I wrote back, in all good faith and simplicity, recommending him to go through a course of comparative anatomy and physiology, and then to study development. I am sorry to say he was very much displeased, as people often are with good advice. Notwithstanding this discouraging result, I venture, as a parting word, to repeat the suggestion, and to say to all the more or less acute lay and clerical "paper-philosophers" ' who venture into the regions of biological controversy – Get a little sound, thorough, practical, elementary instruction in biology.

1 Writers of this stamp are fond of talking about the Baconian method. I beg them therefore to lay to heart these two weighty sayings of the herald of Modern Science: i

"Syllogismus ex propositionibus constat, propositiones ex verbis, verba no- tionum tesserae sunt. Itaque si notiones ipsas (id quod basis rei esf) confuses Bint et temere a rebus abstractse, nihil in iis quas superstruuntur est firmitu dinis." – "Novum Organon," ii. 14.

.'Huic autem vanitati nonnulli exmodernis

summalevitatoitaindulserunt, ut in primo capitulo G-eneseos et in libro Job et aliis scripturis sacris, philosophiam naturalem fundare conati sint; *inter vivas quosrentes mortua."* – Ibid. 65.

10

SECTION 10

XI

ON ELEMENTARY INSTRUCTION IN PHYSIOLOGY
[1877]

THE chief ground upon which I venture to recommend that the teaching of elementary physiology should form an essential part of any organized course of instruction in matters pertaining to domestic economy, is, that a knowledge of even the elements of this subject supplies those conceptions of the constitution and mode of action of the living body, and of the nature of health and disease, which prepare the mind to receive instruction from sanitary science.

It is, I think, eminently desirable that the hygienist and the physician should find something in the public mind to which they can appeal; some little stock of universally acknowledged truths, which may serve as a foundation for their warnings, and predispose toward an intelligent obedience to their recommendations.

Listening to ordinary talk about health, disease, and death, one is often led to entertain a doubt whether the speakers believe that the course of natural causation runs as smoothly in the human body as elsewhere. Indications are too often obvious of a strong, though perhaps an unavowed and half unconscious, under-current of opinion that the phenomena of life are not only widely different, in their superficial characters and in their practical importance, from other natural events, but that they do not follow in that definite order which characterizes the succession of all other occurrences, and the statement of which we call a law of nature.

Hence, I think, arises the want of heartiness of belief in the value of knowledge respecting the laws of health and disease, and of the foresight and care to which knowledge is the essential preliminary, which is so often noticeable; and a corresponding laxity and carelessness In practice, the results of which are too frequently lamentable.

It is said that among the many religious sects of Russia there is one which holds that all disease is brought about by the direct and special interference of the Deity, and which, therefore, looks with repugnance upon both preventive and curative measures as alike blasphemous interferences with the will of God. Among ourselves, the "Peculiar People" are, I believe, the only persons who hold the like doctrine in its integrity, and carry it out with logical rigor. But many of us are old enough to recollect that the administration of chloroform in assuagement of the pangs of childbirth was, at its introduction, strenuously resisted upon similar grounds.

I am not sure that the feeling, of which the doctrine to which I have referred is the full expression, does not lie at the bottom of the minds of a great many people who yet would vigorously object to give a verbal assent to the doctrine itself. However this may be, the main point is, that sufficient knowledge has now been acquired of vital phenomena to justify the assertion that the notion that there is anything exceptional about these phenomena receives not a particle of support from any known fact. On the contrary, there is a vast and anincreasing mass of evidence that birth and death, health and disease, are as much parts of the ordinary stream of events as the rising and setting of the sun, or the changes of the moon; and that the living body is a mechanism, the proper working of which we term health; its disturbance, disease; its stoppage, death. The activity of this mechanism is dependent upon many and complicated conditions, some of which are hopelessly beyond our control, while others are readily accessible, and are capable of being indefinitely modified by our own actions. The business of the hygienist and of the physician is to know the range of these modifiable conditions, and how to influence them toward the maintenance of health and the prolongation of life; the business of the general public is to give an intelligent assent, and a ready obedience based upon that assent, to the rules laid down for their guidance by such experts. But an intelligent assent is an assent based upon - knowledge, and the knowledge which is here in question means an acquaintance with the elements of physiology.

It is not dimcult to acquire such knowledge. What is true, to a certain extent, of all the physical sciences, is eminently characteristic of physiology – the difficulty of the subject begins beyond the stage of elementary knowledge, and increases with every stage of progress. While the most highly trained and the best furnished intellect may find all its resources insufficient, when it strives to reach the heights and penetrate into the depths of the problems of physiology, the elementary and fundamental truths can be made clear to a child.

No one can have any difficulty in comprehending the mechanism of circulation or respiration; or the generalmode of operation of the organ of vision; though the unravelling of all the minutiae of these processes may, for the present, baffle the conjoined attacks of the most accomplished physicists, chemists and mathematicians.

To know the anatomy of the human body, with even an approximation to thoroughness, is the work of a life; but as much as is needed for a sound comprehension of elementary physiological truths may be learned in a week.

A knowledge of the elements of physiology is not only easy of acquirement, but it may be made a real and practical acquaintance with the facts, as far as it goes. The subject of study is always at hand in one's self. The principal constituents of the skeleton, and the changes of form of contracting muscles, may be felt through one's own skin. The beating of one's heart, and its connection with the pulse, may be noted; the influence of the valves of one's own veins may be shown; the movements of respiration may be observed; while the wonderful phenomena of sensation afford an endless field for curious and interesting self-study. The prick of a needle will yield, in a drop of one's own blood, material for microscopic observation of phenomena which lie at the foundation of all biological conceptions; and a cold, with its concomitant coughing and sneezing, may prove the sweet uses of adversity by helping one to a clear conception of what is meant by "reflex action."

Of course there is a limit to this physiological self- examination. But there is so close a solidarity between ourselves and our poor relations of the animal world, that our inaccessible inward parts may be supplemented by theirs. A comparative anatomist knows that a sheep'sheart and lungs, or eye, must not be confounded with those of a man; but, so far as the comprehension of the elementary facts of the physiology of circulation, of respiration, and of vision goes, the one furnishes the needful anatomical data as well as the other.

Thus, it is quite possible to give instruction in elementary physiology in such a manner as not only to confer knowledge, which, for the reason I have mentioned, is useful in itself, but to serve the purposes of a training in accurate observation and in the methods of reasoning of physical science. But that is an advantage which I mention only incidentally, as the present Conference does not deal with education in the ordinary sense of the word.

It will not be suspected that I wish to make physiologists of all the world. It would be as reasonable to accuse an advocate of the "three E's" of a desire to make an orator, an author, and a mathematician of everybody. A stumbling reader, a pot-hook writer, and an arithmetician who has not got beyond the rule of three, is not a person of brilliant acquirements; but the difference between such a member of society and one who can neither read, write, nor cipher is almost inexpressible; and no one nowadays doubts the value of instruction, even if it goes no further.

The saying that a little knowledge is a dangerous thing is, to my mind, a very dangerous adage. If knowledge is real and genuine, I do not believe that it is other than a very valuable possession, however infinitesimal its quantity may be. Indeed, if a little knowledge is dangerous, where is the man who has so much as to be out of danger ?

If "William Harvey's life-long labors had revealed to him a tenth part of that which may be made sound and real knowledge to our boys and girls, he would not only have been what he was, the greatest physiologist of hio age, but he would have loomed upon the seventeenth century as a sort of intellectual portent. Our "little knowledge" would have been to him a great, astounding, unlooked-for vision of scientific truth.

I really see no harm which can come of giving our children a little knowledge of physiology. But then, aa I have said, the instruction must be real, based upon observation, eked out by good explanatory diagrams and models, and conveyed by a teacher whose own knowledge has been acquired by a study of the facts; and not the mere catechismal parrot-work which too often usurps the place of elementary teaching.

It is, I hope, unnecessary for me to give a formal contradiction to the silly fiction, which is assiduously circulated by fanatics who not only ought to know, but do know, that their assertions are untrue, that I have advocated the introduction of that experimental discipline which is absolutely indispensable to the professed physiologist, into elementary teaching.

But while I should object to any experimentation which can justly be called painful, for the purpose of elementary instruction; and while, as a member of a late Royal Commission, I gladly did my best to prevent the infliction of needless pain, for any purpose; I think it is my duty to take this opportunity of expressing my regret at a condition of the law which permits a boy to troll for pike, or set lines with live frog bait, for idle amusement; and, at the same time, lays the teacher of that boy opento the penalty of fine and imprisonment, if he uses the same animal for the purpose of exhibiting one of the most beautiful and instructive "of physiological spectacles, the circulation in the web of the foot. No one could undertake to affirm that a frog is not inconvenienced by being wrapped up in a wet rag and having his toes tied out; and it cannot be denied that inconvenience is a sort of pain. But you must not inflict the least pain on a vertebrated animal for scientific purposes (though you may do a good deal in that way for gain or for sport) without due license of the Secretary of State for the Home Department, granted under the authority of the Vivisection Act.

So it comes about that, in this present year of grace, 1877, two persons may be charged with cruelty to animals. One has impaled a frog, and suffered the creature to writhe about in that condition for hours; the other has pained the animal no more than one of us would be pained by tying strings round his fingers, and keeping him in the position of a hydropathic patient. The first offender says, "I did it because I find fishing very amusing," and the magistrate bids him depart in peace; nay, probably wishes him good sport. The second pleads, "I wanted to impress a scientific truth, with a distinctness attainable in no other way, on the minds of my scholars," and the magistrate fines him five pounds.

I cannot but think that this is an anomalous and not wholly creditable state of things.

XII

ON MEDICAL EDUCATION

[1870]

IT has given me sincere pleasure to be here to-day, at the desire of your highly respected President and the Council of the College. In looking back upon my own past, I am sorry to say that I have found that it ia a quarter of a century since I took part in those hopea and in those fears by which you have all recently been agitated, and which now are at an end. But, although Bo long a time has elapsed since I was moved by the same feelings, I beg leave to assure you that my sympathy with both victors and vanquished remains fresh – so fresh, indeed, that I could almost try to persuade myself, that, after all, it cannot be so very long ago. My business during the last hour, however, has been to show that sympathy with one side only, and I assure you I have done my best to play my part heartily, and to rejoice in the success of those who have succeeded. Still, I should like to remind you at the end of it all, that success on an occasion of this kind, valuable and important as it is, is in reality only putting the foot upon one rung of the ladder which leads upward; and that the rung of a ladder was never meant to rest upon, but only to hold a man's foot long enough to enable him to put the other somewhat higher. I trust that you will all regard these successes as simply reminders that your nextbusiness is, having enjoyed the success of the day, no longer to look at th. at success, but to look forward to the next difficulty that is to be conquered. And now, having had so much to say to the successful candidates, you must forgive me if I add that a sort of under-current of sympathy has been going on in my mind all the time for those who have not been successful, for those valiant knights who have been overthrown in your tourney, and have not made their appearance in public. I trust that, in accordance with old custom, they, wounded and bleeding, have been carried off to their tents, to be carefully tended by the fairest of maidens; and in these days, when the chances are that every one of such maidens will be a qualified practitioner, I have no doubt that all the splinters will have been carefully extracted, and that they are now physically healed. But there may remain some little fragment of moral or intellectual discouragement, and therefore I will take the liberty to remark that your chairman to-day, if he occupied his proper place, would be among them. Your chairman, in virtue of his position, and for the brief hour that he occupies that position, is a person of importance; and it may be some consolation to those who have failed if I say that the quarter of a century which I have been speaking of takes me back to the time when I was up at the University of London, a candidate for honors in anatomy and physiology, and when I was exceedingly well beaten by my excellent friend, Dr. Eansom, of Nottingham. There is a person here who recollects that circumstance very well. I refer to your venerated teacher and mine, Dr. Sharpey. He was at that time one of the examiners in anatomy and physiology, and you may be quite surethat, as he was one of the examiners, there remained not the smallest doubt in my mind of the propriety of his judgment, and I accepted my defeat with the most comfortable assurance that I had thoroughly well earned it. But, gentlemen, the competitor having been a worthy one, and the examination a fair one, I cannot say that I found in that circumstance anything very discouraging. I said to myself, "Never mind; what's the next thing to be done?" And I found that policy of "never minding" and going on to the next thing to be done to be the most important of all policies in the conduct of practical life. It does not matter how many tumbles you have in this life, so long as you do not get dirty when you tumble; it is only the people who have to stop to be washed and made clean who must necessarily lose the race. And I can assure you that there is the greatest practical benefit in making a few failures early in life. You learn that which is of inestimable importance – that there are a great many people in the world who are just as clever as you are. You learn to put your trust, by and by, in an economy and frugality of the exercise of your powers, both moral and intellectual; and you very soon find out, if you have not found it out before, that patience and tenacity of purpose are worth more than twice their weight of cleverness. In fact, if I were to go on discoursing on this subject, I should become almost eloquent in praise of non-success; but, lest so doing should seem, in any way, to wither well-earned laurels, I will turn from that topic, and ask you to accompany me in some considerations touching another subject which has a very profound interest for me, and which I think ought to have an equally profound interest for you.

I presume that the great majority of those whom I address propose to devote themselves to the profession of medicine; and I do not doubt, from the evidences of ability which have been given to-day, that I have before me a number of men who will rise to eminence in that profession, and who will exert a great and deserved influence upon its future. That in which I am interested, and about which *I* wish to speak, is the subject of medical education, and I venture to speak about it for the purpose, if I can, of influencing you, who may have the power of influencing the medical education of the future. You may ask, by what authority do I venture, being a person not concerned in the practice of medicine, to meddle with that subject? I can only tell you it is a fact, of which a number of you I dare say are aware by experience (and I trust the experience has no painful associations), that I have been for a considerable number of years (twelve or thirteen years to the best of my recollection) one of the examiners in the University of London. You are further aware that the men who come up to the University of London are the picked men of the medical schools of London, and therefore such, observations as I may have to make upon the state of knowledge of these gentlemen, if they be justified, in regard to any faults I may have to find, cannot be held to indicate defects in the capacity, or in the power of application of those gentlemen, but must be laid, more or less, to the account of the prevalent system of medical education. I will tell you what has struck me – but in speaking in this frank way, as one always does about the defects of one's friends, I must beg you to disabuse your minds of the notion that I am alluding to any particular school, or to any particular college, or to any particular person; and to believe that if I am silent when I should be glad to speak with high praise, it is because that praise would come too close to this locality. What has struck me, then, in this long experience of the men best instructed in physiology from the medical schools of London is (with the many and brilliant exceptions to which I have referred), taking it as a whole, and broadly, the singular unreality of their knowledge of physiology. Now, I use that word "unreality" advisedly; I do not say "scanty"; on the contrary, there is plenty of it – a great deal too much of it – but it is the quality, the nature of the knowledge, which I quarrel with. I know I used to have – I don't know whether I have now, but I had once upon a time – a bad reputation among students for setting up a very high standard of acquirement, and I dare say you may think that the standard of this old examiner, who happily is now verv nearly an extinct examiner, has been pitched too high. Nothing of the kind, I assure you. The defects I have noticed, and the faults I have to find, arise entirely from the circumstance that my standard is pitched too low. This is no paradox, gentlemen, but quite simply the fact. The knowledge I have looked for was a real, precise, thorough, and practical knowledge of fundamentals; whereas that which the best of the candidates, in a large proportion of cases, have had to give me was a large, extensive, and inaccurate knowledge of superstructure; and' that is what I mean by saying that my demands went too low and not too high. What I have had to complain of is, that a large proportion of the gentlemen who come up for physiology to the University of London do

not know it as they know their anatomy, and have not been taught it as they have been taught their anatomy. Now, I should not wonder at all if I heard a great many "No, noes" here; but I am not talking about University College; as I have told you before, I am talking about the average education of medical schools. What I have found, and found so much reason to lament, is, that while anatomy has been taught as a science ought to be taught, as a matter of autopsy, and observation, and strict discipline; in a very large number of cases, physiology has been taught as if it were a mere matter of books and of hearsay. I declare to you, gentlemen, that I have often expected to be told, when I have asked a question about the circulation of the blood, that Professor Breitkopf is of opinion that it circulates, but that the whole thing is an open question. I assure you that I am hardly exaggerating the state of mind on matters of fundamental importance which I have found over and over again to obtain among gentlemen coming up to that picked examination of the University of London. Now, I do not think that is a desirable state of things. I cannot understand why physiology should not be taught – in fact, you have here abundant evidence that it can be taught – with the same definiteness and the same precision as anatomy is taught. And you may depend upon this, that the only physiology which is to be of any good whatever in medical practice, or in its application . to the study of medicine, is that physiology which a man knows of his own knowledge; just as the only anatomy which would be of any good to the surgeon is the anatomy which he knows of his own knowledge. Another peculiarity I have found in the physiology which hasbeen current, and that is, that in the minds of a great many gentlemen it has been supplanted by histology. They have learned a great deal of histology, and they have fancied that histology and physiology are the same things. I have asked for some knowledge of the physics and the mechanics and the chemistry of tbe human body, and I have been met by talk about cells. I declare to you I believe it will take me two years, at least, of absolute rest from the business of an examiner to hear the word "cell," "germinal matter," or "carmine," without a sort of inward shudder.

Well, now, gentlemen, I am sure my colleagues in this examination will bear me out in saying that I have not been exaggerating the evils and defects which are current – have been current – in a large quantity of the physiological teaching the results of which come before examiners. And it becomes a very interesting question to know how all this comes about, and in what way it can be remedied. How it comes about will be perfectly obvious to any one who has considered the growth of medicine. I suppose that medicine and surgery first began by some savage, more intelligent than the rest, discovering that a certain herb was good for a certain pain, and that a certain pull, somehow or other, set a dislocated joint right. I suppose all things had their humble beginnings, and medicine and surgery were in the same condition. People who wear watches know nothing about watchmaking. A watch goes wrong and it stops; you see the owner giving it a shake, or, if he is very bold, he opens the case, and gives the balance- wheel a push. Gentlemen, that is empirical practice, and you know what are the-results upon the watch. I shouldthink you can divine what are the results of analogous operations upon the human body. And because men of sense very soon found that such were the effects of meddling with very complicated machinery they did not understand, I suppose the first thing, as being the easiest, was to study the nature of the works of the human watch, and the next thing was to study the way the parts worked together, and the way the watch worked. Thus, by degrees, we have had growing up our body of anatomists, or knowers of the construction of the human watch, and our physiologists, who know how the machine works. And just as any sensible man, who has a valuable watch, does not meddle with it himself, but goes to some one who has studied watchmaking, and understands what the effect of doing this or that may be; so, I suppose, the man who, having charge of that valuable machine, his own body, wants to have it kept in good order, comes to a professor of the medical art for the purpose of having it set right, believing that, by deduction from the facts of structure and from the facts of function, the physician will divine what may be the matter with his bodily watch at that particular time, and what may be the best means of setting it right. If that may be taken as a just representation of the relation of the theoretical branches of medicine – what we may call the institutes of medicine, to use an old term – to the practical branches, I think it will be obvious to you that they are of prime and fundamental importance. Whatever tends to effect the teaching of them injuriously must tend to destroy and to disorganize the whole fabric of the medical art. I think every sensible man has seen this long ago; but the difficulties in the way of attaining

good teaching in the different branches of the theory, or institutes, of medicine are very serious. It' is a comparatively easy matter – pray mark that I use the word "comparatively" – it is a comparatively easy matter to learn anatomy and to teach it; it is a very difficult matter to learn physiology and to teach it. It is a very difficult matter to know and to teach those branches of physics and those branches of chemistry which bear directly upon physiology; and hence it is that, as a matter of fact, the teaching of physiology, and the teaching of the physics and the chemistry which bear upon it, must necessarily be in a state of relative imperfection; and there is nothing to be grumbled at in the fact that this relative imperfection exists. But is the relative imperfection which exists only such as is necessary, or is it made worse by our practical arrangements? I believe – and if I did not so believe I should not have troubled you with these observations – I believe it is made infinitely worse by our practical arrangements, or rather, I ought to say, our very unpractical arrangements. Some very wise man long ago affirmed that every question, in the long run, was a question of finance; and there is a good deal to be said for that view. Most assuredly the question of medical teaching is, in a very large and broad sense, a question of finance. What I mean is this: that in London the arrangements of the medical schools, and the number of them, are such as to render it almost impossible that men who confine themselves to the teaching of the theoretical branches of the profession should be able to make their bread by that operation; and, you know, if a man cannot make his bread he cannot teach – at least his

teaching comes to a speedy end. That is a matter of
– Science – 12
physiology. Anatomy is fairly well taught, because it lies in the direction of practice, and a man is all the better surgeon for being a good anatomist. It does not

absolutely interfere with the pursuits of a practical surgeon if he should hold a Chair of Anatomy – though I do not for one moment say that he would not be a better teacher if he did not devote himself to practice. (Applause.) Yes, I know exactly what that cheer means, but I am keeping as carefully as possible from any sort of allusion to Professor Ellis. But the fact is, that even human anatomy has now grown to be so large a matter that it takes the whole devotion of a man's life to put the great mass of knowledge upon that subject into such a shape that it can be teachable to the mind of the ordinary student. What the student wants in a professor is a man who shall stand between him and the infinite diversity and variety of human knowledge, and who shall gather all that together, and extract from it that which is capable of being assimilated by the mind. That function is a vast and an important one, and unless, in such subjects as anatomy, a man is wholly free from other cares, it is almost impossible that he can perform it thoroughly and well. But if it be hardly possible for a man to pursue anatomy without actually breaking with his profession, how is it possible for him to pursue physiology?

I get every year those very elaborate reports of Henle and Meissner – volumes of, I suppose, 400 pages altogether – and they consist merely of abstracts of the memoirs and works which have been written on Anatomy and Physiology – only abstracts of them! How is a man to keep up his acquaintance with all that is doingin the physiological world- – in a world advancing with enormous strides every day and every hour – if he has to be distracted with the cares of practice? You know very well it must be impracticable to do so. Our men of ability join our medical schools with an eye to the future. They take the Chairs of Anatomy or of Physiology; and by and by they leave those Chairs for the more profitable pursuits into which they have drifted by professional success, and so they become clothed, and physiology is bare. The result is that in those schools in which physiology is thus left to the benevolence, Bo to speak, of those who have no time to look to it, the effect of such teaching comes out obviously, and is made manifest in what I spoke of just now – the unreality, the bookishness of the knowledge of the taught. And if this is the case in physiology, still more must it be the case in those branches of physics which are the foundation of physiology; although it may be less the case in chemistry, because for an able chemist a certain honorable and independent career lies in the direction of his work, and he is able, like the anatomist, to look upon what he may teach to the student as not absolutely taking him away from his bread-winning pursuits.

But it is of no use to grumble about this state of things unless one is prepared to indicate some sort of practical remedy. And I believe – and I venture to make the statement because I am wholly independent of all sorts of medical schools, and may, therefore, say what I believe without being supposed to be affected by any personal interest – but I say I believe that the remedy for this state of things, for that imperfection of our theoretical knowledge which keeps down the ability of England at the present time in medical matters, is a mere affair of mechanical arrangement; that so long as you have a dozen medical schools scattered about in different parts of the metropolis, and dividing the students among them, so long, in all the smaller schools at any rate, it is impossible that any other state of things than that which I have been depicting should obtain. Professors must live; to live they must occupy themselves with practice; and if they occupy themselves with practice, the pursuit of the abstract branches of science must go to the wall. All this is a plain and obvious matter of common-sense reasoning. I believe you will never alter this state of things until, either by consent or by *force majeure* – and I should be very sorry to see the latter applied – but until there is some new arrangement, and until all the theoretical branches of the profession, the institutes of medicine, are taught in London in not more than one or two, or at the outside three, central institutions, no good will be effected. If that large body of men, the medical students of London, were obliged in the first place to get a knowledge of the theoretical branches of their profession in two or three central schools, there would be abundant means for maintaining able professors – not, indeed, for enriching them, as they would be able to enrich themselves by practice – but for enabling them to make that choice which such men are so willing to make; namely, the choice between wealth and a modest competency, when that modest competency is to be combined with a scientific career, and the means of advancing knowledge. I do not believe that all the talking about, and tinkering of, medical education will do the slightest good until the fact is clearly recognized that men mustbe thoroughly grounded in the theoretical branches of their profession, and that to this end the teaching of those theoretical branches must be confined to two or three centres.

Now let me add one other word, and that is that, if I were a despot, I would cut down these branches to a very considerable extent. The next thing to be done beyond that which I mentioned just now is to go back to primary education. The great step toward a thorough medical education is to insist upon the teaching of the elements of the physical sciences in all schools, so that medical students shall not go up to the medical colleges utterly ignorant of that with which they have to deal; to insist on the elements of chemistry, the elements of botany, and the elements of physics being taught in our ordinary and common schools, so that there shall be some preparation for the discipline of medical colleges. And, if this reform were once effected, you might confine the "Institutes of Medicine" to physics as applied to physiology – to chemistry as applied to physiology – to physiology itself, and to anatomy. Afterward, the student, thoroughly grounded in these matters, might go to any hospital he pleased for the purpose of studying the practical branches of his profession. The practical teaching might be made as local as you like; and you might use to advantage the opportunities afforded by all these local institutions for acquiring a knowledge of the practice of the profession. But you may say: "This is abolishing a great deal; you are getting rid of botany and Zoology to begin with." I have not a doubt that they 'bught to be got rid of, as branches of special medical education; they ought to be put back to an earlier stage, andmade branches of general education. Let me say, by way of self-denying ordinance, for which you will, I am sure, give me credit, that I believe that comparative anatomy ought to be absolutely abolished. I say so, not without a certain fear of the Vice-Chancellor of the University of London who sits upon my left. But I do not think the charter gives him very much power over me; moreover, I shall soon come to an end of my examinarship, and therefore I am not afraid, but shall go on to say what I was going to say, and that is, that in my belief it is a downright cruelty – I have no other word for it – to require from gentlemen who are engaged in medical studies the pretence – for it is nothing else, and can be nothing else, than a pretence

– of a knowledge of comparative anatomy as part of their medical curriculum. Make it part of their Arts teaching if you like, make it part of their general education if you like, make it part of their qualification for the scientific degree by all means – that is its proper place; but to require that gentlemen whose whole faculties should be bent upon the acquirement of a real knowledge of human physiology should worry themselves with getting up hearsay about the alternation of generations in the Salpae is really monstrous. I cannot characterize it in any other way. And having sacrificed my own pursuit, I am sure I may sacrifice other people's; and I make this remark with all the more willingness because I discovered, on reading the names of your Professors just now, that the Professor of Materia Medica is not present. I must confess, if I had my way I should abolish Materia Medica ' altogether. Irecollect, when I was first under examination at the University of London, Dr. Pereira was the examiner, and you know that Pereira's "Materia Medica" was a book *de omnibus rebus.* I recollect my struggles with that book late at night and early in the morning (I worked very hard in those days), and I do believe that I got that book into my head somehow or other, but then I will undertake to say that I forgot it all a week afterward. Not one trace of a knowledge of drugs has remained in my memory from that time to this; and really, as a matter of common-sense, I cannot understand the arguments for obliging a medical man to know all about drugs and where they come from. Why not make him belong to the Iron and Steel Institute, and learn something about cutlery, because he uses knives ?

1 It will, I hope, be understood that I do not include Therapeutics under this head.

But do not suppose that, after all these deductions, there would not be ample room for your activity. Let us count up what we have left. I suppose all the time for medical education that can be hoped for is, at the outside, about four years. Well, what have you to master in those four years upon my supposition ? Physics applied to physiology; chemistry applied to physiology; physiology; anatomy; surgery; medicine (including therapeutics); obstetrics; hygiene; and medical jurisprudence – nine subjects for four years! And when you consider what those subjects are, and that the acquisition of anything beyond the rudiments of any one of them may tax the energies of a lifetime, I think that even those energies which you young gentlemen have been displaying for the last hour or two might be taxed to keep you thoroughly up to what is wanted for your medical career.

I entertain a very strong conviction that any one whoadds to medical education one iota or tittle beyond what is absolutely necessary is guilty of a very grave offence. Gentlemen, it will depend upon the knowledge that you happen to possess – upon your means of applying it within your own field of action – whether the bills of mortality of your district are increased or diminished; and that, gentlemen, is a very serious consideration indeed. And, under those circumstances, the subjects with which you have to deal being so difficult, their extent so enormous, and the time at your disposal so limited, I could not feel my conscience easy if I did not, on such an occasion as this, raise a protest against employing your energies upon the acquisition of any knowledge which may not be absolutely needed iu your future career.

XIII

THE STATE AND THE MEDICAL PROFESSION

[1884]

AT INTERVALS during the last quarter of a century committees of the Houses of the Legislature and specially appointed commissions have occupied themselves with the affairs of the medical profession. Much evidence has been taken, much wrangling has gone on over the reports of these bodies; and sometimes much trouble has been taken to get measures based upon all this work through Parliament, but very little has been achieved.

The Bill introduced last session was not more fortunate than several predecessors. I suppose that it is not right to rejoice in the misfortunes of anything, even a Bill; but I confess that this event afforded me lively satisfaction, for I was a member of the Royal Commission on the report of which the Bill was founded, and I did my best to oppose and nullify that report.

That the question must be taken up again and finally dealt with by the Legislature before long cannot be doubted; but in the meanwhile there is time for reflection, and I think that the non-medical public would be wise if they paid a little attention to a subject which is really of considerable importance to them.

The first question which a plain man is disposed to ask himself is, Why should the State interfere with theprofession of medicine any more than it does, say, with the profession of engineering ? Anybody who pleases may call himself an engineer, and may practice as such. The State confers no title upon engineers, and does not profess to tell the public that one man is a qualified engineer and that another is not so.

The answers which are given to the question are various, and most of them, I think, are bad. A large number of persons seem to be of opinion that the State is bound no less to take care of the general public than to see that it is protected against incompetent persons, against quacks and medical impostors in general. I do not take that view of the case. I think it is very much wholesomer for the public to take care of itself in this as in all other matters; and although I am not such a fanatic for the liberty of the subject as to plead that interfering with the way in which a man may choose to be killed is a violation of that liberty, yet I do think that it is far better to let everybody do as he likes. Whether that be so or not, I am perfectly certain that, as a matter of practice, it is absolutely impossible to prohibit the practice of medicine by people who have no special qualification for it. Consider the terrible consequences of attempting to prohibit practice by a very large class of persons who are certainly not technically qualified – I am far from saying a word as to whether they are otherwise qualified or not. The number of Ladies Bountiful – grandmothers, aunts, and mothers-in- law – whose chief delight lies in the administration of their cherished provision of domestic medicine, is past computation, and one shudders to think of what might happen if their energies were turned from this innocuous, if not beneficent channel, by the strong arm of the law. But the thing is impracticable.

Another reason for intervention is propounded, I am sorry to say, by some, though not many, members of the medical profession, and is simply an expression of that trades unionism which tends to infest professions no less than trades.

The general practitioner trying to make both ends meet on a poor practice, whose medical training has cost him a good deal of time and money, finds that many potential patients, whose small fees would be welcome as the little that helps, prefer to go and get their shilling's worth of "doctor's stuff" and advice from the chemist and druggist round the corner, who has not paid sixpence for his medical training, because he has never had any.

The general practitioner thinks this is very hard upon him and ought to be stopped. It is perhaps natural that he should think so, though it would be very difficult for Mm to justify his opinion on any ground of public policy. But the question is really not worth discussion, as it is obvious that it would be utterly impracticable to stop the practice "over the counter" even if it were desirable.

Is a man who has a sudden attack of pain in tooth or stomach not to be permitted to go to the nearest druggist's shop and ask for something that will relieve him ? The notion is preposterous. But if this is to be legal, the whole principle of the permissibility of counter practice is granted.

In my judgment the intervention of the State in the affairs of the medical profession can be justified not uponany pretence of protecting the public, and still less upon that of protecting the medical profession, but simply and solely upon the fact that the State employs medical men for certain purposes, and, as employer, has a right to define the conditions on which it will accept service. It is for the interest of the community that no person shall die without there being some official recognition of the cause of his death. It is a matter of the highest importance to the community that, in civil and criminal cases, the law shall be able to have recourse to persons whose evidence may be taken as that of experts; and it will not be doubted that the State has a right to dictate the conditions under which it will appoint persons to the vast number of naval, military, and civil medical offices held directly or indirectly under the Government. Here, and here only, it appears to me, lies the justification for the intervention of the State in medical affairs. It says, or, in my judgment, should say, to the public, "Practice medicine if you like – go to be practiced upon by anybody"; and to the medical practitioner, "Have a qualification, or do not have a qualification if people don't mind it; but if the State is to receive your certificate of death, if the State is to take your evidence as that of an expert, if the State is to give you any kind of civil, or military, or naval appointment, then we" can call upon you to comply with our conditions, and to produce evidence that you are, in our sense of the word, qualified. Without that we will not place you in that position." As a matter of fact, that is the relation of the State to the medical profession in this country. For my part, I think it an extremely healthy relation; and it is one that I should be very sorry to see altered, exceptin so far that it would certainly be better if greater facilities were given for the swift and sharp punishment of those who profess to have the State qualification when, in point of fact, they do not possess it. They are simply cheats and swindlers, like other people who profess to be what they are not, and should be punished as such.

But supposing we are agreed about the justification of State intervention in medical affairs, new questions arise as to the manner in which that intervention should take place and the extent to which it should go, on which the divergence of opinion is even greater than it is on the general question of intervention.

It is now, I am sorry to say, something over forty years since I began my medical studies; and, at that time, the state of affairs was extremely singular. I should think it hardly possible that it could have obtained anywhere but in such a country as England, which cherishes a fine old crusted abuse as much as it does its port wine. At that time there were twenty- one licensing bodies – that is to say, bodies whose certificate was received by the State as evidence that the persons who possessed that certificate were medical experts. How these bodies came to possess these powers is a very curious chapter in history, on which it would be out of place to enlarge. They were partly universities, partly medical guilds and corporations, partly the Archbishop of Canterbury. Those were the three sources from which the license to practice came in that day. There was no central authority, there was nothing to prevent any one of those licensing authorities from granting a license to any one upon any conditions it thoughtfit. The examination might be a sham, the curriculum might be a sham, the certificate might be bought and sold like anything in a shop; or, on the other hand, the examination might be fairly good and the diploma correspondingly valuable; but there was not the smallest guarantee, except the personal character of the people who composed the administration of each of these licensing bodies, as to what might happen. It was possible for a young man to come to London and to spend two years and six months of the time of his compulsory three years "walking the hospitals" in idleness or worse; he could then, by putting himself in the hands of a judicious "grinder" for the remaining six months, pass triumphantly through the ordeal of one hour's *vivd voce* examination, which was all that was absolutely necessary, to enable him to be turned loose upon the public, like death on the pale horse, "conquering and to conquer," with the fall sanction of the law, as a "qualified practitioner."

It is difficult to imagine, at present, such a state of things, still more difficult to depict the consequences of it, because they would appear like a gross and malignant caricature; but it may be said that there was never a system, or want of system, which was better calculated to ruin the students who came under it, or to degrade the profession as a whole. My memory goes back to a time when models from whom the Bob Sawyer of the "Pickwick Papers" might have been drawn were anything but rare.

Shortly before my student days, however, the dawn of a better state of things in England began to be visible, in consequence of the establishment of the University of London, and the comparatively very high standard which it placed before its medical graduates.

I say comparatively high standard, for the requirements of the University in those days, and even during the twelve years at a later period, when I was one of the examiners of the medical faculty, were such as would not now be thought more than respectable, and indeed were in many respects very imperfect. But, relatively to the means of learning, the standard was high, and none but the more able and ambitious of the students dreamed of passing the University. Nevertheless, the fact that many men of this stamp did succeed in obtaining their degrees, led others to follow in their steps, and slowly but surely reacted upon the standard of teaching in the better medical schools. Then came the Medical Act of 1858. That Act introduced two immense improvements: one of them was the institution of what is called the Medical Eegister, upon which the names of all persons recognized by the State as medical practitioners are entered; and the other was the establishment of the Medical Council, which is a kind of Medical Parliament, composed of representatives of the licensing bodies and of leading men in the medical profession nominated by the Crown. The powers given by the Legislature to the Medical Council were found practically to be very limited, but I think that no fair observer of the work will doubt that this much attacked body has exerted no small influence in bringing about the great change for the better, which has been effected in the training of men for the medical profession within my recollection.

Another source of improvement must be recognized in the Scottish Universities, and especially in the medical faculty of the University of Edinburgh. The medical education and examinations of this body were for manyyears the best of their kind in these islands,' and I doubt if, at the present moment, the three kingdoms can show a better school of medicine than that of Edinburgh. The vast number of medical students at that University is sufficient evidence of the opinion of those most interested in this subject.

Owing to all these influences, and to the revolution which has taken place in the course of the last twenty years in our conceptions of the proper method of teaching physical science, the training of the medical student in a good school, and the examination test applied by the great majority of the present licensing bodies, reduced now to nineteen, in consequence of the retirement of the Archbishop and the fusion of two of the other licensing bodies, are totally different from what they were even twenty years ago.

I was perfectly astonished, upon one of my sons commencing his medical career the other day, when I contrasted the carefully-watched courses of theoretical and practical instruction, which he is expected to follow with regularity and industry, and the number and nature of the examinations which he will have to pass before he can receive his license, not only with the monstrous laxity of my own student days, but even with the state of things which obtained when my term of office as examiner in the University of London expired some sixteen years ago.

I have no hesitation in expressing the opinion, which is fully borne out by the evidence taken before the late Royal Commission, that a large proportion of the existing licensing bodies grant their license on conditions which insure quite as high a standard as it is practicable oradvisable to exact under present circumstances, and that they show every desire to keep pace with the improvements of the times. And I think there can be no doubt that the great majority have so much improved their ways, that their standard is far above that of the ordinary qualification thirty years ago, and I cannot see what excuse there would be for meddling with them if it were not for two other defects which have to be remedied.

Unfortunately there remain two or three black sheep – licensing bodies which simply trade upon their privilege, and sell the cheapest wares they can for shame's sake supply to the bidder. Another defect in the existing system, even where the examination has been so greatly improved as to be good of its kind, ia that there are certain licensing bodies which give a qualification for an acquaintance with either medicine or surgery alone, and which more or less ignore obstetrics. This is a revival of the archaic condition of the profession when surgical operations were mostly left to the barbers and obstetrics to the midwives, and when the physicians thought themselves, and were considered by the world, the "superior persons" of the profession. I remember a story was current in my young days of a great court physician who was travelling with a friend, like himself, bound on a visit to a country house. The friend fell down in an apoplectic fit, and the physician refused to bleed him because it was contrary to professional etiquette for a physician to perform that operation. Whether the friend died or whether he got better because he was not bled I do not remember, but the moral of the story is the same. On the other hand, a famous surgeon was asked whether he meant to bring up hisson to his own calling, "No," he said, "he is such a fool, I mean to make a physician of him."

Nowadays, it is happily recognized that medicine is one and indivisible, and that no one can properly practice one branch who is not familiar with at any rate the principles of all. Thus the two great things that are wanted now are, in the first place, some means of enforcing such a degree of uniformity upon all the examining bodies that none should present a disgracefully low minimum or pass examination; and the second point is that somebody or other shall have the power of enforcing upon every candidate for the license to practice the study of the three branches – what is called the tripartite qualification. All the members of the late commission were agreed that these were the main points to be attended to in any proposals for the further improvement of medical training and qualification.

But such being the ends in view, our notions as to the best way of attaining them were singularly divergent; so that it came about that eleven commissioners made seven reports. There was one main majority report and six minor reports, which differed more or less from it, chiefly as to the best method of attaining these two objects.

The majority report recommended the adoption of what is known as the conjoint scheme. According to this plan the power of granting a license to practice is to be taken away from all the existing bodies, whether they have done well or ill, and to be placed in the hands of a body of delegates (divisional boards), one for each of the three kingdoms. The license to practice is to be conferred by passing the delegate examination. The licenseemay afterward, if he pleases, go before any of the existing bodies and indulge in the luxury of another examination and the payment of another fee in order to obtain a title, which does not legally place him in any better position than that which he would occupy without it.

Under these circumstances, of course, the only motive for obtaining the degree of a University or the license of a medical corporation would be the prestige of these bodies. Hence the "black sheep" would certainly be deserted, while those bodies which have acquired a reputation by doing their duty would suffer less.

But, as the majority report proposes that the existing bodies should be compensated for any loss they might suffer out of the fees of the examiners for the State license, the curious result would be brought about that the profession of the future would be taxed, for all time,' for the purpose of handing over to wholly irresponsible bodies a sum, the amount of which would be large for those who had failed in their duty and small for those who had done it.

The scheme in fact involved a perpetual endowment of the "black sheep," calculated on the maximum of their ill-gained profits.1 I confess that I found myself unable to assent to a plan which, in addition to the rewarding the evil-doers, proposed to take away the privileges of a number of examining bodies which confessedly weredoing their duty well, for the sake of getting rid of a. few who had failed. It was too much like the Chinaman's device of burning down his house to obtain a poor dish of roast pig – uncertain whether in the end he might not find a mere mass of cinders. What we do know is that the great majority of the existing licensing bodies have marvellously improved in the course of the last twenty years, and are improving. What we do not know is that the complicated scheme of the divisional boards will ever be got to work at all.

1 The fees to be paid by candidates for admission to the examinations of the Divisional Board should be of such an amount as will be sufficient to cover the cost of the examinations and the other expenses of the Divisional Board, *and also to provide the sum required to compensate the medical authorities, or such of them as may be entitled to compensation, for any pecuniary losses they may hereafter sustain by reason of the abolition of their privilege of conferring a license to practice. Report* 50, p. xii.

My own belief is that every necessary reform may be effected, without any interference with vested interests, without any unjust interference with the prestige of institutions which have been, and still are, extremely valuable, without any question of compensation arising, and by an extremely simple operation. It is only necessary in fact to add a couple of clauses to the Medical Act to this effect: (1) That from and after such a date no person shall be placed upon the Medical Eegister unless he possesses the threefold qualification. (2) That from and after this date no examination shall be accepted as satisfactory from any licensing body except such aa has been carried on in part by examiners appointed by the licensing body, and in part by coadjutor-examiners of equal authority appointed by the Medical Council or other central authority, and acting under their instructions.

In laying down a rule of this kind the State confiscates nothing, and meddles with nobody, but simply acts within its undoubted right of laying down the conditions under which it will confer certain privileges upon medical practitioners. No one can say that the State has notthe right to do this; no one can say that the State interferes with any private enterprise or corporate interest unjustly, in laying down its own conditions for its own service. The plan would have the further advantage that all those corporate bodies which have obtained (as many of them have) a great and just prestige by the admirable way in which they have done their work would reap their just reward in the thronging of students, thenceforward as formerly, to obtain their qualifications; while those who have neglected their duties, who have in some one or two cases, I am sorry to say, absolutely disgraced themselves, would sink into oblivion, and come to a happy and natural euthanasia, in which their misdeeds and themselves would be entirely forgotten.

Two of my colleagues, Professor Turner and Mr. Bryce, M. P., whose practical familiarity with examinations gave their opinions a high value, expressed their substantial approval of this scheme, and I am unable to see the weight of the objections urged against it. It is urged that the difficulty and expense of adequately inspecting so many examinations and of guaranteeing their efficiency would be great, and the difficulty in the way of a fair adjustment of the representation of existing interests and of the representation of new interests upon the general Medical Council would be almost insuperable.

The latter objection is unintelligible to me. I am not aware that any attempt at such adjustment has been fairly discussed, and until that has been done it may be well not to talk about insuperable difficulties. As to the notion that there is any difficulty in getting the coadjutor- examiners, or that the expense will be overwhelming, we have the experience "of Scotland, in which every CJniversity does, at the present time, appoint its coadjutor- examiners, who do their work just in the way proposed.

Whether in the way I have proposed, or by the Conjoint Scheme, however, this is perfectly certain: the two things I refer to have to be done: you must have the threefold qualification; you must have the limitation of the minimum qualification also; and any scheme for the improvement of the relations of the State to medicine which does not profess to do these two things thoroughly and well has no chance of finality.

But when these reforms are witnessed, when there is a Medical Council armed with a more real authority than it at present possesses; when a license to practice cannot be obtained without the threefold qualification; and when an even minimum of qualification is exacted for every license, is there anything else that remains that any one seriously interested in the welfare of the medical profession, as I may most conscientiously declare myself to be, would like to see done? I think there are three things.

In the first place, even now, when a four years' curriculum is required, the time allotted for medical education is too brief. A young man of eighteen beginning to study medicine is probably absolutely ignorant of the existence of such a thing as anatomy, or physiology, or indeed of any branch of physical science. He comes into an entirely new world; he addresses himself to a kind of work of which he has not the smallest experience. Up to that time his work has been with books; he rushes suddenly into work with things, which is as different from work with books as anything can well be. I am quite sure that a very considerable number of young men spend a very large portion of their first session in simply learning how to learn subjects which are entirely new to them. And yet recollect that in this period of four years they have to acquire a knowledge of all the branches of a great and responsible practical calling of medicine, surgery, obstetrics, general pathology, medical jurisprudence, and so forth. Anybody who knows what these things are, and who knows what is the kind of work which is necessary to give a man the confidence which will enable him to stand at the bedside and say to the satisfaction of his own conscience what shall be done, and what shall not be done, must be aware that if a man has only four years to do all that in he will not have much time to spare. But that is not all. As I have said, the young man comes up, probably ignorant of the existence of science; he has never heard a word of chemistry, he has never heard a word of physics, he has not the smallest conception of the outlines of biological science; and all these things have to be learned as well and crammed into the time which in itself is barely sufficient to acquire a fair amount of that knowledge which is requisite for the satisfactory discharge of his professional duties.

Therefore it is quite clear to me that, somehow or other, the curriculum must be lightened. It is not that any of the subjects which I have mentioned need not to be studied, and may be eliminated. The only alternative therefore is to lengthen the time given to study. Everybody will agree with me that the practical necessities of life in this country are such that, for the average medical practitioner at any rate, it is hopeless to think of extending the period of professional study beyond theage of twenty-two. So that, as the period of study cannot be extended forward, the only thing to be done is to extend it backward.

The question is how this can be done. My own belief is that if the Medical Council, instead of insisting upon that examination in general education which I am sorry to say I believe to be entirely futile, were to insist upon a knowledge of elementary physics, and chemistry, and biology, they would be taking one of the greatest steps which at present can be made for the improvement of medical education. And the improvement would be this. The great majority of the young men who are going into the profession have practically completed their general education – or they might very well have done so – by the age of sixteen or seventeen. If the interval between this age and that at which they commence their purely medical studies were employed in obtaining a practical acquaintance with elementary physics, chemistry, and biology, in my judgment it would be as good as two years added to the course of medical study. And for two reasons: in the first place, because the subject-matter of that which they would learn is germane to their future studies, and is so much gained; in the second place, because you might clear out of the course of their professional study a great deal which at present occupies time and attention; and last, but not least – probably most – they would then come to their medical studies prepared for that learning from Nature which is what they have to do in the course of becoming skilful medical men, and for which at present they are not in the slightest degree prepared by their previous education.

The second wish I have to express concerns London especially, and I may speak of it briefly as a more economical use of the teaching power in the medical schools. At this present time every great hospital in London – and there are ten or eleven of them – has its complete medical school, in which not only are the branches of practical medicine taught, but also those studies in general science, such as chemistry, elementary physics, general anatomy, and a variety of other topics which are what used to be called (and the term was an extremely useful one) the institutes of medicine. That was all very well half a century ago; it is all very ill now, simply because those general branches of science, such as anatomy, physiology, chemistry, physiological chemistry, physiological physics, and so forth, have now become so large, and the mode of teaching them is so completely altered, that it is absolutely impossible for any man to be a thoroughly competent teacher of them, or for any student to be effectually taught without the devotion of the whole time of the person who is engaged in teaching. I undertake to say that it is hopelessly impossible for any man at the present time to keep abreast with the progress of physiology unless he gives his whole mind to it; and the bigger the mind is, the more scope he will find for its employment Again, teaching has become, and must become still more, practical, and that also involves a large expenditure of time. But if a man is to give his whole time to my business he must live by it, and the resources of the schools do not permit them to maintain ten or eleven physiological specialists.

If the students in their first one or two years were

VIII – Science – 13

taught the institutes of medicine, in two or three central institutions, it would be perfectly easy to have those subjects taught thoroughly and effectually by persons who gave their whole mind and attention to the subject; while at the same time the medical schools at the hospitals would remain what they ought to be – great institutions in which the largest possible opportunities are laid open for acquiring practical acquaintance with the phenomena of disease. So that the preliminary or earlier half of medical education would take place in the central institutions, and the final half would be devoted altogether to practical studies in the hospitals.

I happen to know that this conception has been entertained, not only by myself, but by a great many of those persons who are most interested in the improvement of medical study for a considerable number of years. I do not know whether anything will come of it this half- century or not; but the thing has to be done. It is not a speculative notion; it lies patent to everybody who is accustomed to teaching, and knows what the necessities of teaching are; and I should very much like to see the first step taken – people making up their minds that it has to be done somehow or other.

The last point to which I may advert is one wnich concerns the action of the profession itself more than anything else. We have arrangements for teaching, we have arrangements for the testing of qualifications, we have marvellous aids and appliances for the treatment of disease in all sorts of ways; but I do not find in London at the present time, in this little place of four or five million inhabitants which supports so many things, any organization or any arrangement for advancing the scienceof medicine, considered as a pure science. I am quite aware that there are medical societies of various kinds; I am not ignorant of the lectureships at the College of Physicians and the College of Surgeons; there is the Brown Institute; and there is the Society for the Advancement of Medicine by . Research, but there is no means, so far as I know, by which any person who has the inborn gifts of the investigator and discoverer of new truth, and who desires to apply that to the improvement of medical science, can carry out his intention. In Paris there is the University of Paris, which gives degrees; but there are also the Sorbonne and the College de France, places in which professoriates are established for the express purpose of enabling men who have the power of investigation, the power of advancing knowledge and thereby reacting on practice, to do that which it is their special mission to do. I do not know of anything of the kind in London; and if it should so happen that a Claude Bernard or a Ludwig should turn up in London, I really have not the slightest notion of what we could do with him. We could not turn him to account, and I think we should have to export him to Germany or France.

I doubt whether that is a good or a wise condition of things. I do not think it is a condition of things which can exist for any great length of time, now that people are every day becoming more and more awake to the importance of scientific investigation and to the astounding and unexpected manner in which it everywhere reacts upon practical pursuits. I should look upon the establishment of some institution of that kind as a recognition, on the part of the medical profession ingeneral, that if their great and beneficent work is to be carried on, they must, like other people who have great and beneficent work to do, contribute to the advancement of knowledge in the only way in which experience shows that it can be advanced.

11

SECTION 11

XIV

THE CONNECTION OF THE BIOLOGICAL SCIENCES WITH MEDICINE
[1881]

THE GREAT body of theoretical and practical knowledge which has been accumulated by the labors of some eighty generations, since the dawn of scientific thought in Europe, has no collective English name to which an objection may not be raised; and I use the term "medicine" as that which is least likely to be misunderstood; though, as every one knows, the name is commonly applied, in a narrower sense, to one of the chief divisions of the totality of medical science.

Taken in this broad sense, "medicine" not merely denotes a kind of knowledge, but it comprehends the various applications of that knowledge to the alleviation of the sufferings, the repair of the injuries, and the conservation of the health, of living beings. In fact, the practical aspect of medicine so far dominates over every other that the "Healing Art" is one of its most widely- received synonyms. It is so difficult to think of medicine otherwise than as something which is necessarily connected with curative treatment that we are apt to forget that there must be, and is, such a thing as a pure science of medicine – a "pathology" which has no more necessary subservience to practical ends than has zoology or botany.

The logical connection between this purely scientific doctrine of disease, or pathology, and ordinary biology, is easily traced. Living matter is characterized by its innate tendency to exhibit a definite series of the morphological and physiological phenomena which constitute organization and life. Given a certain range of conditions, and these phenomena remain the same, within narrow limits, for each kind of living thing. They furnish the normal and typical character of the species, and, as such, they are the subject-matter of ordinary biology.

Outside the range of these conditions, the normal course of the cycle of vital phenomena is disturbed; abnormal structure makes its appearance, or the proper character and mutual adjustment of the functions cease to be preserved. The extent and the importance of these deviations from the typical life may vary indefinitely. They may have no noticeable influence on the general well-being of the economy, or they may favor it. On the other hand, they may be of such a nature as to impede the activities of the organism, or even to involve its destruction.

In the first case, these perturbations are ranged under the wide and somewhat vague category of "variations"; in the second, they are called lesions, states of poisoning, or diseases; and, as morbid states, they lie within the province of pathology. No sharp line of demarcation can be drawn between the two classes of phenomena. No one can say where anatomical variations end and tumors begin, nor where modification of function, which may at first promote health, passes into disease. All that can be said is, that whatever change of structure or function is hurtful belongs to pathology. Hence it is obvious thatpathology is a branch of biology; it is the morphology, the physiology, the distribution, the aetiology of abnormal life.

However obvious this conclusion may be now, it was nowise apparent in the infancy of medicine. For it is a peculiarity of the physical sciences that they are independent in proportion as they are imperfect; and it is only as they advance that the bonds which really unite them all become apparent. Astronomy had no manifest connection with terrestrial physics before the publication of the "Principia"; that of chemistry with physics is of still more modern revelation; that of physics and chemistry with physiology has been stoutly denied within the recollection of most of us, and perhaps still may be.

Or, to take a case which affords a closer parallel with that of medicine. Agriculture has been cultivated from the earliest times, and, from a remote antiquity, men have attained considerable practical skill in the cultivation of the useful plants, and have empirically established many scientific truths concerning the conditions under which they flourish. But it is within the memory of many of us that chemistry on the one hand, and vegetable physiology on the other, attained a stage of development such that they were able to furnish a sound basis for scientific agriculture. Similarly, medicine took its rise in the practical needs of mankind. At first, studied without reference to any other branch of knowledge, it long maintained, indeed still to some extent maintains, that independence. Historically, its connection with the biological sciences has been slowly established, and the full extent and intimacy of that connection are only now beginning to be apparent. I trust I have not been mistaken in supposing that an attempt to give a brief sketch of the steps by which a philosophical necessity has become a historical reality may not be devoid of interest, possibly of instruction, to the members of this great Congress, profoundly interested as all are in the scientific development of medicine.

The history of medicine is more complete and fuller than that of any other science, except, perhaps, astronomy; and, if we follow back the long record as far as clear evidence lights us, we find ourselves taken to the early stages of the civilization of Greece. The oldest hospitals were the temples of Isculapius; to these As- clepiea, always erected on healthy sites, hard by fresh springs and surrounded by shady groves, the sick and the maimed resorted to seek the aid of the god of health. Votive tablets or inscriptions recorded the symptoms, no less than the gratitude, of those who were healed; and, from these primitive clinical records, the half-priestly, half-philosophic caste of the Asclepiads compiled the data upon which the earliest generalizations of medicine, as an inductive science, were based.

In this state, pathology, like all the inductive sciences at their origin, was merely natural history; it registered the phenomena of disease, classified them, and ventured upon a prognosis wherever the observation of constant coexistences and sequences suggested a rational expectation of the like recurrence under similar circumstances.

Further than tlr. s it hardly went. In fact, in the then state of knowledge, and in the condition of philosophical speculation at that time, neither the causes of the morbid state, nor the *rationale* of treatment, were likely to be sought for as we seek for them now. The anger of a godwas a sufficient reason for the existence of a malady, and a dream ample warranty for therapeutic measures; that a physical phenomenon must needs have a physical cause was not the implied or expressed axiom that it is to us moderns.

The great man whose name is inseparably connected with the foundation of medicine, Hippocrates, certainly knew very little, indeed practically nothing, of anatomy or physiology; and he would, probably, have been perplexed even to imagine the possibility of a connection between the zoological studies of his contemporary De- mocritus and medicine. Nevertheless, in so far as he, and those who worked before and after him, in the same spirit, ascertained, as matters of experience, that a wound, or a luxation, or a fever, presented such and such symptoms, and that the return of the patient to health was facilitated by such and such measures, they established laws of nature, and began the construction of the science of pathology. All true science begins with empiricism – though all true science is such exactly, in so far as it strives to pass out of the empirical stage into that of the deduction of empirical from more general truths. Thus, it is not wonderful that the early physicians had little or nothing to do with the development of biological science; and, on the other hand, that the early biologists did not much concern themselves with medicine. There is nothing to show that the Asclepiads took any prominent share in the work of founding anatomy, physiology, zoology, and botany. Rather do these seem to have sprung from the early philoso- phers, who were essentially natural philosophers, animated by the characteristically Greek thirst for knowledge as such. Pythagoras, Alemeon, Democritus, Diogenes of Apollonia, are all credited with anatomical and physiological investigations; and, though Aristotle is said to have belonged to an As- clepiad family, and not improbably owed his taste for anatomical and zoological inquiries to the teachings of his father, the physician Nicomachus, the "Historia Ani- malium," and the treatise "De Partibus

Animalium," are as free from any allusion to medicine as if they had issued from a modern biological laboratory.

It may be added, that it is not easy to see in what way it could have benefited a physician of Alexander's time to know all that Aristotle knew on these subjects. His human anatomy was too rough to avail much in diagnosis; his physiology was too erroneous to supply data for pathological reasoning. - But when the Alexandrian school, with Erasistratus and Herophilus at their head, turned to account the opportunities of studying human structure, afforded to them by the Ptolemies, the value of the large amount of accurate knowledge thus obtained to the surgeon for his operations, and to the physician for his diagnosis of internal disorders, became obvious, and a connection was established between anatomy and medicine which has ever become closer and closer. Since the revival of learning, surgery, medical diagnosis, and anatomy have gone hand in hand. Mor- gagni called his great work, "De sedibus et causis mor- borum per anatomen indagatis," and not only showed the way to search out the localities and the causes of disease by anatomy, but himself travelled wonderfully far upon the road. Bichat, discriminating the grosser constituents of the organs and parts of the body, one from another, pointed out the direction which modernresearch must take; until, at length, histology, a science of yesterday, as it seems to many of us, has carried the work of Morgagni as far as the microscope can take us, and has extended the realm of pathological anatomy to the limits of the invisible world.

Thanks to the intimate alliance of morphology with medicine, the natural history of disease has, at the present day, attained a high degree of perfection. Accurate regional anatomy has rendered practicable the exploration of the most hidden parts of the organism, and the determination, during life, of morbid changes in them; anatomical and histological post-mortem investigations have supplied physicians with a clear basis upon which to rest the classification of diseases, and with unerring tests of the accuracy or inaccuracy of their diagnoses.

If men could be satisfied with pure knowledge, the extreme precision with which, in these days, a sufferer may be told what is happening, and what is likely to happen, even in the most recondite parts of his bodily frame, should be as satisfactory to the patient as it is to the scientific pathologist who gives him the information. But I am afraid it is not; and even the practicing physician, while nowise underestimating the regulative value of accurate diagnosis, must often lament that so much of his knowledge rather prevents him from doing wrong than helps him to do right.

A scorner of physic once said that nature and disease may be compared to two men fighting, the doctor to a blind man with a club, who strikes into the m$Zee, sometimes hitting the disease, and sometimes hitting nature. The matter is not mended if you suppose the blind man's hearing to be so acute that he can register everystage of the struggle, and pretty clearly predict how it will end. He had better not meddle at all, until his eyes are opened, until he can see the exact position of the antagonists, and make sure of the effect of his blows. But that which it behooves the physician to see, not, indeed, with his bodily eye, but with clear, intellectual vision, is a process, and the chain of causation involved in that process. Disease, as we have seen, is a perturbation of the normal activities of a living body, and it is, and must remain, unintelligible, so long as we are ignorant of the nature of these normal activities. In other words, there could be no real science of pathology until the science of physiology had reached a degree of perfection unattained, and indeed unattainable, until quite recent times.

So far as medicine is concerned, I am not sure that physiology, such as it was down to the time of Harvey, might as well not have existed. Nay, it is perhaps no exaggeration to say that, within the memory of living men, justly renowned practitioners of medicine and surgery knew less physiology than is now to be learned from the most elementary text-book; and, beyond a few broad facts, regarded what they did know as of extremely little practical importance. Nor am I disposed to blame them for this conclusion; physiology must be useless, or worse than useless, to pathology, so long as its fundamental conceptions are erroneous.

Harvey is often said to be the founder of modern physiology; and there can be no question that the elucidations of the function of the heart, of the nature of the pulse, and of the course of the blood, put forth in the ever-memorable little essay, "De motu cordis," directlyworked a revolution in men's views of the nature and of the concatenation of some of the most important physiological processes among the higher animals; while, indirectly, their influence was perhaps even more remarkable.

But, though Harvey made this signal and perennially important contribution to the physiology of the moderns, his general conception of vital processes was essentially identical with that of the ancients; and, in the "Exercita- tiones de generatione," and notably in the singular chapter "De calido innato," he shows himself a true son of Galen and of Aristotle.

For Harvey, the blood possesses powers superior to those of the elements; it is the seat of a soul which is not only vegetative, but also sensitive and motor. The blood maintains and fashions all parts of the body, "idque summa cum providentia" et intellectu in flnem certum agens, quasi ratiocinio quodam uteretur."

Here is the doctrine of the "pneuma," the product of the philosophical mold into which the animism of primitive men ran in Greece, in full force. Nor did its strength abate for long after Harvey's time. The same ingrained tendency of the human mind to suppose that a process ia explained when it is ascribed to a power of which nothing is known except that it is the hypothetical agent of the process, gave rise, in the next century, to the animism of Stahl; and, later, to the doctrine of a vital principle, that "asylum ignorantiae" of physiologists, which has so easily accounted for everything and explained nothing, down to our own times.

Now the essence of modern, as contrasted with ancient, physiological science appears to me to lie in its antagonism to animistic hypotheses and animisticphraseology. It offers physical explanations of vital phenomena, or frankly confesses that it has none to offer. And, so far as I know, the first person who gave expression to this modern view of physiology, who was bold enough to enunciate the proposition that vital phenomena, like all the other phenomena of the physical world, are, in ultimate analysis, resolvable into matter and motion, was Rene Descartes.

The fifty-four years of life of this most original and powerful thinker are widely overlapped, on both sides, by the eighty of Harvey, who survived his younger contemporary by seven years, and takes pleasure in acknowledging the French philosopher's appreciation of his great discovery.

In fact, Descartes accepted the doctrine of the circulation as propounded by "Harvaeus medecin d'Angleterre," and gave a full account of it in his first work, the famous "Discours de la Me'thode," which was published in 1637, only nine years after the exercitation "De motu cordis"; and, though differing from Harvey on some important points (in which it may be noted, in passing, Descartes was wrong and Harvey right), he always speaks of him with great respect. And so important does the subject seem to Descartes that he returns to it in the "Traite des Passions," and in the "Traite" de FHomme."

It is easy to see that Harvey's work must have had a peculiar significance for the subtle thinker, to whom we owe both the spiritualistic and the materialistic philosophies of modern times. It was in the very year of its publication, 1628, that Descartes withdrew into that life of solitary investigation and meditation of which his philosophy was the fruit. And, as the course of his speculations led him to establish an absolute distinction of nature between the material and the mental worlds, he was logically compelled to seek for the explanation of the phenomena of the material world within itself; and having allotted the realm of thought to the soul, to see nothing but extension and motion in the rest of nature. Descartes uses "thought" as the equivalent of our modern term "consciousness." Thought is the function of the soul, and its only function. Our natural heat and all the movements of the body, says he, do not depend on the soul. Death does not take place from any fault of the soul, but only because some of the principal parts of the body become corrupted. The body of a living man differs from that of a dead man in the same way as a watch or other automaton (that is to say, a machine which moves of itself) when it is wound up and has, in itself, the physical principle of the movements which the mechanism is adapted to perform, differs from the same watch, or other machine, when it is broken, and the physical principle of its movement no longer exists. All the actions which are common to us and the lower animals depend only on the conformation of our organs, and the course which the animal spirits take in the brain, the nerves, and the muscles; in the same way as the movement of a watch is produced by nothing but the force of its spring and the figure of its wheels and other parts.

Descartes's "Treatise on Man" is a sketch of human physiology, in which a bold attempt is made to explain all the phenomena of life, except those of consciousness, by physical reasonings. To a mind turned in this direction, Harvey's exposition of the heart and vessels as a hydraulic mechanism must have been supremely welcome.

Descartes was not a mere philosophical theorist, but a hardworking dissector and experimenter, and he held the strongest opinion respecting the practical value of the new conception which he was introducing. He speaks of the importance of preserving health, and of the dependence of the mind on the body being so close that, perhaps, the only way of making men wiser and better than they are, is to be sought in medical science. "It is true," says he, "that as medicine is now practiced it contains little that is very useful; but without any desire to depreciate, I am sure that there is no one, even among professional men, who will not declare that all we know is very little as compared with that which remains to be known; and that we might escape an infinity of diseases of the mind, no less than of the body, and even perhaps from the weakness of old age, if we had sufficient knowledge of their causes, and of all the remedies with which nature has provided us." ' So strongly impressed was Descartes with this, that he resolved to spend the rest of his life in trying to acquire such a knowledge of nature as would lead to the construction of a better medical doctrine. The anti-Cartesians found material for cheap ridicule in these aspirations of the philosopher; and it is almost needless to say that, in the thirteen years which elapsed between the publication of the "Discours" and the death of Descartes, he did not contribute much to their realization. But, for the next century, all progress in physiology took place along the lines which Descartes laid down.

The greatest physiological and pathological work of the seventeenth century, Borelli's treatise "De Motu Animalium," is, to all intents and purposes, a development of Descartes's fundamental conception; and the same may be said of the physiology and pathology of Boer- haave, whose authority dominated in the medical world of the first half of the eighteenth century.

1 "Discours de la Methode," 6" partie, Ed. Cousin, p. 193. 8 Ibid. pp. 193 and 211.

With the origin of modern chemistry, and of electrical science, in the latter half of the eighteenth century, aids in the analysis of the phenomena of life, of which Descartes could not have dreamed, were offered to the physiologist. And the greater part of the gigantic progress which has been made in the present century is a justification of the prevision of Descartes. For it consists, essentially, in a more and more complete resolution of the grosser organs of the living body into physico-chemical mechanisms.

"I shall try to explain our whole bodily machinery in such a way that it will be no more necessary for us to suppose that the soul produces such movements as are not voluntary than it is to think that there is in a clock a soul which causes it to show the hours." ' These words of Descartes might be appropriately taken as a motto by the author of any modern treatise on physiology.

But though, as I think, there is no doubt that Descartes was the first to propound the fundamental conception of the living body as a physical mechanism, which is the distinctive feature of modern as contrasted with ancient physiology, he was misled by the natural temptation to carry out, in all its details, a parallel between the machines with which he was familiar, such as clocks and pieces of hydraulic apparatus, and the living machine. In all such machines there is a central source of power, and the parts of the machine are merely passive distributors of that power. The Cartesian school conceived of the living body as a machine of this kind; and herein they might have learned from Galen, who, whatever ill use he may have made of the doctrine of "natural faculties," nevertheless had the great merit of perceiving that looal forces play a great part in physiology.

1 "De la Formation du Foetus."

The same truth was recognized by Glisson, but it was first prominently brought forward in the Hallerian doctrine of the "vis insita" of muscles. If muscle can contract without nerve, there is an end of the Cartesian mechanical explanation of its contraction by the influx of animal spirits.

The discoveries of Trembley tended in the same direction. In the fresh-water *Hydra* no trace was to be found of that complicated machinery upon which the performance of the functions in the higher animals was supposed to depend. And yet the hydra moved, fed, grew, multiplied, and its fragments exhibited all the powers of the whole. And, finally, the work of Caspar F. Wolff," by demonstrating the fact that the growth and development of both plants and animals take place antecedently to the existence of their grosser organs, and are, in fact, the causes and not the consequences of organization (as then understood), sapped the foundations of the Cartesian physiology as a complete expression of vital phenomena.

For Wolff, the physical basis of life is a fluid, pos sessed of a "vis essentialis" and a "solidescibilitas," in

"Theoria Generationis," 1759.

virtue of which it gives rise to organization; and, as he points out, this conclusion strikes at the root of the whole iatro-mechanical system.

In this country, the great authority of John Hunter exerted a similar influence; though it must be admitted that the too sibylline utterances which are the outcome of Hunter's struggles to define his conceptions are often susceptible of more than one interpretation. Nevertheless, on some points Hunter is clear enough. For example, he is of opinion that "Spirit is only a property of matter" ("Introduction to Natural History," page 6), he is prepared to renounce animism (*I. e.* page 8), and his conception of life is so completely physical that he thinks of it as something which can exist in a state of combination in the food. "The aliment we take in has in it, in a fixed state, the real life; and this does not become active until it has got into the lungs; for there it is freed from its prison" (Observations on Physiology," page 113). He also thinks that "It is more in accord with the general principles of the animal machine to suppose that none of its effects are produced from any mechanical principle whatever; and that every effect is produced from an action in the part; which action is produced by a stimulus upon the part which acts, or upon some other part with which this part sympathizes so as to take up the whole action" (*I. e.* page 152).

And Hunter is as clear as Wolff, with whose work he was probably unacquainted, that "whatever life is, it most certainly does not depend upon structure or organization" (*I. e.* page 114).

Of course it is impossible that Hunter could have intended to deny the existence of purely mechanical operations in the animal body. But while, with Borelli and Boerhaave, he looked upon absolution, nutrition, and secretion as operations effected by means of the small vessels, he differed from the mechanical physiologists, who regarded these operations as the result of the mechanical properties of the small vessels, such as the size, form and disposition of their canals and apertures. Hunter, on the contrary, considers them to be the effect of properties of these vessels which are not mechanical but vital. "The vessels," says he, "have more of the polypus in them than any other part of the body," and he talks of the "living and sensitive principles of the arteries," and even of the "dispositions or feelings of the arteries." "When the blood is good and genuine, the sensations of the arteries, or the dispositions for sensation, are agreeable. ... It is then they dispose of the blood to the best advantage, increasing the growth of the whole, supplying any losses, keeping up a due succession," etc. (*l. c.* page 133).

If we follow Hunter's conceptions to their logical issue, the life of one of the higher animals is essentially the sum of the lives of all the vessels, each of which is a sort of physiological unit, answering to a polype; and, as health is the result of the normal "action of the vessels," so is disease an effect of their abnormal action. Hunter thus stands in thought, as in time, midway between Borelli on the one hand and Bichat on the other.

The acute founder of general anatomy, in fact, outdoes Hunter in his desire to exclude physical reasonings from the realm of life. Except in the interpretation of the action of the sense organs, he will not allow physics to have anything to do with physiology.

"To apply the physical sciences to physiology is to explain the phenomena of living bodies by the laws of inert bodies. Now this is a false principle, hence all its consequences are marked with the same stamp. Let us leave to chemistry its affinity; to physics, its elasticity and its gravity. Let us invoke for physiology only sensibility and contractility." '

Of all the unfortunate dicta of men of eminent ability this seems one of the most unhappy, when we think of what the application of the methods and the data of physics and chemistry has done toward bringing physiology into its present state. It is not too much to say that one-half of a modern text-book of physiology consists of applied physics and chemistry; and that it is exactly in the exploration of the phenomena of sensibility and contractility that physics and chemistry have exerted the most potent influence.

Nevertheless, Bichat rendered a solid service to physiological progress by insisting upon the fact that what we call life, in one of the higher animals, is not an indivisible unitary archajus dominating, from its central seat, the parts of the organism, but a compound result of the synthesis of the separate lives of those parts.

"All animals," says he, "are assemblages of different organs, each of which performs its function and concurs, after its fashion, in the preservation of the whole. They are so many special machines in the general machine which constitutes the individual. But each of these special machines is itself compounded of many tissues of very different natures, which in truth constitute the elements of those organs" *(I. e.* lxxix.). "The conceptionof a proper vitality is applicable only to these simple tissues, and not to the organs themselves" *(I. e.* lxxxiv.).

1 "Anatomie generate," i. p. liv.

And'Bichat proceeds to make the obvious application of this doctrine of synthetic life, if I may so call it, to pathology. Since diseases are only alterations of vital properties, and the properties of each tissue are distinct from those of the rest, it is evident that the diseases of each tissue must be different from those of the rest Therefore, in any organ composed of different tissues, one may be diseased and the other remain healthy; and this is what happens in most cases (Z. c. lxxxv.).

In a spirit of true prophecy, Bichat says, "We have arrived at an epoch in which pathological anatomy should start afresh." For, as the analysis of the organs had led him to the tissues as the physiological units of the organism; so, in a succeeding generation, the analysis of the tissues led to the cell as the physiological element of the tissues. The contemporaneous study of development brought out the same result; and the zoologists and botanists, exploring the simplest and the lowest forms of animated beings, confirmed the great induction of the cell theory. Thus the apparently opposed views, which have been battling with one another ever since the middle of the last century, have proved to be each half the truth.

The proposition of Descartes that the body of a living man is a machine, the actions of which are explicable by the known laws of matter and motion, is unquestionably largely true. But it is also true that the living body is a synthesis of innumerable physiological elements, each of which may nearly be described, in "Wolff's words, as a fluid possessed of a "vis essentialis" and a "solidescibilitas" or, in modern phrase, as protoplasm susceptible of structural metamorphosis and functional metabolism: and that the only machinery, in the precise sense in which the Cartesian school understood mechanism, is that which co-ordinates and regulates these physiological units into an organic whole.

In fact, the body is a machine of the nature of an army, not of that of a watch or of a hydraulic apparatus. Of this army each cell is a soldier, an organ a brigade, the central nervous system headquarters and field telegraph, the alimentary and circulatory system the commissariat. Losses are made good by recruits born in camp, and the life of the individual is a campaign, conducted successfully for a number of years, but with certain defeat in the long run.

The efficacy of an army, at any given moment, depends on the health of the individual soldier, and on the perfection of the machinery by which he is led and brought into action at the proper time; and, therefore, if the analogy holds good, there can be only two kinds of diseases, the one dependent on abnormal states of the physiological units, the other on perturbations of their co-ordinating and alimentative machinery.

Hence, the establishment of the cell theory, in normal biology, was swiftly followed by a "cellular pathology," as its logical counterpart. I need not remind you how great an instrument of investigation this doctrine has proved in the hands of the man of genius to whom its development is due, and who would probably be the last to forget that abnormal conditions of the co-ordinative and distributive machinery of the body are no less important factors of disease.

Henceforward, as it appears to me, the connection of medicine with the biological sciences is clearly indicated. Pure pathology is that branch of biology which defines the particular perturbation of cell-life, or of the coordinating machinery, or of both, on which the phenomena of disease depend.

Those who are conversant with the present state of biology will hardly hesitate to admit that the conception of the life of one of the higher animals as the summation of the lives of a cell aggregate, brought into harmonious action by a co-ordinative machinery formed by some of these cells, constitutes a permanent acquisition of physiological science. But the last form of the battle between the animistic and the physical views of life is seen in the contention whether the physical analysis of vital phenomena can be carried beyond this point or not.

There are some to whom living protoplasm is a substance, even such as Harvey conceived the blood to be, "summa cum providentia et intellectu in finem certum agens, quasi ratiocinio quodam"; and who look with as little favor as Bichat did upon any attempt to apply the principles and the methods of physics and chemistry to the investigation of the vital processes of growth, metabolism, and contractility.

They stand upon the ancient ways; only, in accordance with that progress toward democracy, which a great political writer has declared to be the fatal characteristic of modern times, they substitute a republic formed by a few billion of "animuloe" for the monarchy of the all-pervading "anima."

Others, on the contrary, supported by a robust faith in the universal applicability of the principles laid down by Descartes, and seeing that the actions called "vital"are, so far as we have any means of knowing, nothing but changes of place of particles of matter, look to molecular physics to achieve the analysis of the living protoplasm itself into a molecular mechanism. If there is any truth in the received doctrines of physics, that contrast between living and inert matter, on which Bichat lays so much stress, does not exist. In nature, nothing is fit rest, nothing is amorphous; the simplest particle of that which men in their blindness are pleased to call "brute matter" is a vast aggregate of molecular mechanisms performing complicated movements of immense rapidity, and sensitively adjusting themselves to every change in the surrounding world. Living matter differs from other matter in degree and not in kind; the microcosm repeats the macrocosm; and one chain of causation connects the nebulous original of suns and planetary systems with the protoplasmic foundation of life and organization.

From this point of view, pathology is the analogue of the theory of perturbations in astronomy; and therapeutics resolves itself into the discovery of the means by which a system of forces competent to eliminate any given perturbation may be introduced into the economy. And, as pathology bases itself upon normal physiology, so therapeutics rests upon pharmacology; which is, strictly speaking, a part of the great biological topic of the influence of conditions on the living organism, and has no scientific foundation apart from physiology.

It appears to me that there is no more hopeful indication of the progress of medicine toward the ideal of Descartes than is to be derived from a comparison of the state of pharmacology, at the present day, with that

VIII – Science – 14

which existed forty years ago. If we consider the knowledge positively acquired, in this short time, of the *modus operandi* of urari, of atropia, of physostigmin, of veratria, of casca, of strychnia, of bromide of potassium, of phosphorus, there can surely be no ground for doubting that, sooner or later, the pharmacologist will supply the physician with the means of affecting, in any desired sense, the functions of any physiological element of the body. It will, in short, become possible to introduce into the economy a molecular mechanism which, like a very cunningly-contrived torpedo, shall find its way to some particular group of living elements, and cause an explosion among them, leaving the rest untouched.

The search for the explanation of diseased states in modified cell-life; the discovery of the important part played by parasitic organisms in the aetiology of disease; the elucidation of the action of medicaments by the methods and the data of experimental physiology; appear to me to be the greatest steps which have ever been made toward the establishment of medicine on a scientific basis. I need hardly say they could not have been made except for the advance of normal biology.

There can be no question, then, as to the nature or the value of the connection between medicine and the biological sciences. There can be no doubt that the future of pathology and of therapeutics, and, therefore, that of practical medicine, depends upon the extent to which those who occupy themselves with these subjects are trained in the methods and impregnated with the fundamental truths of biology.

And, in conclusion, I venture to suggest that the collective sagacity of this congress could occupy itselfwith no more important question than with this: How is medical education to be arranged so that, without entangling the student in those details of the systematist which are valueless to him, he may be enabled to obtain a firm grasp of the great truths respecting animal and vegetable life, without which, notwithstanding all the progress of scientific medicine, he will still find himself an empiric?

12

SECTION 12

XV

THE SCHOOL BOARDS: WHAT THEY CAN DO, AND WHAT THEY MAY
DO

[1870]

AN ELECTIONEERING manifesto would be out of place in the pages of this Review; but any suspi- cion that may arise in the mind of the reader that the following pages partake of that nature will be dispelled, if he reflect that they cannot be published ' until after the day on which the ratepayers of the metropolis will have decided which candidates for seats upon the Metropolitan School Board they will take, and which they will leave.

As one of those candidates, I may be permitted to say that I feel much in the frame of mind of the Irish bricklayer's laborer, who bet another that he could not carry him to the top of the ladder in his hod. The challenged hodman won his wager, but as the stakes were handed over, the challenger wistfully remarked, "I'd great hopes of falling at the third round from the top." And, in view of the work and the worry which awaits the members of the School Boards, I must confess to an occasional ungrateful hope that the friends who are toiling upward with me in their hod may, whenthey reach "the third round from the top," let me fall back into peace and quietness.

1 Notwithstanding Mr. Huxley's intentions, the Editor took upon himself, in what seemed to him to be the public interest, to send an extract from this article to the newspapers – before the day of the election of the School Board. – Editor of the "Contemporary Review."

But whether fortune befriend me in this rough method or not, I should like to submit to those of whom I am a potential, but of whom I may not be an actual, colleague, and to others who may be interested in this most important problem – how to get the Education Act to work efficiently – some considerations as to what are the duties of the members of the School Boards, and what are the limits of their power.

I suppose no one will be disposed to dispute the proposition that the prime duty of every member of such a Board is to endeavor to administer the Act honestly; -or in accordance, not only with its letter, but with its spirit. And if so, it would seem that the first step toward this very desirable end is to obtain a clear notion of what that letter signifies, and what that spirit implies; or, in other words, what the clauses of the Act are intended to enjoin and to forbid. So that it is really not admissible, except for factious and abusive purposes, to assume that any one who endeavors to get at this clear meaning is desirous only of raising quibbles and making difficulties.

Reading the Act with this desire to understand it, I find that its provisions may be classified, as might naturally be expected, under two heads: the one set relating to the subject-matter of education; the other to the establishment, maintenance, and administration of the schools in which that education is to be conducted.

Now it is a most important circumstance that all the sections of the Act, except four, belong to the latter division; that is, they refer to mere matters of administration. The four sections in question are the seventh, the fourteenth, the sixteenth, and the ninety-seventh. Of these, the seventh, the fourteenth, and the ninety-seventh deal with the subject-matter of education, while the sixteenth defines the nature of the relations which are to exist between the "Education Department" (a euphemism for the future Minister of Education) and the School Boards. It is the sixteenth clause which is the most important, and, in some respects, the most remarkable of all. It runs thus:

"If the School Board do, or permit, any act in contravention of, or fail to comply with, the regulations, according to which a school provided by them is required by this Act to be conducted, the Education Department may declare the School Board to be, and such Board shall accordingly be deemed to be, a Board in default, and the Education Department may proceed accordingly; and every act, or omission, of any member of the School Board, or manager appointed by them, or any person under the control of the Board, shall be deemed to be permitted by the Board, unless the contrary be proved.

"If any dispute arises as to whether the School Board Uave done, or permitted, any act in contravention of, or have failed to comply with, the said regulations, *the matter shall be referred to the Education Department, whose decision thereon shall be final.*"

It will be observed that this clause gives the Minister of Education absolute power over the doings of the School Boards. He is not only the' administrator of the Act, but he is its interpreter. I had imagined that on the occurrence of a dispute, not as regards a question of pure administration, but as to the meaning of a clauseof the Act, a case might be taken and referred to a court of justice. But I am led to believe that the

Legislature has, in the present instance, deliberately taken this power out of the hands of the judges and lodged it in those of the Minister of Education, who, in accordance with our method of making Ministers, will necessarily be a political partisan, and who may be a strong theological sectary into the bargain. And I am informed by members of Parliament who watched the progress of the Act, that the responsibility for this unusual state of things rests, not with the Government, but with the Legislature, which exhibited a singular disposition to accumulate power in the hands of the future Minister of Education, and to evade the more troublesome difficulties of the education question by leaving them to be settled between that Minister and the School Boards.

I express no opinion whether it is, or is not, desirable that such powers of controlling all the School Boards in the country should be possessed by a person who may be, like Mr. Eorster, eminently likely to use these powers justly and wisely, but who also may be quite the reverse. I merely wish to draw attention to the fact that such powers are given to the Minister, whether he be fit or unfit. The extent of these powers becomes apparent when the other sections of the Act referred to are considered. The fourth clause of the seventh section says:

"The school shall be conducted in accordance with the conditions required to be fulfilled by an elementary school in order to obtain an annual Parliamentary grant."

What these conditions are appears from the following clauses of the ninety-seventh section:

"The conditions required to be fulfilled by an elementary school in order to obtain an annual Parliamentary grant shall be those contained in the minutes of the Education Department in force for the time being. . . . Provided that no such minute of the Education Department, not in force at the time of the passing of this Act, shall be deemed to be in force until it has lain for not less than one month on the table of both Houses of Parliament."

Let us consider how this will work in practice. A school established by a School Board may receive support from three sources – from the rates, the school fees, and the Parliamentary grant. The latter may be as great as the two former taken together; and as it may be assumed, without much risk of error, that a constant pressure will be exerted by the ratepayers on the members who represent them to get as much out of the Government, and as little out of the rates, as possible, the School Boards will have a very strong motive for shaping the education they give, as nearly as may be, on the model which the Education Minister offers for their imitation, and for the copying of which he is prepared to pay.

The Revised Code did not compel any schoolmaster to leave off teaching anything; but, by the very simple process of refusing to pay for many kinds of teaching, it has practically put an end to them. Mr. Forster is said to be engaged in revising the Revised Code; a successor of his may re-revise it – and there will be no sort of check upon these revisions and counter revisions, except the possibility of a Parliamentary debate, when the revised, or added, minutes are laid upon the table. What chance is there that any such debate will take place on a matter of detail relating to elementary education – a subject with which members of the Legislature, having been, for the most part, sent to our public schools thirty years ago, have not the least practical acquaintance, and for which they care nothing, unless it derives a political value from its connection with sectarian politics ?

I cannot but think, then, that the School Boards will have the appearance, but not the reality, of freedom of action, in regard to the subject-matter of what is commonly called "secular" education.

As respects what is commonly called "religious" education, the power of the Minister of Education is even more despotic. An interest, almost amounting to pathos, attaches itself, in my mind, to the frantic exertions which are at present going on in almost every school division to elect certain candidates whose names have never before been heard of in connection with education, and who are either sectarian partisans, or nothing. In my own particular division, a body organized *ad hoc* is moving heaven and earth to get the seven seats filled by seven gentlemen, four of whom are good Churchmen, and three no less good Dissenters. But why should this seven times heated fiery furnace of theological zeal be so desirous to shed its genial warmth over the London School Board ? Can it be that these zealous sectaries mean to evade the solemn pledge given in the Act?

"No religious catechism or religious formulary which is distinctive of any particular denomination shall be taught in the school."

I confess I should have thought it my duty to reject any such suggestion, as dishonoring to a number of worthy persons, if it had not been for a leading article andsome correspondence which appeared in the "Guardian" of November 9th, 1870.

The "Guardian" is, as everybody knows, one of the best of the "religious" newspapers; and, personally, I have every reason to speak highly of the fairness, and indeed kindness, with which the editor is good enough to deal with a writer who must, in many ways, be so objectionable to him as myself. I quote the following passages from a leading article on a letter of mine, therefore, with all respect, and with a genuine conviction that the course of conduct advocated by the writer must appear to him in a very different light from that under which I see it:

" The first of these points is the interpretation which Professor Huxley puts on the ' Cowper-Temple clause.' It is, in fact, that which we foretold some time ago as likely to be forced upon it by those who think with him. The clause itself was one of those compromises which it is very difficult to define or to maintain logically. On the one side was the simple freedom to School Boards to establish what schools they pleased, which Mr. Forster originally gave, but against which the Nonconformists lifted up their voices, because they conceived it likely to give too much power to the Church. On the other side there was the proposition to make the schools secular – intelligible enough, but in the consideration of public opinion simply impossible – and there was the vague impracticable idea, which Mr. Gladstone thoroughly tore to pieces, of enacting that the teaching of all schoolmasters in the new schools should be strictly 'undenominational.' The Cowper-Temple clause was, we repeat, proposed simply to tide over the difficulty. It was to satisfy the Nonconformists and the 'unsectarian,' as distinct from the secular party of the League, by forbidding all distinctive 'catechisms and formularies,' which might havethe effect of openly assigning the schools to this or that religious body. It refused, at the same time, to attempt the impossible task of defining what was undenominational; and its author even contended, if we understood him correctly, that it would in no way, even indirectly, interfere with the substantial teaching of any master in any school. This assertion we always believed to be untenable; we could not see how, in" the face of this clause, a distinctly denominational tone could be honestly given to schools nominally general. But beyond this mere suggestion of an attempt at a general tone of comprehensiveness in religious teaching it was not intended to go, and only because such was its limitation was it accepted by the Government and by the House.

"But now we are told that it is to be construed as doing precisely that which it refused to do. A "formulary,' it seems, is a collection of formulas, and formulas are simply propositions of whatever kind touching religious faith. All such propositions, if they cannot be accepted by all Christian denominations, are to be proscribed; and it is added significantly that the Jews also are a denomination, and so that any teaching distinctively Christian is perhaps to be excluded, lest it should interfere with their freedom and rights. Are we then to fall back on the simple reading of the letter of the Bible? No! this, it is granted, would be an 'unworthy pretence.' The teacher is to give 'grammatical, geographical, or historical explanations'; but he is to keep 'clear of 'theology proper,' because, as Professor Huxley takes great pains to prove, there is no theological teaching which is not opposed by some sect or other, from Ro- man Catholicism on the one hand to Unitarianism on the other. It was not, perhaps, hard to see that this difficulty would be started; and to those who, like Professor Huxley, look at it theoretically, without much practical experience of schools, it may appear serious or unanswerable. But there is very little in it practically; when it is faced deter- minately and handled firmly, it will soon shrink into its truedimensions. The class who are least frightened at it are the school teachers, simply because they know most about it. It is quite clear that the school managers must be cautioned against allowing their schools to be made places of prose- lytism; but when this is done, the case is simple enough. Leave the masters under this general understanding to teach freely; if there is ground of complaint, let it be made, but leave the *onus probandi* on the objectors. For extreme peculiarities of belief or unbelief there is the Conscience Clause; as to the mass of parents, they will be more anxious to have religion taught than afraid of its assuming this or that particular shade. They will trust the school managers and teachers till they have reason to distrust them, and experience has shown that they may trust them safely enough. Any attempt to throw the burden of making the teaching undenominational upon the managers must be sternly resisted: it is simply evading the intentions of the Act in an elaborate attempt to carry them out. We thank Professor Huxley for the warning. To be forewarned is to be forearmed."

A good deal of light seems to me to be thrown on the practical significance of the opinions expressed in the foregoing extract by the following interesting letter, which appeared in the same paper:

" Sib – I venture to send to you the substance of a correspondence with the Education Department upon the question of the lawfulness of religious teaching in rate schools under section 14 (2) of the Act. I asked whether the words 'which is distinctive,' etc., taken grammatically as limiting the prohibition of any religious formulary, might be construed as allowing (subject, however, to the other provisions of the Act) any religious formulary common to any two denominations anywhere in England to be taught in such schools; and if practically the limit could not be so extended, but would have to be fixed according to the special circumstances of each district, then what degree of general acceptance in a district would exempt such a formulary from the prohibition? The answer to this was as follows; 'It was understood, when clause 14 of the Education Act was discussed in the House of Commons, that, according to a well-known rule of interpreting Acts of Parliament, "denomination" must be held to include "denominations." When any dispute is referred to the Education Department under the last paragraph of section 16, it will be dealt with according to the circumstances of the case.'

"Upon my asking further if I might hence infer that the lawfulness of teaching any religious formulary in a rate school would thus depend *exclusively* on local circumstances, and would accordingly be so decided by the Education Department in case of dispute, I was informed in explanation that 'their lordships' ' letter was intended to convey to me that no general rule, beyond that stated in the first paragraph of their letter, could at present be laid down by them; and that their decision in each particular case must depend on the special circumstances accompanying it.

"I think it would appear from this that it may yet be in many cases both lawful and expedient to teach religious formularies in rate schools. H. I.

"steynino, *Novembers, 1870.*"

Of course I do not mean to suggest that the editor of the "Guardian" is bound by the opinions of his correspondent; but I cannot help thinking that I do not misrepresent him when I say that he also thinks "that it may yet be, in many cases, both lawful and expedient to teach religious formularies in rate schools under these circumstances."

It is not uncharitable, therefore, to assume that, the express words of the Act of Parliament notwithstanding, all the sectaries who are toiling so hard for seats in the London School Board have the lively hope of the gentleman from Steyning, that it may be "both lawful and expedient to teach religious formularies in rate schools"; and that they mean to do their utmost to bring this happy consummation about.'

Now the pathetic emotion to which I have referred, as accompanying my contemplations of the violent struggles of so many excellent persons, is caused by the circumstance that, so far as I can judge, their labor is in vain.

Supposing that the London School Board contains, as it probably will do, a majority of sectaries; and that they carry, over the heads of a minority, a resolution that certain theological formulas, about which they all happen to agree – say, for example, the doctrine of the Trinity – shall be taught in the schools. Do they fondly imagine that the minority will not at once dispute their interpretation of the Act, and appeal to the Education Department to settle that dispute? And if so, do they suppose that any Minister of Education, who wants to keep his place, will tighten boundaries which the Legislature has left loose; and will give a "final decision" which shall be offensive to every Unitarian and to every Jew in the Uouse of Commons, besides creating a precedent which will afterward be used to the injury of every Nonconformist ? The editor of the "Guardian" tells his friends sternly to resist every attempt to throw the burden of snaking the teaching undenominational on the managers, and thanks me for the warning I have given him. I return the thanks, with interest, for *his* warning, as to the course the party he represents intends to pursue, and for enabling me thus to draw public attention to a perfectly constitutional and effectual mode of checkmating them.

1 A passage iu an article on the "Working of the Education Act," in the "Saturday Review" for November 19, 1870, completely justiSes this anticipation of the line of action which the sectaries mean to take. After commending the Liverpool compromise, the writer goes on to say:

"If this plan is fairly adopted in Liverpool, the fourteenth clause of the Act will in effect be restored to its original form, and the majority of the ratepayers in each district be permitted to decide to what denomination the school shall belong."

In a previous paragraph the writer speaks of a possible "mistrust" of one another by the members of the Board, and seems to anticipate "accusations of dishonesty." If any of the members of the Board adopt his views, I think it highly probable that he may turn out to be a true prophet.

And, in truth, it is wonderful to note the surprising entanglement into which our able editor gets himself in the struggle between his native honesty and judgment and the necessities of his party. "We could not see," says he, "in the face of this clause how a distinct denominational tone could be honestly given to schools nominally general." There speaks the honest and clearheaded man. "Any attempt to throw the burden of making the teaching undenominational must be sternly resisted." There speaks the advocate holding a brief for his party. "Verily," as Trinculo says, "the monster hath two mouths": the one, the forward mouth, tells us very justly that the teaching cannot "honestly" be "distinctly denominational"; but the other, the backward mouth, asserts that-it must by no manner of means be "undenominational." Putting the two utterances together, I can only interpret them to mean that the teaching is to be "indistinctly denominational." If the editor of the "Guardian" had not shown signs of anger at my use of the term "theological fog," I should have been temptedto suppose it must have been what he had in his mind, under the name of "indistinct denominationalism." But this reading being plainly inadmissible, I can only imagine that he inculcates the teaching of formulas common to a number of denominations.

But the Education Department has already told the gentleman from Steyriing that any such proceeding will be illegal. "According to a well-known rule of interpreting Acts of Parliament, 'denomination' would be held to include 'denominations.' " In other words, we must read the Act thus:

"No religious catechism or religious formulary which is distinctive of any particular *denominations* shall be taught."

Thus we are really very much indebted to the editor of the "Guardian" and his correspondent. The one has shown us that the sectaries mean to try to get as much denominational teaching as they can agree upon among themselves forced into the elementary schools; while the other has obtained a formal declaration from the Educational Department that any such attempt will contravene the Act of Parliament, and that, therefore, the unsecta- rian, law-abiding members of the School Boards may safely reckon upon bringing down upon their opponents the heavy hand of the Minister of Education.1

1 Since this paragraph was written, Mr. Forster, in speaking at the Birkbeck Institution, has removed all doubt as to what his "final decision" will be in the case of

such disputes being referred to him: "I have the fullest confidence that in the reading and explaining of the Bible what the children will be taught will be the great truths of Christian life and conduct, which all of us desire they should know, and that no effort will be made to cram into their poor little minds theological dogmas which their tender age prevents them from under-

So much for the powers of the School Boards. Limited as they seem to be, it by no means follows that euch Boards, if they are composed of intelligent and practical men, really more in earnest about education than about sectarian squabbles, may not exert a very great amount of influence. And, from many circumstances, this is especially likely to be the case with the London School Board, which, if it conducts itself wisely, may become a true educational parliament, as subordinate in authority to the Minister of Education, theoretically, as the Legislature is to the Crown, and yet, like the Legislature, possessed of great practical authority. And I suppose that no Minister of Education would be other than glad to have the aid of the deliberations of such a body, or fail to pay careful attention to its recommendations.

What, then, ought to be the nature and scope of the education which a School Board should endeavor to give to every child–/under its influence, and for which it should try to obtain the aid of the Parliamentary grants ? In my judgment it should include at least the following kinds of instruction and of discipline:

1. Physical training and drill, as part of the regular business of the school.

It is impossible to insist too much on the importance of this part of education for the children of the poor of great towns. All the conditions of their lives are unfavorable to their physical well-being. They are badly lodged, badly housed, badly fed, and live from one year's end to another in bad air, without chance of a change. They have no playgrounds; they amuse themselves with marbles and chuck-farthing, instead of cricketor hare-and-hpunds; and if it were not for the wonderful instinct which leads all poor children of tender years to run under the feet of cab-horses whenever they can, I know not how they would learn to use their limbs with agility.

Now there is no real difficulty about teaching drill and the simpler kinds of gym- nastics. It is done admirably well, for example, in the North Surrey Union schools; and a year or two ago, when I had an opportunity of inspecting these schools, I was greatly struck with the effect of such training upon the poor little waifs and strays of humanity, mostly picked out of the gutter, who are being made into cleanly, healthy, and useful members of society in that excellent institution.

Whatever doubts people may entertain about the efficacy of natural selection, there can be none about artificial selection; and the breeder who should attempt to make, or keep up, a fine stock of pigs, or sheep, under the conditions to which the children of the poor are exposed, would be the laughing-stock even of the bucolic mind. Parliament has already done something in this direction by declining to be an accomplice in the asphyxiation of school children. It refuses to make any grant to a school in which the cubical contents of the schoolroom are inadequate to allow of proper respiration. I should like to see it make another step in the same direction, and either refuse to give a grant to a school in which physical training is not a part of the programme, or, at any rate, offer to pay upon such training. If something of the kind is not done, the English physique, which has been, and is still, on. the whole, a grand one, will become as extinct as the dodo in the great towns.

And then the moral and intellectual effect of drill, as an introduction to, and aid of, all other sorts of training, must not be overlooked. If you want to break in a colt, surely the first thing to do is to catch him and get him quietly to face his trainer; to know his voice and bear his hand; to learn that colts have something else to do with their heels than to kick them up whenever they feel so inclined; and to discover that the dreadful human figure has no desire to devour, or even to beat him, but that, in case of attention and obedience, he may hope for patting and even a sieve of oats.

But, your "street Arabs," and other neglected poor children, are rather worse and wilder than colts; for the reason that the horse-colt has only his animal instincts in him, and his mother, the mare, has been always tender over him, and never came home drunk and kicked him in her life; while the man-colt is inspired by that very real devil, perverted manhood, and *his* mother may have done all that and more. So, on the whole, it may probably be even more expedient to begin your attempt to get at the higher nature of the child, than at that of the colt, from the physical side.

2. Next in order to physical training I put the instruction of children, and especially of girls, in the elements of household work and of domestic economy; in the first place for their own sakes, and in the second for that of their future employers.

Every one who knows anything of the life of the English poor is aware of the misery and waste caused by their want of knowledge of domestic economy, and by their lack of habits of frugality and method. I suppose it is no exaggeration to say that a poor Frenchwomanwould make the money which the wife of a poor Englishman spends in food go twice as far, and at the same time turn out twice as palatable a dinner. Why Englishmen, who are so notoriously fond of good living, should be so hopelessly incompetent in the art of cookery is one of the great mysteries of nature; but from the varied abominations of the railway refreshment-rooms to the monotonous dinners of the poor, English feeding is either wasteful or nasty, or both.

And as to domestic service, the groans of the housewives of England ascend to heaven! In five cases out of six the girl who takes a "place" has to be trained by her mistress in the first rudiments of decency and order; and it is a mercy if she does not turn up her nose at anything like the mention of an honest and proper economy. Thousands of young girls are said to starve, or worse, yearly in London; and at the same time thousands of mistresses of households are ready to pay high wages for a decent housemaid, or cook, or a fair workwoman; and can by no means get what they want.

Surely, if the elementary schools are worth anything, they may put an end to a state of things which is demoralizing the poor, while it is wasting the lives of those better off in small worries and annoyances.

3. But the boys and girls for whose education the School Boards have to provide have not merely to discharge domestic duties, but each of them is a member of a social and political organization of great complexity, and has, in future life, to fit himself into that organization, or be crushed by it. To this end it is surely needful, not only that they should be made acquainted with the elementary laws of conduct, but that their affectionsshould be trained so as to love with all their hearts that conduct which

tends to the attainment of the highest good for themselves and their fellowmen, and to hate with all their hearts that opposite course of action which is fraught with evil.

So far as the laws of conduct are determined by the intellect, I apprehend that they belong to science, and to that part of science which is called morality. But the engagement of the affections in favor of that particular kind of conduct which we call good seems to me to be something quite beyond mere science. And I cannot but think that it, together with the awe and reverence which have no kinship with base fear, but arise whenever one tries to pierce below the surface of things, whether they be material or spiritual, constitutes all that has any unchangeable reality in religion.

And just as I think it would be a mistake to confound the science, morality, with the affection, religion; so do I conceive it to be a most lamentable and mischievous error that the science, theology, is so confounded in the minds of many – indeed, I might say, of the majority of men.

I do not express any opinion as to whether theology is a true science, or whether it does not come under the apostolic definition of "science falsely so called"; though I may be permitted to express the belief that if the Apostle to whom that much-misapplied phrase is due could make the acquaintance of much of modern theology, he would not hesitate a moment in declaring that it is exactly what he meant the words to denote.

But it is at any rate conceivable that the nature of the Deity, and his relations to the universe, and moreespecially to mankind, are capable of being ascertained, either inductively or deductively, or by both processes. And, if they have been ascertained, then a body of science has been formed which is very properly called theology.

Further, there can be no doubt that affection for the Being thus defined and described by theologic science would be properly termed religion; but it would not be the whole of religion. The affection for the ethical ideal defined by moral science would claim equal if not superior rights. For suppose theology established the existence of an evil deity – and some theologies, even Christian ones, have come very near this – is the religious affection to be transferred from the ethical ideal to any such omnipotent demon? I trow not. Better a thousand times that the human race should perish under his thunderbolts than it should say, "Evil, be thou my good."

There is nothing new, that I know of, in this statement of the relations of religion with the science of morality on the one hand and that of theology on the other. But I believe it to be altogether true, and very needful, at this time, to be clearly and emphatically recognized as such by those who have to deal with the education question.

We are divided into two parties – the advocates of so- called "religious" teaching on the one hand, and those of so-called "secular" teaching on the other. And both parties seem to me to be not only hopelessly wrong, but in such a position that if either succeeded completely, it would discover, before many years were over, that it hall made a great mistake and done serious evil to the cause of education.

For, leaving aside the more farseeing minority on each side, what the "religious" party is crying for is mere theology, under the name of religion; while the "secularists" have unwisely and wrongfully admitted the assumption of their opponents, and demand the abolition of all "religious" teaching, when they only want to be free of theology – Burning your ship to get rid of the cockroaches!

But my belief is, that no human being, and no society composed of human beings, ever did, or ever will, come to much, unless their conduct was governed and guided by the love of some ethical ideal. Undoubtedly, your gutter child may be converted by mere intellectual drill into "the subtlest of all the beasts of the field"; but we know what has become of the original of that description, and there is no need to increase the number of those who imitate him successfully without being aided by the rates. And if I were compelled to choose for one of my own children, between a school in which real religious instruction is given, and one without it, I should prefer the former, even though the child might have to take a good deal of theology with it. Nine-tenths of a dose of bark is mere half-rotten wood; but one swallows it for the sake of the particles of quinine, the beneficial effect of which may be weakened, but is not destroyed, by the wooden dilution, unless in a few cases of exceptionally tender stomachs.

Hence, when the great mass of the English people declare that they want to have the children in the elementary schools taught the Bible, and when it is plain from the terms of the Act, the debates in and out of Parliament, and especially the emphatic declarations of the Vice-President of the Council, that it was intended that such Bible-reading should be permitted,' unless good cause for prohibiting it could be shown, I do not see what reason there is for opposing that wish. Certainly, I, individually, could with no shadow of consistency oppose the teaching of the children of other people to do that which my own children are taught to do. And, even if the reading the Bible were not, as I think it is, consonant with political reason and justice, and with a desire to act in the spirit of the education measure, I am disposed to think it might still be well to read that book in the elementary schools.

I have always been strongly in favor of secular education, in the sense of education without theology; but I must confess I have been no less seriously perplexed to know by what practical measures the religious feeling, which is the essential basis of conduct, was to be kept up, in the present utterly chaotic state of opinion on these matters, without the use of the Bible. The Pagan moralists lack life and color, and even the noble Stoic, Marcus Antonius, is too high and refined for an ordinary child. Take the Bible as a whole; make the severest deductions which fair criticism can dictate for shortcomings and positive errors; eliminate, as a sensible lay-teacher would do, if left to himself, all that it is not desirable for children to occupy themselves with; and there still remains in this old literature a vast residuum of moral beauty and grandeur. And then consider the great historical fact that, for three centuries, this book has been woven into the life of all that is best and noblest in English history; that it has become the national epic of Britain, and is as familiar to noble and simple, from John-o'-Groat's House to Land's End, as Dante and Tasso once were to the Italians; that it is written in the noblest and purest English, and abounds in exquisite beauties of mere literary form; and, finally, that it forbids the veriest hind who never left his village to be ignorant of the existence of other countries and other civilizations, and of a great past, stretching back to Lhe furthest limits of the oldest nations in the world. By the study of what other book could children be so much humanized and made to feel that each figure in that vast historical procession fills, like themselves, but a momentary space in the interval between two eternities; and earns the blessings or the curses of all time, according to its effort to do good and hate evil, even as they also are earning their payment for their work?

On the whole, then, I am in favor of reading the Bible, with such grammatical, geographical, and historical explanations by a lay-teacher as may be needful, with rigid exclusion of any further theological teaching than that contained in the Bible itself. And in stating what this is, the teacher would do well not to go beyond the precise words of the Bible; for if he does, he will, in the first place, undertake a task beyond his strength, seeing that all the Jewish and Christian sects have been at work upon that subject for more than two thousand years, and have not yet arrived, and are not in the least likely to arrive, at an agreement; and, in the second place, he will certainly begin to teach something distinctively denominational, and thereby come into violent collision with the Act of Parliament.

4. The intellectual training to be given in the elementary schools must of course, in the first place, consist

VIII – Science – 15

in learning to use the means of acquiring knowledge, or reading, writing, and arithmetic; and it will be a great matter to teach reading so completely that the act shall have become easy and pleasant. If reading remains "hard," that accomplishment will not be much resorted to for instruction, and still less for amusement – which last is one of its most valuable uses to hard-worked people. But along with a due proficiency in the use of the means of learning, a certain amount of knowledge, of intellectual discipline, and of artistic training should be conveyed in the elementary schools; and in this direction – for reasons which I am afraid to repeat, having urged them so often – I can conceive no subject-matter of education Bo appropriate and so important as the rudiments of physical science, with drawing, modelling, and singing. Not only would such teaching afford the best possible preparation for the technical schools about which so much is now said, but the organization for carrying it into effect already exists. The Science and Art Department, the operations of which have already attained considerable magnitude, not only offers to examine and pay the results of such examination in elementary science and art, but it provides what is still more important; viz., a means of giving children of high natural ability, who are just as abundant among the poor as among the rich, a helping hand. A good old proverb tells us that "One should not take a razor to cut a block": the razor is soon spoiled, and the block is not so well cut as it would be with a hatchet. But it is worse economy to prevent a possible Watt from being anything but a stoker, or to give a possible Faraday no chance of doing anything but to bind books. Indeed, the loss in such cases of mistaken vocation has no measure; it is absolutely infinite and irreparable. And among the arguments in favor of the interference of the State in education, none seems to be stronger than this – that it is the interest of every one that ability should be neither wasted, nor misapplied, by any one; and, therefore, that every one's representative, the State, is necessarily fulfilling the wishes of its constituents when it is helping the capacities to reach their proper places.

It may be said that the scheme of education here sketched is too large to be effected in the time during which the children will remain at school; and, secondly, that even if this objection did not exist it would cost too much.

I attach no importance whatever to the first objection tintil the experiment has been fairly tried. Considering how much catechism, lists of the kings of Israel, geography of Palestine, and the like, children are made to swallow now, I cannot believe there will be any difficulty hi inducing them to go through the physical training, which is more than half play; or the instruction in household work, or in those duties to one another and to themselves which have a daily and hourly practical interest. That children take kindly to elementary science and art no one can doubt who has tried the experiment properly. And if Bible-reading is not accompanied by constraint and solemnity, as if it were a sacramental operation, I do not believe there is anything in which children take more pleasure. At least I know that some of the pleasantest recollections of my childhood are connected with the voluntary study of an ancient Bible which belonged to my grandmother. There were splendidpictures in it, to be sure; but I recollect little or nothing about them save a portrait of the high priest in his vestments. What come vividly back on my mind are remembrances of my delight in the histories of Joseph and of David; and of my keen appreciation of the chivalrous kindness of Abraham in his dealing with Lot. Like a sudden flash there returns back upon me my utter scorn of the pettifogging meanness of Jacob, and my sympathetic grief over the heartbreaking lamentation of the cheated Esau, "Hast thou not a blessing for me also, O my father?" And I see, as in a cloud, pictures of the grand phantasmagoria of the Book of Revelation.

I enumerate, as they issue, the childish impressions which come crowding out of the pigeon-holes in my brain, in which they have lain almost undisturbed for forty years. I prize them as an evidence that a child of five or six years old, left to his own devices, may be deeply interested in the Bible, and draw sound moral sustenance from it. And I rejoice that I was left to deal with the Bible alone; for if I had had some theological "explainer" at my side, he might have tried, as such do, to lessen my indignation against Jacob, and thereby have warped my moral sense forever; while the great apocalyptic spectacle of the ultimate triumph of right and justice might have been turned to the base purposes of a pious lampooner of the Papacy.

And as to the second objection – costliness – the reply is, first, that the rate and the Parliamentary grant together ought to be enough, considering that science and art teaching is already provided for; and, secondly, that if they are not, it may be well for the educational parliament to consider what has become of those endowmentswhich were originally intended to be devoted, more or less largely, to the education of the poor.

When the monasteries were spoiled, some of their endowments were applied to the foundation of cathedrals; and in all such cases it was ordered that a certain portion of the endowment should be applied to the purposes of education. How much is so applied? Is that which may be so applied given to help the poor, who cannot pay for education, or does it virtually subsidize the comparatively rich, who can? How are Christ's Hospital and Alleyn's foundation securing their right purposes, or how far are they perverted into contrivances for affording relief to the classes who can afford to pay for education ? How – But this paper is already too long, and, if I begin, I may find it hard to stop asking questions of this kind, which after all are worthy only of the lowest of Radicals.

13

SECTION 13

XVI

TECHNICAL EDUCATION

[1877]

ANY CANDID observer of the phenomena of modern society will readily admit that bores must be classed among the enemies of the human race; and a little consideration will probably lead him to the further admission that no species of that extensive genus of noxious creatures is more objectionable than the educational bore. Convinced as I am of the truth of this great social generalization, it is not without a certain trepidation that I venture to address you on an educational topic. For, in the course of the last ten years, to go back no further, I am afraid to say how often I have ventured to speak of education, from that given in the primary schools to that which is to be had in the universities and medical colleges; indeed, the only part of this wide region into which, as yet, I have not adventured is that into which I propose to intrude to-day.

Thus, I cannot but be aware that I am dangerously near becoming the thing which all men fear and fly. But *I* have deliberately elected to run the risk. For when you did me the honor to ask me to address you, an unexpected circumstance had led me to occupy myself seriously with the question of technical education; and I had acquired the conviction that there are few subjects respecting which it is more important for all classes of the community to have clear and just ideas than this; while, certainly, there is none which is more deserving of attention by the Working Men's Club and Institute Union.

It is not for me to express an opinion whether the considerations, which I am about to submit to you, will be proved by experience to be just or not, but I will do my best to make them clear. Among the many good things to be found in Lord Bacon's works, none is more full of wisdom than the saying that "truth more easily comes out of error than out of confusion." Clear and consecutive wrong-thinking is the next best thing to right-thinking; so that, if I succeed in clearing your ideas on this topic, I shall have wasted neither your time nor my own.

"Technical education," in the sense in which the term is ordinarily used, and in which I am now employing it, means that sort of education which is specially adapted to the needs of men whose business in life it is to pursue some kind of handicraft; it is, in fact, a fine Greco-Latin equivalent for what in good vernacular English would be called "the teaching of handicrafts." And probably, at this stage of our progress, it may occur to many of you to think of the story of the cobbler and his last, and to say to yourselves, though you will be too polite to put the question openly to me, What does the speaker know practically about this matter? What is his handicraft? I think the question is a very proper one, and unless I were prepared to answer it, I hope satisfactorily, I should have chosen some other theme.

The fact is. I am, and have been, any time these thirty years, a man who works with his hands – a handicraftsman. I do not say this in the broadly metaphorical sense in which fine gentlemen, with all the delicacy of Agag about them, trip to the hustings about election time, and protest that they too are working men. I really mean my words to be taken in their direct, literal, and straightforward sense. In fact, if the most nimble- fingered watch-maker among you will come to my workshop, he may set me to put a watch together, and I will set him to dissect, say, a blackbeetle's nerves. I do not wish to vaunt, but I am inclined to think that I shall manage my job to his satisfaction sooner than he will do his piece of work to mine.

In truth, anatomy, which is iny handicraft, is one of the most difficult kinds of mechanical labor, involving, as it does, not only lightness and dexterity of hand, but sharp eyes and endless patience. And you must not suppose that my particular branch of science is especially distinguished for the demand it makes upon skill in manipulation. A similar requirement is made upon all students of physical science. The astronomer, the electrician, the chemist, the mineralogist, the botanist, are constantly called upon to perform manual operations of exceeding delicacy. The progress of all branches of physical science depends upon observation, or on that artificial observation which is termed experiment, of one kind or another; and the further we advance, the more practical difficulties surround the investigation of the conditions of the problems offered to us; so that mobile and yet steady hands, guided by clear vision, are more and more in request in the workshops of science.

Indeed, it has struck me that one of the grounds of that sympathy between the handicraftsmen of this country and the men of science, by which it has so often been my good fortune to profit, may, perhaps, lie here. You feel and we feel that, among the so-called learned folk, we alone are brought into contact with tangible facts in the way that you are. You know well enough that it is one thing to write a history of chairs in general, or to address a poem to a throne, or to speculate about the occult powers of the chair of St. Peter; and quite another thing to make with your own hands a veritable chair, that will stand fair and square, and afford a safe and satisfactory resting-place to a frame of sensitiveness and solidity.

So it is with us, when we look out from our scientific handicrafts upon the doings of our learned brethren, whose work is untrammelled by anything "base and mechanical," as handicrafts used to be called when the world was younger, and, in some respects, less wise than now. We take the greatest interest in their pursuits; we are edified by their histories and are charmed with their poems, which sometimes illustrate so remarkably the powers of man's imagination; some of us admire and even humbly try to follow them in their high philosophical excursions, though we know the risk of being snubbed by the inquiry whether grovelling dissectors of monkeys and blackbeetles can hope to enter into the empyreal kingdom of speculation. But still we feel that our business is different; humbler if you will, though the diminution of dignity is, perhaps, compensated by the increase of reality; and that we, like you, have to get our work done in a region where little avails, if the power of dealing with practical tangible facts is wanting. You know that clever talk touching joinery will not make a chair; and I know that it is of about as much value in the physical sciences. Mother Nature is serenely obdurate to honeyed words; only those who understand the ways of things, and can silently and effectually handle them, get any good out of her.

And now, having, as I hope, justified my assumption of a place among handicrafts-men, and put myself right with you as to my qualification, from practical knowledge, to speak about technical education, I will proceed to lay before you the results of my experience as a teacher of a handicraft, and tell you what sort of education I should think best adapted for a boy whom one wanted to make a professional anatomist.

I should say, in the first place, let him have a good English elementary education. I do not mean that he shall be able to pass in such and such a standard – that may or may not be an equivalent expression – but that his teaching shall have been such as to have given him command of the common implements of learning and to have created a desire for the things of the understanding.

Further, I should like him to know the elements of physical science, and especially of physics and chemistry, and I should take care that this elementary knowledge was real. I should like my aspirant" to be able to read a scientific treatise in Latin, French, or German, because an enormous amount of anatomical knowledge is locked up in those languages. And especially, I should require some ability to draw – I do not mean artistically, for that is a gift which may be cultivated but cannot be learned, but with fair accuracy. I will not say that everybody can learn even this; for the negative development of the faculty of drawing in some people is almost miraculous. Still everybody, or almost everybody, can learn to write; and, as writing is a kind of drawing, I suppose that the majority of the people who say they cannot draw, and give copious evidence of the accuracy of their assertion, could draw, after a fashion, if they tried. And that "after a fashion" would be better than nothing for my purposes.

Above all things, let my imaginary pupil have preserved the freshness and vigor of youth in his mind as well as his body. The educational abomination of desolation of the present day is the stimulation of young people to work at high pressure by incessant competitive examinations. Some wise man (who probably was not an early riser) has said of early risers in general, that they are conceited all the forenoon and stupid all the afternoon. Now whether this is true of early risers in the common acceptation of the word or not, I will not pretend to say; but it is too often true of the unhappy children who are forced to rise too early in their classes. They are conceited all the forenoon of life, and stupid all its afternoon. The vigor and freshness, which should have been stored up for the purposes of the hard struggle for existence in practical life, have been washed out of them by precocious mental debauchery – by book gluttony and lesson bibbing. Their faculties are worn out by the strain put upon their callow brains, and they are demoralized by worthless childish triumphs before the real work of life begins. I have no compassion for sloth, but youth has more need for intellectual rest than age; and the cheerfulness, the tenacity of purpose, the power of work which make many a successful man what he is, must often be placed to the credit, not of his hours of industry, but to that of his hours of idleness, in boyhood. Even the hardest worker of us all, if he has to deal with anything above mere details, will do well, now and again, to let his brain lie fallow for a space. The next crop of thought will certainly be all the fuller in the ear and the weeds fewer.

This is the sort of education which I should like any one who was going to devote himself to my handicraft to undergo. As to knowing anything about anatomy itself, on the whole I would rather he left that alone until he took it up seriously in my laboratory. It is hard work enough to teach, and I should not like to have superadded to that the possible need of unteaching.

Well, but, you will say, this is Hamlet with the Prince of Denmark left out; your "technical education" is simply a good education, with more attention to physical science, to drawing, and to modern languages than is common, and there is nothing specially technical about it.

Exactly so; that remark takes us straight to the heart of what I have to say; which is, that, in my judgment, the preparatory education of the handicraftsman ought to have nothing of what is ordinarily understood by "technical" about it.

The workshop is the only real school for a handicraft. The education which precedes that of the workshop shoxild be entirely devoted to the strengthening of the body, the elevation of the moral faculties, and the cultivation of the intelligence; and, especially, to the imbuing the mind with a broad and clear view of the laws of that natural world with the components of which the handicraftsman will have to deal. And, the earlier the period of life at which the handicraftsman has to enter into actual practice of his craft, the more important is it that he should devote the precious hours of preliminary education to things of the mind, which have no direct and immediate bearing on his branch of industry, though they lie at the foundation of all realities.

Now let me apply the lessons I have learned from my handicraft to yours. If any of you were obliged to take an apprentice, I suppose you would like to get a good healthy lad, ready and willing to learn, handy, and with his fingers not all thumbs, as the saying goes. You would like that he should read, write, and cipher well; and, if you were an intelligent master, and your trade involved the application of scientific principles, as so many trades do, you would like him to know enough of the elementary principles of science to understand what was going on. I suppose that, in nine trades out of ten, it would be useful if he could draw; and many of you must have lamented your inability to find out for yourselves what foreigners are doing or have done. So that some knowledge of French and German might, in many cases, be very desirable.

So it appears to me that what you want is pretty much what I want; and the practical question is, How are you to get what you need, under the actual limitations and conditions of life of handicraftsmen in this country ?

I think I shall have the assent both of the employers of labor and of the employed as to one of these limitations; which is, that no scheme of technical education is likely to be seriously entertained which will delay the entrance of boys into working life, or prevent them fromcontributing toward their own support, as early as they do at present. Not only do I believe that any such scheme could not be carried out, but I doubt its desirableness, even if it were practicable.

The period between childhood and manhood is full of difficulties and dangers, under the most favorable circumstances; and, even among the well-to-do, who can afford to surround their children with the most favorable conditions, examples of a career ruined, before it has well begun, are but too frequent. Moreover, those who have to live by labor must be shaped to labor early. The colt that is left at grass too long makes but a sorry draught- horse, though his way of life does not bring him within the reach of artificial temptations. Perhaps the most valuable result of all education is the ability to make yourself do the thing you have to do, when it ought to be done, whether you like it or not; it is the first lesson that ought to be learned; and, however early a man's training begins, it is probably the last lesson that he learns thoroughly.

There is another reason, to which I have already adverted, and which I would reiterate, why any extension of the time devoted to ordinary schoolwork is undesirable. In the newly-awakened zeal for education, we run some risk of forgetting the truth that while under- instruction is a bad thing, over-instruction may possibly be a worse.

Success in any kind of practical life is not dependent, solely, or indeed chiefly, upon knowledge. Even in the learned professions, knowledge alone is of less consequence than people are apt to suppose. And, if much expenditure of bodily energy is involved in the day'swork, mere knowledge is of still less importance when weighed against the probable cost of its acquirement. To do a fair day's work with his hands, a man needs, above all things, health, strength, and the patience and cheerfulness which, if they do not always accompany these blessings, can hardly in the nature of things exist without them; to which we must add honesty of purpose and a pride in doing what is done well.

A good handicraftsman can get on very well without genius, but he will fare badly without a reasonable share of that which is a more useful possession for workaday life, namely, mother-wit; and he will be all the better for a real knowledge, however limited, of the ordinary laws of nature, and especially of those which apply to his own business.

Instruction carried so far as to help the scholar to turn his store of mother-wit to account, to acquire c, fair amount of sound elementary knowledge, and to use his hands and eyes; while leaving him fresh, vigorous, and with a sense of the dignity of his own calling, whatever it may be, if fairly and honestly pursued, cannot fail to be of invaluable service to all those who come under its influence.

But, on the other hand, if school instruction is carried so far as to encourage bookishness; if the ambition of the scholar is directed, not to the gaining of knowledge, but to the being able to pass examinations successfully; especially if encouragement is given to the mischievous delusion that brainwork is, in itself, and apart from its quality, a nobler or more respectable thing than handiwork – such education may be a deadly mischief to the workman, and lead to the rapid ruin of the industries it is intended to serve.

I know that I am expressing the opinion of some of the largest as well as the most enlightened employers of labor when I Bay that there is a real danger that, from the extreme of no education, we may run to the other extreme of over-education of handicraftsmen. And I apprehend that what is true for the ordinary handworker is true for the foreman. Activity, probity, knowledge of men, ready mother-wit, supplemented by a good knowledge of the general principles involved in his business, are the making of a good foreman. If he possess these qualities, no amount of learning will fit him better for his position; while the course of life and the habit, of mind required for the attainment of such learning may, in various direct and indirect ways, act as direct disqualifications for it.

Keeping in mind, then, that the two things to be avoided are, the delay of the entrance of boys into practical life, and the substitution of exhausted bookworms for shrewd, handy men, in our works and factories, let us consider what may be wisely and safely attempted in the way of improving the education of the handicraftsman.

First, I look to the elementary schools now happily established all over the country. I am not going to criticise or find fault with them; on the contrary, their establishment seems to me to be the most important and the most beneficial result of the corporate action of the people in our day. A great deal is said of British interests just now, but, depend upon it, that no Eastern difficulty needs our intervention as a nation so seriously as the putting down both the Bashi-Bazouks of ignorance and the Cossacks of sectarianism at home. What hasalready been achieved in these directions is a great thing; you must have lived some time to know how great. An education, better in its processes, better in its substance, than that which was accessible to the great majority of well-to-do Britons a quarter of a century ago, is now obtainable by every child in the land. Let any man of my age go into an ordinary elementary school, and unless he was unusually fortunate in his youth, he will tell you that the educational method, the intelligence, patience, and good temper on the teacher's part, which are now at the disposal of the veriest waifs and wastrels of society, are things of which he had no experience in those costly, middle-class schools, which were so ingeniously contrived as to combine all the evils and shortcomings of the great public schools with none of their advantages. Many a man, whose so-called education cost a good deal of valuable money and occupied many a year of invaluable time, leaves the inspection of a well-ordered elementary school devoutly wishing that, in his young days, he had had the chance of being as well taught as these boys and girls are.

But while, in view of such an advance in general education, I willingly obey the natural impulse to be thankful, I am not willing altogether to rest. I want to see instruction in elementary science and in art more thoroughly incorporated in the educational system. At present, it is being administered by driblets, as if it were a potent medicine, "a few drops to be taken occasionally in a teaspoon." Every year I notice that that earnest and untiring friend of yours and of mine, Sir John Lubbock, stirs up the Government of the day in the House of Commons on this subject; and also thatevery year he and the few members of the House of Commons, such as Dr. Playfair, who sympathize with him, are met with expressions of warm admiration for science in general, and reasons at large for doing nothing in particular. But now that Mr. Forster, to whom the education of the country owes so much, has announced his conversion to the right faith, I begin to hope that, sooner or later, things will mend.

I have given what I believe to be a good reason for the assumption that the keeping at school of boys who are to be handicraftsmen beyond the age of thirteen or fourteen is neither practicable nor desirable; and, as it is quite certain, that, with justice to other and no less important branches of education, nothing more than the rudiments of science and art teaching can be introduced into elementary schools, we must seek elsewhere for a supplementary training in these subjects, and, if need be, in foreign languages, which may go on after the workman's life has begun.

The means of acquiring the scientific and artistic part of this training already exists in full working order, in the first place, in the classes of the Science and Art Department, which are, for the most part, held in the evening, so as to be accessible to all who choose to avail themselves of them after working hours. The great advantage of these classes is that they bring the means of instruction to the doors of the factories and workshops; that they are no artificial creations, but by their very existence prove the desire of the people for them; and finally, that they admit of indefinite development in proportion as they are wanted. I have often expressed the opinion, and I repeat it here, that, during the eighteenyears they have been in existence, these classes have done incalculable good; and I can say, of my own knowledge, that the Department spares no pains and trouble in trying to increase their usefulness and insure the soundness of their work.

No one knows better than my friend Colonel Donnelly, to whose clear views and great administrative abilities so much of the successful working of the science classes is due, that there is much to be done before the system can be said to be thoroughly satisfactory. The instruction given needs to be made more systematic and especially more practical; the teachers are of very unequal excellence, and not a few stand much in need of instruction themselves, not only in the subject which they teach, but in the objects for which they teach. I dare say you have heard of that proceeding, reprobated by all true sportsmen, which is called "shooting for the pot." Well, there is such a thing as "teaching for the pot" – teaching, that is, not that your scholar may know, but that he may count for payment among those who pass the examination; and there are some teachers, happily not many, who have yet to learn that the examiners of the Department regard them as poachers of the worst description.

Without presuming in any way to speak in the name of the Department, I think I may say, as a matter which has come under my own observation, that it is doing its best to meet all these difficulties. It systematically promotes practical instruction in the classes; it affords facilities to teachers who desire to learn their business thoroughly; and it is always ready to aid in the suppression of pot-teaching.

All this is, as you may imagine, highly satisfactory to me. I see that spread of scientific education, about which I have so often permitted myself to worry the public, become, for all practical purposes, an accomplished fact. Grateful as I am for all that is now being done, in the same direction, in our higher schools and universities, I have ceased to have any anxiety about the wealthier classes. Scientific knowledge is spreading by what the alchemists called a "distillatio per ascensum"; and nothing now can prevent it from continuing to distil upward and permeate English society, until, in the remote future, there shall be no member of the legislature who does not know as much of science as an elementary schoolboy; and even the heads of houses in our venerable seats of learning shall acknowledge that natural science is not merely a sort of University back-door through which inferior men may get at their degrees. Perhaps this apocalyptic vision is a little wild; and I feel I ought to ask pardon for an outbreak of enthusiasm, which, I assure you, is not my commonest failing.

I have said that the Government is already doing a great deal in aid of that kind of technical education for handicraftsmen which, to my mind, is alone worth seeking. Perhaps it is doing as much as it ought to do, even in this direction. Certainly there is another kind of help of the most important character, for which we may look elsewhere than to the Government. The great mass of mankind have neither the liking, nor the aptitude, for either literary, or scientific, or artistic pursuits; nor, indeed, for excellence of any sort. Their ambition is to go through life with moderate exertion and a fair share of ease, doing common things in a common way. And a great blessing and comfort it is that the majority of men are of this mind; for the majority of things to be done are common things, and are quite well enough done when commonly done. The great end of life is not knowledge but action. What men need is, as much knowledge as they can assimilate and organize into a basis for action; give them more and it may become injurious. One knows people who are as heavy and stupid from undigested learning as others are from overfulness of meat and drink. But a small percentage of the population is born with that most excellent quality, a desire for excellence, or with special aptitudes of some sort or another; Mr. Gal ton tells us that not more than one in four thousand may be expected to attain distinction, and not more than one in a million some share of that intensity of instinctive aptitude, that burning thirst for excellence, which is called genius.

Now, the most important object of all educational schemes is to catch these exceptional people, and turn them to account for the good of society. No man can say where they will crop up; like their opposites, the fools and knaves, they appear sometimes in the palace, and sometimes in the hovel; but the great thing to be aimed at, I was almost going to say the most important end of all social arrangements, is to keep these glorious sports of Nature from being either corrupted by luxury or starved by poverty, and to put them into the position in which they can do the work for which they are especially fitted.

Thus, if a lad in an elementary school showed signs of special capacity, I would try to provide him with the means of continuing his education after his daily workinglife had begun; if in the evening classes he developed special capabilities in the direction of science or of drawing, I would try to secure him an apprenticeship to some trade in which those powers would have applicability. Or, if he chose to become a teacher, he should have the chance of so doing. Finally, to the lad of genius, the one in a million, I would make accessible the highest and most complete training the country could afford. "Whatever that might cost, depend upon it the investment would be a good one. I weigh my words when I say that if the nation could purchase a potential Watt, or Davy, or Faraday, at the cost of a hundred thousand pounds down, he would be dirt-cheap at the money. It is a mere commonplace and every-day piece of knowledge that what these three men did has produced untold millions of wealth, in the narrowest economical sense of the word.

Therefore, as the sum and crown of what is to be done for technical education, I look to the provision of a machinery for winnowing out the capacities and giving them scope. When I was a member of the London School Board, I said, in the course of a speech, that our business was to provide a ladder, reaching from the gutter to the university, along which every child in the three kingdoms should have the chance of climbing as far as he was fit to go. This phrase was so much bandied about at the time, that, to say truth, I am rather tired of it; but I know of no other which so fully expresses my belief, not only (about education in general, but about technical education in particular.

The essential foundation of all the organization needed for the promotion of education among handicraftsmenwill, I believe, exist in this country, when every working lad can feel that society has done as much as lies in its powerto remove all needless and artificial obstacles from his path; that there is no barrier, except such as exists in the nature of things, between himself and whatever place in the social organization he is fitted to fill; and, more than this, that, if he has capacity and industry, a hand is held out to help him along any path which is wisely and honestly chosen.

I have endeavored to point out to you that a great deal of such an organization already exists; and I am glad to be able to add that there is a good prospect that what is wanting will, before long, be supplemented.

Those powerful and wealthy societies, the livery companies of the City of London, remembering that they are the heirs and representatives of the trade guilds of the Middle Ages, are interesting themselves in the question. So far back as 1872 the Society of Arts organized a system of instruction in the technology of arts and manufactures, for persons actually employed in factories and workshops, who desired to extend and improve their knowledge of the theory and practice of their particular avocations;[1] and a considerable subsidy, in aid of the efforts of the Society, was liberally granted by the Clothworkers' Company. We have here the hopeful commencement oi a rational organization for the promotion of excellence among handicraftsmen. Quite recently, other of the livery companies have determined upon giving their powerful, and, indeed, almost boundless, aid to the improvement of the teaching of handicrafts. They havealready gone so far as to appoint a committee to act for them; and I betray no confidence in adding that, some time since, the committee sought the advice and assistance of several persons, myself among the number.

1 See the "Programme" for 1878, issued by the Society of Arts, p. 14.

Of course I cannot tell you what may be the result of the deliberations of the committee; but we may all fairly hope that, before long, steps which will have a weighty and a lasting influence on the growth and spread of sound and thorough teaching among the handicraftsmen1 of this country will be taken by the livery companies of London.

[This hope has been fully justified by the establishment of the Cowper Street Schools, and that of the Central Institution of the City and Guilds of London Institute, September, 1881.]

1 It is perhaps advisable to remark that the important question of the professional education of managers of industrial works is not touched in the foregoing remarks.

14

SECTION 14

XVII

ADDRESS ON BEHALF OF THE NATIONAL ASSOCIATION FOR THE PRO-
MOTION OF TECHNICAL EDUCATION

M'

[1887]

E. MAYOE AND GENTLEMEN – It must be a matter of sincere satisfaction
to those who, like myself, have for many years past been convinced of the vital
importance of technical education to thia country to see that that subject is now being
taken up by some of the most important of our manufacturing towns. The evidence
which is afforded of the public interest in the matter by such meetings as those at
Liverpool and Newcastle, and, last but not least, by that at which I have the honor to
be present to-day, may convince us all, I think, that the question has passed out of the
region of speculation into that of action. I need hardly say to any one here that the
task which our Association contemplates is not only one of primary importance – I
may say of vital importance – to the welfare of the country; but that it is one of great
extent and of vast difficulty. There is a well-worn adage that those who set out upon
a great enterprise would do well to count the cost. I am not sure that this is always

true. I think that some of the very greatest enterprises in this world have been carried out successfully simply because

the people who undertook them did not count the cost;

(361) Vill – Science – 16

and I am much of opinion that, in this very case, the most instructive consideration for us is the cost of doing nothing. But there is one thing that is perfectly certain, and it is that, in undertaking all enterprises, one of the most important conditions of success is to have a perfectly clear comprehension of what you want to do – to have that before your minds before you set out, and from that point of view to consider carefully the measures which are best adapted to the end.

Mr. Acland has just given you an excellent account of what is properly and strictly understood by technical education; but I venture to think that the purpose of this Association may be stated in somewhat broader terms, and that the object we have in view is the development of the industrial productivity of the country to the uttermost limits consistent with social welfare. And you will observe that, in thus widening the definition of our object, I have gone no further than the Mayor in his speech, when he not obscurely hinted – and most justly hinted – that in dealing with this question there are other matters than technical education, in the strict sense, to be considered.

It would be extreme presumption on my part if I were to attempt to tell an audience of gentlemen intimately acquainted with all branches of industry and commerce, such as I see before me, in what manner the practical details of the operations that we propose are to be carried out. I am absolutely ignorant both of trade and of commerce, and upon such matters I cannot venture to say a solitary word. But there is one direction in which I think it possible I may be of service – not much perhaps, but still of some – because this matter, in the first place, involves the consideration of methods of education with which it has been my business to occupy myself during the greater part of my life; and, in the second place, it involves attention to some of those broad facts and laws of nature with which it has been my business to acquaint myself to the best of my ability. And what I think may be possible is this, that if I succeed in putting before you – as briefly as I can, but in clear and connected shape – what strikes me as the programme that we have eventually to carry out, and what are the indispensable conditions of success, that that proceeding, whether the conclusions at which I arrive be such as you approve or as you disapprove, will nevertheless help to clear the course. In this and in all complicated matters we must remember a saying of Bacon, which may be freely translated thus: "Consistent error is very often vastly more useful than muddle- headed truth." At any rate, if there be any error in the conclusions I shall put before you, I will do my best to make the error perfectly clear and plain.

Now, looking at the question of what we want to do in this broad and general way, it appears to me that it is necessary for us, in the first place, to amend and improve our system of primary education in such a fashion as will make it a proper preparation for the business of life. In the second place, I think we have to consider what measures may best be adopted for the development to its uttermost of that which may be called technical skill; and, in the third place, I think we have to consider what other matters there are for us to attend to, what other arrangements have to be kept carefully in sight in order that, while . pursuing these ends, we donot forget that which is the end of civil existence; I mean a stable social state without which all other measures are merely futile, and, in etfect, modes of going faster to ruin.

You are aware – no people should know the fact better than Manchester people – that, within the last seventeen years, a vast system of primary education has been created and extended over the whole country. I had some part in the original organization of this system in London, and I am glad to think that, after all these years, I can look back upon that period of my life as perhaps the part of it least wasted.

No one can doubt that this system of primary education has done wonders for our population; but, from our point of view, I do' not think anybody can doubt that it still has very considerable defects. It has the defect which is common to all the educational systems which we have inherited – it is too bookish, too little practical. The child is brought too little into contact with actual facts and things, and as the system stands at present it constitutes next to no education of those particular faculties which are of the utmost importance to industrial life – I mean the faculty of observation, the faculty of working accurately, of dealing with things instead of with words.

I do not propose to enlarge upon this topic, but I would venture to suggest that there are one or two remedial measures which are imperatively needed; indeed, they have already been alluded to by Mr. Acland. Those which strike me as of the greatest importance are two, and the first of them is the teaching of drawing. In my judgment, there is no mode of exercising the facultyof observation and the faculty of accurate reproduction of that which is observed, no discipline which so readily tests error in these matters, as drawing properly taught. And by that I do not mean artistic drawing; I mean figuring natural objects: making plans and sections, approaching geometrical rather than artistic drawing. I do not wish to exaggerate, but I declare to you that, in my judgment, the child who has been taught to make an accurate elevation, plan and section of a pint pot has had an admirable training in accuracy of eye and hand. I am not talking about artistic education. That is not the question. Accuracy is the foundation of everything else, and instruction in artistic drawing is something which may be put off till a later stage. Nothing has struck me more in the course of my life than the loss which persons, who are pursuing scientific knowledge ot any kind, sustain from the difficulties which arise because they never have been taught elementary drawing; and I am glad to say that in Eton, a school of whose governing body I have the honor of being a member, we some years ago made drawing imperative on the whole school.

The other matter in which we want some systematic and good teaching is what I have hardly a name for, but which may best be explained as a sort of developed object-lessons such as Mr. Acland adverted to. Anybody who knows his business in science can make anything subservient to that purpose. You know it was said of Dean Swift that he could write an admirable poem upon a broomstick, and the man who has a real knowledge of science can make the commonest object in the world subservient to an introduction to the principles andgreater truths of natural knowledge. It is in that way that your science must be taught if it is to be of real service. Do not suppose any amount of book work, any repetition by rote of catechisms and other abominations of that kind are of value for our object. That is mere wasting of time. But take the commonest object and lead the child from that foundation to such truths of a higher order as may be within his grasp. With regard to drawing, I do not think there is any practical difficulty; but in respect to the scientific object lessons you want teachers trained in a manner different from that which now prevails.

If it is found practicable to add further training of the hand and eye by instruction in modelling or in simple carpentry, well and good. But I should stop at this point. The elementary schools are already charged with quite as much as they can do properly; and I do not believe -that any good can come of burdening them with special technical instruction. Out of that, I think, harm would come.

Now let me pass to my second point, which is the development of technical skill. Everybody here is aware that at this present moment there is hardly a branch of trade or of commerce which does not depend, more or less directly, upon some department or other of physical science, which does not involve, for its successful pursuit, reasoning from scientific data. Our machinery, our chemical processes or dyeworks, and a thousand operations which it is not necessary to mention, are all directly and immediately connected with science. You have to look among your workmen and foremen for persons who shall intelligently grasp the modifications, based uponscience, which are constantly being introduced into these industrial processes. I do not mean that you want professional chemists, or physicists, or mathematicians, or the like, but you want people sufficiently familiar with the broad principles which underlie industrial operations to be able to adapt themselves to new conditions. Such qualifications can only be secured by a sort of scientific instruction which occupies a midway place between those primary notions given in the elementary schools and those more advanced studies which would be carried out in the technical schools.

You are aware that, at present, a very large machinery is in operation for the purpose of giving this instruction. I don't refer merely to such work as is being done at Owens College here, for example, or at other local colleges. I allude to the larger operations of the Science and Art Department, with which I have been connected for a great many years. I constantly hear a great many objections raised to the work of the Science and Art Department. If you will allow me to say so-, my connection with that department – 'Which, I am happy to say, remains, and which I am very proud of – is purely honorary; and, if it appeared to me to be right to criticise that department with merciless severity, the Lord President, if he were inclined to resent my proceedings, could do nothing more than dismiss me. Therefore you may believe that I speak with absolute impartiality. My impression is this, not that it is faultless, nor that it has not various defects, nor that there are not sundry *lacunae* which want filling up; but that, if we consider the conditions under which the department works, we shall see that certain defects are inseparable from those conditions. People talk of the want of flexibility of the department, of its being bound by strict rules. Now, will any man of common-sense who has had anything to do with the administration of public funds or knows the humor of the House of Commons on these matters – will any man who is in the smallest degree acquainted with the practical working of State departments of any kind, imagine that such a department could be other than bound by minutely denned regulations ? Can he imagine that the work of the department should go on fairly and in such a manner as to be free from just criticism, unless it were bound by certain definite and fixed rules ? I cannot imagine it.

The next objection of importance that *I* have heard commonly repeated is that the teaching is too theoretical, that there is insufficient practical teaching. I venture to say that there is no one who has taken more pains to insist upon the comparative uselessness of scientific teaching without practical work than I have; I venture to say that there are no persons who are more cognizant of these defects in the work of the Science and Art Department than those who administer it. But those who talk in this way should acquaint themselves with the fact that proper practical instruction is a matter of no small difficulty in the present scarcity of properly taught teachers, that it is very costly, and that, in some branches of science, there are other difficulties which I won't allude to. But it is a matter of fact that, wherever it has been possible, practical teaching has been introduced, and has been made an essential element in examination; and no doubt if the House of Commons would grant unlimited means, and if proper teachers were to hand, as thick asblackberries, there would not be much difficulty in organizing a complete system of practical instruction and examination ancillary to the present science classes. Those who quarrel with the present state of affairs would be better advised if, instead of groaning over the shortcomings of the present system, they would put before themselves these two questions – Is it possible under the conditions to invent any better system ? Is it possible under the conditions to enlarge the work of practical teaching and practical examination which is the one desire of those who administer the department? That is all I have to say upon that subject.

Supposing we have this teaching of what I may call intermediate science, what we want next is technical instruction, in the strict sense of the word technical; I mean instruction in that kind of knowledge which is essential to the successful prosecution of the several branches of trade and industry. Now, the best way of obtaining this end is a matter about which the most experienced persons entertain very diverse opinions. I do not for one moment pretend to dogmatize about it; I can only tell you what the opinion is that I have formed from hearing the views of those who are certainly best qualified to judge, from those who have tested the various methods of conveying this instruction. I think we have before us three possibilities. We have, in the first place, trade schools – I mean schools in which branches of trade are taught. We have, in the next place, schools attached to factories for the purpose of instructing young apprentices and others who go there, and who aim at becoming intelligent workmen and capable foremen. We have, lastly, the system of day classes and eveningclasses. "With regard to the first there is this objection, that they can be attended only by those who are not obliged to earn their bread, and consequently that they will reach only a very small fraction of the population. Moreover, the expense of trade schools is enormous, and those who are best able to judge assure me that, inasmuch as the work which they do is not done under conditions of pecuniary success or failure, it is apt to be too amateurish and speculative, and that it does not prepare the worker for the real conditions under which he will have to carry out his work. In any case, the fact that the schools are very expensive, and the fact that they are accessible only to a small portion of the population, seem to me to constitute a very serious objection to them. I suppose the best of all possible organizations is that of a school attached to a factory, where the employer has an interest in seeing that the instruction given is of a thoroughly practical kind, and where the pupils pass gradually by successive stages to the position of actual workmen. Schools of this kind exist in various parts of the country, but it is obvious that they are not likely to be reached by any large part of the population; so that it appears to me we are shut up practically to schools accessible to those who are earning their bread, and in such cases they must be essentially evening classes. I am strongly of opinion that classes of this kind do an immense amount of good; that they have this admirable quality, that they involve voluntary attendance, take no man out- of his position, but enable any who chooses to make the best of the position he happens to occupy.

Suppose that all these things are desirable, what isthe best way of obtaining them? I must confess that I have a strong -prejudice in favor of carrying out undertakings of this kind, which at first, at any rate, must be to a great extent tentative and experimental, by private effort. I don't believe that the man lives at this present time who is competent to organize a final system of technical education. I believe that all attempts made in that direction must for many years to come be experimental, and that we must get to success through a series of blunders. Now that work is far better performed by private enterprise than in any other way. But there is another method which I think is permissible, and not only permissible but highly recommendable in this case, and that is the method of allowing the locality itself in which any branch of industry is pursued to be its own judge of its own wants, and to tax itself under certain conditions for the purpose of carrying out any scheme of technical education adapted to its needs. I am aware that there are many extreme theorists of the individualist school who hold that all this is very wicked and very wrong, and that by leaving things to themselves they will get right. Well, my experience of the world is that things left to themselves don't get right. I believe it to be sound doctrine that a municipality – and the State itself for that matter – is a corporation existing for the benefit of its members, and that here, as in all other cases, it is for the majority to determine that which is for the good of the whole, and to act upon that. That is the principle which underlies the whole theory of government in this country, and if it is wrong we shall have to go back a long way. But you may ask me, "This process of local taxation can only be carried out under the authority of an Act of Parliament, and do you propose to let any municipality or any local authority have *carte blanche* in these matters; is the Legislature to allow it to tax the whole body of its members to any extent it pleases and for any purposes it pleases ?" I should reply, certainly not.

Let me point out to you that at this present moment it passes the wit of man, so far as I know, to give a legal definition of technical education. If you expect to have an Act of Parliament with a definition which shall include all that ought to be included, and exclude all that ought to be excluded, I think you will have to wait a very long time. I imagine the whole matter is in a tentative state. You don't know what you will be called upon to do, and so you must try and you must blunder. Under these circumstances it is obvious that there are two alternatives. One of these is to give a free hand to each locality. "Well, it is within my knowledge that there are a good many people with wonderful, strange, and wild notions as to what ought to be done in technical education, and it is quite possible that in some places, and especially in small places, where there are few persons who take an interest in these things, you will have very remarkable projects put forth, and in that case the sole court of appeal for those taxpayers, who did not approve of such projects, would be a court of law. I suppose the judges would have to settle what is technical education. That would not be an edifying process, I think, and certainly it would be a very costly one. The other alternative is the principle adopted in the bill of last year now abandoned. I don't say whether the bill was right or wrong in detail. I am dealing nowonly with the principle of the bill, which appears to me to have been very often misunderstood. It has been said that it gave the whole of technical education into. the hands of the Science and Art Department. It appears to me nothing could be more unfounded than that assertion. All *I* understand the Government proposed to do was to provide some authority who should have power to say in case any scheme was proposed, "Well, this comes within the four corners of the Act of Parliament, work it as you like"; or, if it was an obviously questionable project, should take upon itself the responsibility of saying, "No, that is not what the Legislature intended; amend your scheme." There was no initiative, no control; there was simply this power of giving authority to decide upon the meaning of the Act of Parliament to a particular department of the State, whichever it might be; and it seems to me that that is a very much simpler and better process than relegating the whole question to the law courts. I think that here, or anywhere else, people must be extremely sanguine if they suppose that the House of Commons and the House of Lords will ever dream of giving any local authority unlimited power to tax the inhabitants of a district for any object it pleases. I should say that was not in the range of practical politics. Well, I put that before you as a matter for your consideration.

Another very important point 4n this connection is the question of the supply of teachers. I should say that is one of the greatest difficulties which beset the whole problem before us. I do not wish in'the slightest degree to criticise the'existing system of preparing teachers for ordinary school work. I have nothing to sayabout it. But what I do wish to say, and what I trust I may impress on your minds firmly, is this, that for the purpose of obtaining persons competent to teach science or to act as technical teachers, a different system must be adopted. For this purpose a man must know what he is about thoroughly, and be able to deal with his subject as if it were the business of his ordinary life. For this purpose, for the obtaining of teachers of science and of technical classes, the system of catching a boy or girl young, making a pupil teacher of him, compelling the poor little mortal to pour from his little bucket, into a still smaller bucket, that which has just been poured into it out of a big bucket; and passing him afterward through the training college, where his life is devoted to filling the bucket from the pump from morning till night, without time for thought or reflection, is a system which should not continue. Let me assure you that it will not do for us, that you had better give the attempt up than try that system. I remember somewhere reading of an interview between the poet Southey and a good Quaker. Southey was a man of marvellous powers of work. He had a habit of dividing his time into little parts each of which was filled up, and he told the Quaker what he did in this hour and that, and so on through the day until far into the night. The Quaker listened, and at the close said, "Well, but, friend Southey, when dost thee think?" The system which I am now adverting to is arraigned and condemned by putting that question to it. When does the unhappy pupil teacher, or over-drilled student of a training college, find any time to think? I am sure if I were in their place I could not. I repeat, that kind of thing will not do for science teachers. For scienceteachers must have knowledge, and knowledge is not to be acquired on these terms. The power of repetition is, but that is not knowledge. The knowledge which is absolutely requisite in dealing with young children is the knowledge you possess, as you would know your own business, and which you can just turn about as if you were explaining to a boy a matter of every-day life.

So far as science teaching and technical education are concerned, the most important of all things is to provide the machinery for training proper teachers. The Depart-' ment of Science and Art has been at that work for years and years, and though unable under present conditions to do so much as could be wished, it has, I believe, already begun to leaven the lump to a very considerable extent. If technical education is to be carried out on the scale at present contemplated, this particular necessity must be specially and most seriously provided for. And there is another difficulty, namely, that when you have got your science or technical teacher it may not be easy to keep him. You have educated a man – a clever fellow very likely – on the understanding that he is to be a teacher. But the business of teaching is not a very lucrative and not a very attractive one, and an able man who has had a good training is under extreme temptations to carry his knowledge and his skill to a better market, in which case you have had all your trouble for nothing. It has often occurred to me that probably nothing would be of more service in this matter than the creation of a number of not very large bursaries or exhibitions, to be gained by persons nominated by the authorities of the various science colleges and schools of the country – persons such as they thought to be well qualified for the teaching

business – and to be held for a certain term of years, during which the holders should be bound to teach. I believe that some measure of this kind would do more to secure a good supply of teachers than anything else. Pray note that I do not suggest that you should try to get hold of good teachers by competitive examination. That is not the best way of getting men of that special qualification. An effectual method would be to ask professors and teachers of any institution to recommend men who, to their own knowledge, are worthy of such support, and are likely to turn it to good account.

I trust I am not detaining you too long; but there remains yet one other matter which I think is of profound importance, perhaps of more importance than all the rest, on which I earnestly beg to be permitted to say some few words. It is the need, while doing all these things, of keeping an eye, and an anxious eye, upon those measures which are necessary for the preservation of that stable and sound condition of the whole social organism which is the essential condition of real progress, and a chief end of all education. You will all recollect that some time ago there was a scandal and a great outcry about certain cutlasses and bayonets which had been supplied to our troops and sailors. These warlike implements were polished as bright as rubbing could make them; they were very well sharpened; they looked lovely. But when they were applied to the test of the work of war they broke and they bent, and proved more likely to hurt the hand of him who used them than to do any harm to the enemy. Let me apply that analogy to the effect of education, which is a sharpening and polishing of the mind. You may develop the intellectual side ofpeople as far as you like, and you may confer upon them all the skill that training and instruction can give; but, if there is not, underneath all that outside form and superficial polish, the firm fibre of healthy manhood and earnest desire to do well, your labor is absolutely in vain.

Let me further call your attention to the fact that the terrible battle of competition between the different nations of the world is no transitory phenomenon, and does not depend upon this or that fluctuation of the market, or upon any condition that is likely to pass away. It is the inevitable result of that which takes place throughout nature and affects man's part of nature as much as any other; namely, the struggle for existence, arising out of the constant tendency of all creatures in the animated world to multiply indefinitely. It is that, if you look at it, which is at the bottom of all the great movements of history. It is that inherent tendency of the social organism to generate the causes of its own destruction, never yet counteracted, which has been at the bottom of half the catastrophes which have ruined States. "We are at present in the swim of one of those vast movements in which, with a population far in excess of that which we can feed, we are saved from a catastrophe, through the impossibility of feeding them, solely by our possession of a fair share of the markets of the world. And in order that that fair share may be retained, it is absolutely necessary that we should be able to produce commodities which we can exchange with food-growing people, and which they will take, rather than those of our rivals, on the ground of their greater cheapness or of their greater excellence. That is the whole story. And our course, let me say, is not actuated by mere motives of ambition or by mere motives of greed. Those doubtless are visible enough on the surface of these great movements, but the movements themselves have far deeper sources. If there were no such things as ambition and greed in this world, the struggle for existence would arise from the same causes.

Our sole chance of succeeding in a competition, which must constantly become more and more severe, is that our people shall not only have the knowledge and the skill which are required, but that they shall have the will and the energy and the honesty, without which neither knowledge nor skill can be of any permanent avail. This is what I mean by a stable social condition, because any other condition than this, any social condition in which the development of wealth involves the misery, the physical weakness, and the degradation of the worker, is absolutely and infallibly doomed to collapse. Your bayonets and cutlasses will break under your hand, and there will go on accumulating in society a mass of hopeless, physically incompetent, and morally degraded people, who are, as it were, a sort of dynamite which, sooner or later, when its accumulation becomes sufficient and its tension intolerable, will burst the whole fabric.

I am quite aware that the problem which I have put before you and which you know as much about as I do, and a great deal more probably, is one extremely difficult to solve. 1 am fully aware that one great factor in industrial success is reasonable cheapness of labor. That has been pointed out over and over again, and is in itself an axiomatic proposition. And it seems to me that of all the social questions which face us at this present time, the most serious is how to steer a clear course between the two horns of an obvious dilemma. One of these is the constant tendency of competition to lower wages beyond a point at which man can remain man – below a point at which decency and cleanliness and order and habits of morality and justice can reasonably be expected to exist. And the other horn of the dilemma is the difficulty of maintaining wages above this point consistently with success in industrial competition. I have not the remotest conception how this problem will eventually work itself out; but of this I am perfectly convinced, that the sole course compatible with safety lies between the two extremes; between the Scylla of successful industrial production with a degraded population, on the one side, and the Charybdis of a population, maintained in a reasonable and decent state, with failure in industrial competition, on the other side. Having this strong conviction, which, indeed, I imagine must be that of every person who has ever thought seriously about these great problems, I have ventured to put it before you in this bare and almost cynical fashion because it will justify the strong appeal, which I make to all concerned in this work of promoting industrial education, to have a care, at the same time, that the conditions of industrial life remain those in which the physical energies of the population may be maintained at a proper level; in which their moral state may be cared for; in which there may be some rays of hope and pleasure in their lives; and in which the sole prospect of a life of labor may not be an old age of penury.

These are the chief suggestions I have to offer toyou, though I have omitted much that I should like to have said, had time permitted. It may be that some of you feel inclined to look upon them as the Utopian dreams of a student. If there be such, let me tell you that there are, to my knowledge, manufacturing towns in this country, not one-tenth the size, or boasting one- hundredth part of the wealth, of Manchester, in which I do not say that the programme that I have put before you is completely carried out, but in which, at any rate, a wise and intelligent effort had been made to realize it, and in which the main parts of the programme are in course of being worked out. This is not the first time that I have had the privilege and pleasure of addressing a Manchester audience. I have often enough, before now, thrown myself with entire confidence upon the hard- headed intelligence and the very soft-hearted kindness of Manchester people, when I have had a difficult and complicated scientific argument to put before them. If, after the considerations which I have put before you – ' and which, pray be it understood, I by no means claim particularly for myself, for I presume they must be in the minds of a large number of people who have thought about this matter – if it be that these ideaa commend themselves to your mature reflection, then I am perfectly certain that my appeal to you to carry them into practice, with that abundant energy and will which have led you to take a foremost part in the great social movements of our country many a time beforehand, will not be made in vain. I therefore confidently appeal to you to let those impulses once more have full sway, and not to rest until you have done something better and greater than has yet been done in this country in the directionin which we are now going. I heartily thank you for the attention which you have been kind enough to bestow upon me. The practice of public speaking is one I must soon think of leaving off, and I count it a special and peculiar honor to have had the opportunity of speaking to you on this subject to-day.

The borrower must return this item on or before the last date stamped below. If another user places a recall for this item, the borrower will be notified of the need for an earlier return.

Non-receipt of overdue notices does not exempt the borrower from overdue fines.
Harvard College Widener Library Cambridge, MA 02138 617-495-2413
are.
Please handle
Thank you for helping to preserve
library collections at Harvard.

Lightning Source UK Ltd.
Milton Keynes UK
UKOW05f2029100114

224380UK00001B/27/P